International Business

An introduction

Radha Jethu-Ramsoedh LLM
Maud Hendrickx Bsc

First edition

Noordhoff Publishers Groningen/Houten

Cover design: Studio Frank & Lisa, Groningen
Cover illustration: Getty images

If you have any comments or queries about this or any other publication, please contact Noordhoff Uitgevers BV, Afdeling Hoger Onderwijs, Antwoordnummer 13, 9700 VB Groningen, The Netherlands, e-mail: info@noordhoff.nl

With regard to some of the texts and/or illustration materials, despite painstaking efforts to this end, the publishers did not succeed in tracing all possible copyright holders. Should you in your opinion have any copyright applicable to texts and/or illustration materials in this publication, we request that you contact the publisher.

The utmost care has been devoted to the creation of this publication. The author(s), editorial office and publisher accept no responsibility for any information included that is nonetheless incomplete or incorrect. They are always ready to make corrections to any of the included data.

0 1 2 3 4 5 / 15 14 13 12 11

ISBN 978-90-01-80503-6
NUR 801

Preface

The open nature of the economy and the internationalisation of trade and industry have resulted in a growing need for well-trained students with a broad knowledge of the different aspects of international business. In our opinion, a book for English-language bachelor courses in higher education describing the basic principles of international business was not available. Therefore, we deemed it necessary to compile a guideline that provides an introduction to international business for students who encounter the subject regularly in their curriculum. Students are made aware of the fact that international business transactions are not only based on abstract theories, but that day-to-day reality plays an important part as well. Facts, figures and relevant case studies have been added to explain the text material.

Theories and general principles serve as an introductory explanation of the dynamic international environment. The book has been written in industry-wide terms, which means the book provides suitable textmaterial for various forms of higher professional training, in which international business, international trade, international management and globalisation are part of the curriculum. As nearly all companies have suppliers or customers of foreign origin, this book is recommended to anyone working in an international company with hardly any expertise in the field of conducting business in an international environment.

We would appreciate receiving remarks and comments of students and lecturers so that we can improve the quality level of this book. Finally, we would like to express our thanks to all those who have supported us with their advice and suggestions: Martin Zuurhout MBA (Martin Delta), Louise van Weerden (Saxion University, the Netherlands) Sharro Jethu (Optimal Synergy), Marijn Mulders (Avans University of Applied Sciences, the Netherlands), Hendrie van Maanen (Christian University of Applied Sciences, the Netherlands), Ron Harmsen (Radio Gelderland), Vishwa Jethu, Jennifer Evans (students of the Economics & Business Faculty at the Utrecht University, the Netherlands) and our colleagues at the European Fashion Business School. Furthermore, we wish to thank all those from the business community who offered us practical advice: Eric Verbeek (AON Insurance company). A special word of thanks goes to Irene Sueters, Reshmi Nannan Panday and Ageeth Bergsma (Noordhoff Publishers) our excellent coach, and to our families for their encouragement.

Radha Jethu-Ramsoedh
Maud Hendrickx

Contents

Effective studying

38 © Noordhoff Uitgevers bv

Apple admits to using child labour

2

Apple has admitted that child labour was used at the factories that build its computers, iPods and mobile phones. At least eleven 15-year-old children were discovered to be working in three factories that supply Apple last year.
The company did not name the offending factories, or say where they were based, but the majority of its goods are assembled in China. Apple also has factories in Taiwan, Singapore, the Philippines, Malaysia, Thailand, the Czech Republic and the United States.
Apple said the child workers are now no longer being used, or are no longer underage. "In each of the three facilities, we required a review of all employment records for the year as well as a complete analysis of the hiring process to clarify how underage people had been able to gain employment," Apple said, in an annual report on its suppliers.

Apple has been repeatedly criticized for using factories that abuse workers and where conditions are poor. Last year, an employee at Foxconn, the Taiwanese company that is one of Apple's biggest suppliers, committed suicide after being accused of stealing a prototype for the iPhone.
China Labor Watch, a New York-based NGO, accused Foxconn of having an "inhumane and militant" management, which neglects basic human rights. Apple admitted that at least 55 of the 102 factories that produce its goods were ignoring Apple's rule that staff cannot work more than 60 hours a week.
The technology companies own guidelines are already in breach of China's widely ignored labour law, which sets out a maximum 49-hour week for workers. Apple also said that one of its factories had repeatedly falsified its records. "When we investigated, we uncovered records and conducted worker interviews that revealed excessive working hours and seven days of continuous work." Only 65 per cent of the factories were paying their staff the correct wages and benefits, and Apple found 24 factories where workers had not even been paid China's minimum wage of around 800 Yuan a month.

Edited source: The Telegraph, 27 February 2010

Case at the beginning of each chapter

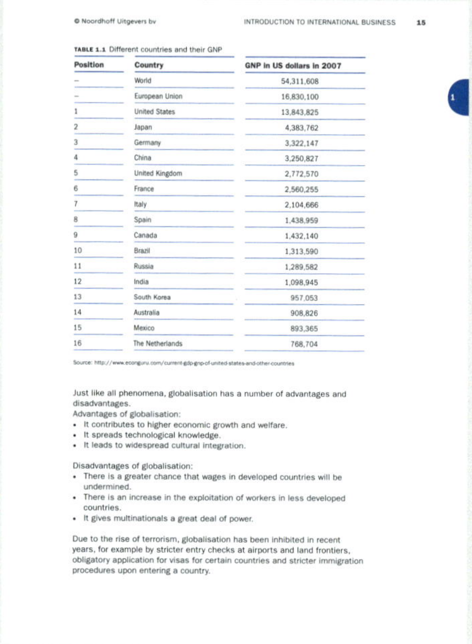

© Noordhoff Uitgevers bv INTRODUCTION TO INTERNATIONAL BUSINESS 15

TABLE 1.1 Different countries and their GNP

Position	Country	GNP in US dollars in 2007
–	World	54,311,608
–	European Union	16,830,100
1	United States	13,843,825
2	Japan	4,383,762
3	Germany	3,322,147
4	China	3,250,827
5	United Kingdom	2,772,570
6	France	2,560,255
7	Italy	2,104,666
8	Spain	1,438,959
9	Canada	1,432,140
10	Brazil	1,313,590
11	Russia	1,289,582
12	India	1,098,945
13	South Korea	957,053
14	Australia	908,826
15	Mexico	893,365
16	The Netherlands	768,704

Source: http://www.econguru.com/current-gdp-gnp-of-united-states-and-other-countries

1

Just like all phenomena, globalisation has a number of advantages and disadvantages.
Advantages of globalisation:
- It contributes to higher economic growth and welfare.
- It spreads technological knowledge.
- It leads to widespread cultural integration.

Disadvantages of globalisation:
- There is a greater chance that wages in developed countries will be undermined.
- There is an increase in the exploitation of workers in less developed countries.
- It gives multinationals a great deal of power.

Due to the rise of terrorism, globalisation has been inhibited in recent years, for example by stricter entry checks at airports and land frontiers, obligatory application for visas for certain countries and stricter immigration procedures upon entering a country.

Facts and figures from international industry

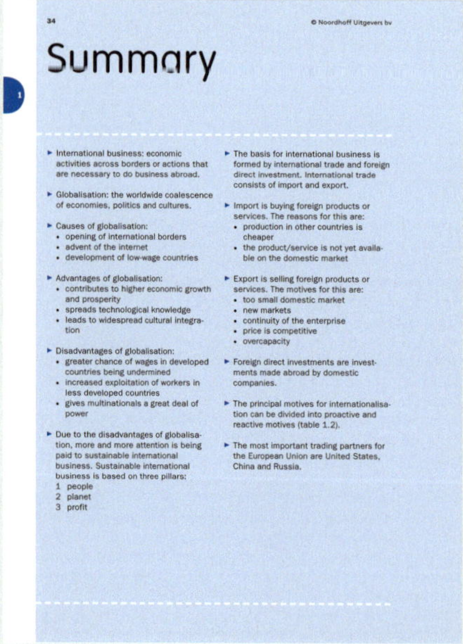

34 © Noordhoff Uitgevers bv

Summary

1

- International business: economic activities across borders or actions that are necessary to do business abroad.
- Globalisation: the worldwide coalescence of economies, politics and cultures.
- Causes of globalisation:
  - opening of international borders
  - advent of the internet
  - development of low-wage countries
- Advantages of globalisation:
  - contributes to higher economic growth and prosperity
  - spreads technological knowledge
  - leads to widespread cultural integration
- Disadvantages of globalisation:
  - greater chance of wages in developed countries being undermined
  - increased exploitation of workers in less developed countries
  - gives multinationals a great deal of power
- Due to the disadvantages of globalisation, more and more attention is being paid to sustainable international business. Sustainable international business is based on three pillars:
  1 people
  2 planet
  3 profit
- The basis for international business is formed by international trade and foreign direct investment. International trade consists of import and export.
- Import is buying foreign products or services. The reasons for this are:
  - production in other countries is cheaper
  - the product/service is not yet available on the domestic market
- Export is selling foreign products or services. The motives for this are:
  - too small domestic market
  - new markets
  - continuity of the enterprise
  - price is competitive
  - overcapacity
- Foreign direct investments are investments made abroad by domestic companies.
- The principal motives for internationalisation can be divided into proactive and reactive motives (table 1.2).
- The most important trading partners for the European Union are United States, China and Russia.

Summary

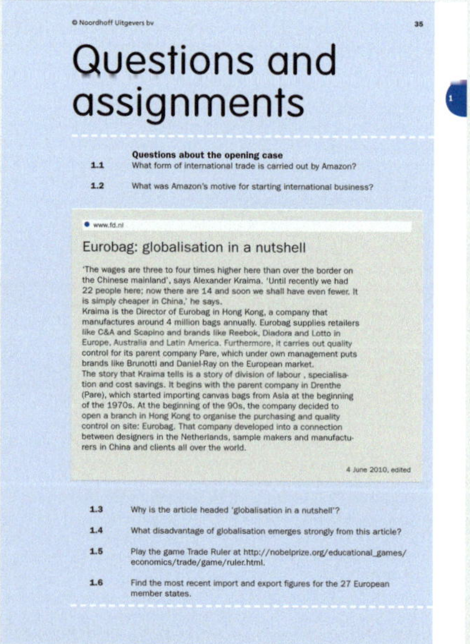

© Noordhoff Uitgevers bv 35

Questions and assignments

1

Questions about the opening case

1.1 What form of international trade is carried out by Amazon?

1.2 What was Amazon's motive for starting international business?

www.fd.nl

Eurobag: globalisation in a nutshell

'The wages are three to four times higher here than over the border on the Chinese mainland', says Alexander Kraima. 'Until recently we had 22 people here; now there are 14 and soon we shall have even fewer. It is simply cheaper in China,' he says.
Kraima is the Director of Eurobag in Hong Kong, a company that manufactures around 4 million bags annually. Eurobag supplies retailers like C&A and Scapino and brands like Reebok, Diadora and Lotto in Europe, Australia and Latin America. Furthermore, it carries out quality control for its parent company Pare, which under own management puts brands like Brunotti and Daniel-Ray on the European market.
The story that Kraima tells is a story of division of labour , specialisation and cost savings. It begins with the parent company in Drenthe (Pare), which started importing canvas bags from Asia at the beginning of the 1970s. At the beginning of the 90s, the company decided to open a branch in Hong Kong to organise the purchasing and quality control on site: Eurobag. That company developed into a connection between designers in the Netherlands, sample makers and manufacturers in China and clients all over the world.

4 June 2010, edited

1.3 Why is the article headed 'globalisation in a nutshell'?

1.4 What disadvantage of globalisation emerges strongly from this article?

1.5 Play the game Trade Ruler at http://nobelprize.org/educational_games/economics/trade/game/ruler.html.

1.6 Find the most recent import and export figures for the 27 European member states.

Questions and assignments in each chapter

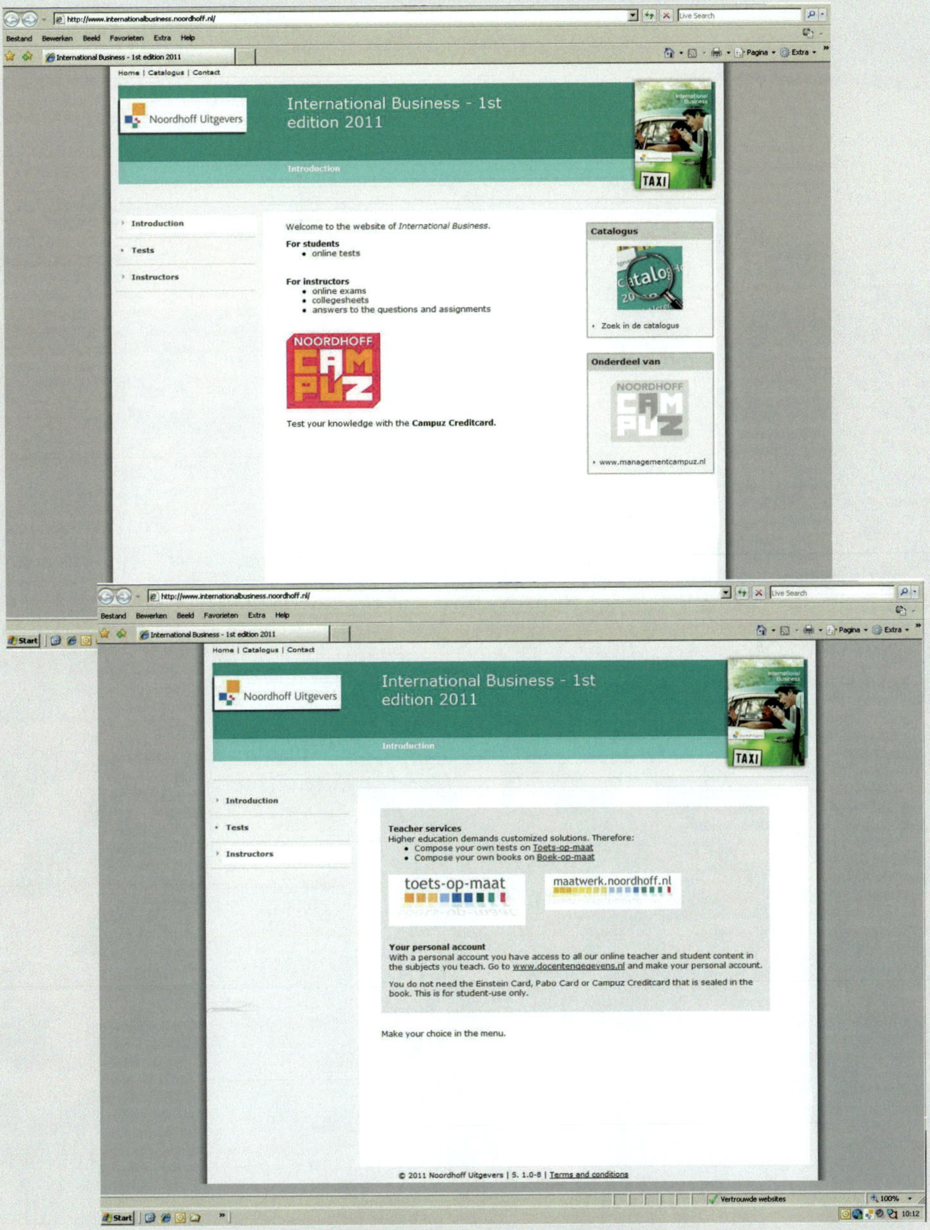

website www.internationalbusiness.noordhoff.nl with test questions for students.

1 Introduction to international business

In this introductory chapter, we discuss the essence of international business and its context. Furthermore, we look at what motivates companies to cross borders. A number of terms that will repeatedly occur in this book, such as import and export, are discussed here. Finally, we zoom in on the performance of the European Union member states concerning international business.

1

Amazon seeks to expand globally

Amazon says it plans to revamp its international e-commerce platform to make it easier for the company to reach customers in new markets.
The online retailer, the world's largest by number of visitors, operates online businesses in six countries outside the US. It says it has set up a new team that will create "the architectural underpinnings to greatly simplify country expansions", by translating content into different languages and adjusting taxes, prices and delivery options to better suit customers' locations.
The move underlines the increasing globalisation of online retailing, as companies such as Gap, the US clothing retailer, and Walmart, the world's largest retailer by sales, seek to use e-commerce sites and cross-border shipping to reach a wider audience.
Walmart, one of Amazon's main online rivals in the US, has invested heavily in a global e-commerce platform over the past two years, which it says it plans to use to reach customers both in existing markets and in countries where it has no physical stores.

Japan's largest online retailer, Rakuten, has also recently acquired or launched sites in the US, Europe and China for its Ebay-style online marketplaces.
Amazon operates websites in Canada, China, Japan, the UK, Germany and France, and offers customers ordering from other countries the ability to pay for purchases in their own currencies. But it has not entered a new country since 2004, when it acquired Joyo.com, its Chinese site. Instead, it has focused on steadily expanding the new product categories on its range of global sites.
The retailer is now seeking to recruit senior software engineers for what it says is "a new team that is gearing up to make a substantial impact on how Amazon does business around the world".
A job posting says the team is "tackling interesting problems like rendering content in multiple languages and calculating tax, price and shipping variations on the fly based on the customer's preferred shipping destination".
Gap has recently launched a UK-based e-commerce site aimed both at the UK and other western European countries, although customers can only pay in sterling, not Euros. Gap has recently launched its first e-commerce sites in Canada and China, while Walmart has said it will shortly open an e-commerce site for its Sam's Club discount warehouse stores in China. Marks and Spencer, the UK general retailer, has said it hopes to use e-commerce to expand its international sales, once its current agreement to rely on a site run by Amazon expires in 2013. Tesco, the UK supermarket group, also said this month that it planned to open e-commerce sites in China, Poland and the Czech Republic.

Edited source: www.ft.com, 23 December 2010

1.1 What is international business?

If European consumers consider the origin of their products, they rapidly become aware that few products are manufactured in Europe. 'Made in China' is a common label in or on various products. The market for products and services is not limited to European borders, but extends across the whole world. Furthermore, there are many foreign companies that operate worldwide. These companies are called multinationals. They include Daimler, Suez, BP en Metro. But even small and medium-size companies are not limited to doing business in their own country any longer. Gradually small companies are venturing across their national borders: for example, through web shops that are set up abroad.

● www.bndestem.nl

Source: Qilai Shen/EPA

Made in China

SHANGHAI – A man waits for the opening of the 20th East China Fair in Shanghai among an array of colourful storage jars.
With around 6,000 exhibitors, this is China's largest trade show for consumer articles and is primarily focused on export. Last year, around 50,000 buyers from more than 100 countries came to the show.

4 March 2010

International business

International business is a broad definition. It covers more than marketing and selling goods and services abroad. It is also related to the development of international commerce or the actions that are necessary to do business on an international level. Companies increasingly seek collaborations with partners abroad. They outsource activities to low-wage countries to increase their productivity or reduce their labour costs. They share knowledge with foreign partners to obtain a stronger competitive position, or they work with others to realise economies of scale. Since international business is much more complicated than national business, we wish to focus with as many aspects as possible which differ from domestic business practice.

Low-wage countries

1.1.1 Globalisation

Why has international business expanded so enormously? Due to the opening of borders, it has become increasingly easy to buy products or services from, or sell them to, other countries. The advent of the internet has made a significant contribution to this. It has become easier and cheaper to be connected worldwide. Due to the industrialisation process of low-wage countries such as China, India and Bangladesh, manufacturing can be done more cheaply. Globalisation does refer to goods and services but also to capital, knowledge and labour which find their way around the globe. Due to the abolition of frontiers, people travel more than ever. Because of this, political systems, economies and cultures influence each other. This can be seen in metropolises: more and more cities are starting to look alike. Look, for example, at McDonald's, which has an outlet in every metropolis.

Globalisation

The last ten years often referred to as 'the age of globalisation'. However, globalisation is not a phenomenon of recent decades. Nevertheless, its development has changed in the last decade. Considering the growth of the Gross National Product (GNP) of countries together, we notice that more than half of this growth comes from the new industrial countries (emerging markets). These countries play an increasingly important role in globalisation – the BRIC countries (Brazil, Russia, India and China) in particular, where enormous growth in GNP is expected in the coming years. This is in contrast to Western countries, whose economies have stagnated, due to the effects of the current credit crisis.

Gross National Product

BRIC countries

Gross National Product (GNP)

The extent to which a country participates in international trade depends primarily on its GNP. The Gross National Product of a country is the total of what is produced in that country in terms of goods and services by firms that are nationally owned, plus the income derived from nationally-owned firms abroad, which is received as a reward for making production facilities available. GNP is an important measure of the economic performance of a country. Table 1.1 lists several countries and their GNP.

TABLE 1.1 Different countries and their GNP

Position	Country	GNP in US dollars in 2007
–	World	54,311,608
–	European Union	16,830,100
1	United States	13,843,825
2	Japan	4,383,762
3	Germany	3,322,147
4	China	3,250,827
5	United Kingdom	2,772,570
6	France	2,560,255
7	Italy	2,104,666
8	Spain	1,438,959
9	Canada	1,432,140
10	Brazil	1,313,590
11	Russia	1,289,582
12	India	1,098,945
13	South Korea	957,053
14	Australia	908,826
15	Mexico	893,365
16	The Netherlands	768,704

Source: http://www.econguru.com/current-gdp-gnp-of-united-states-and-other-countries

Just like all phenomena, globalisation has a number of advantages and disadvantages.
Advantages of globalisation:

- It contributes to higher economic growth and welfare.
- It spreads technological knowledge.
- It leads to widespread cultural integration.

Disadvantages of globalisation:

- There is a greater chance that wages in developed countries will be undermined.
- There is an increase in the exploitation of workers in less developed countries.
- It gives multinationals a great deal of power.

Due to the rise of terrorism, globalisation has been inhibited in recent years, for example by stricter entry checks at airports and land frontiers, obligatory application for visas for certain countries and stricter immigration procedures upon entering a country.

1.1.2 Europe and globalisation

How globalised is Europe, with its open and developed economy and multicultural society? From figure 1.1 it can be observed that Europe is very globalised.

FIGURE 1.1 KOF Index of Globalisation 2007

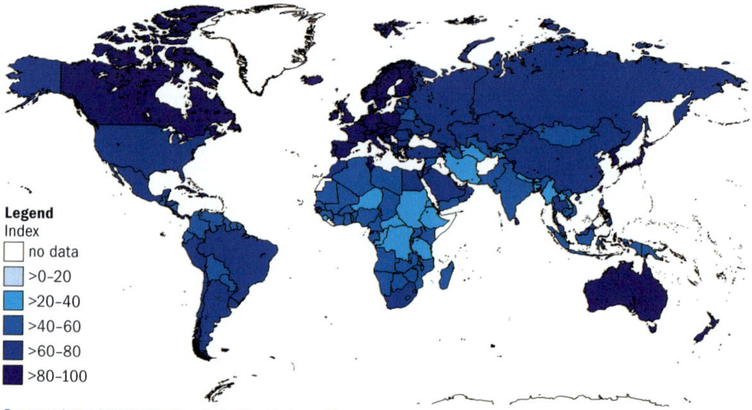

Source: http://globalization.kof.ethz.ch/map/#

From an investigation by the KOF Swiss Economic Institute in 2010, it seems that Belgium comes first in the globalization stakes. Austria, which was in 3rd place last year, now ranks 2nd. The Netherlands ranks 3rd. This year's fast climber is Luxembourg, which advanced from 21st place to 14th place. Switzerland still comes 4th on the globalization index. The emerging markets in Eastern Europe and Central Asia are recording the biggest jump on the KOF Globalization Index. Although the degree of globalization is highest in the industrialised nations and Western Europe, it has stagnated for quite some time. In East Asia and the Pacific region, the globalization process has slowed down compared to the previous year, while index rankings actually went down in the Near East and North Africa.

While economic and political globalization is advancing, social globalization is stagnating. The economic dimension of the KOF Index quantifies not only actual trade and investment flows, but also the extent to which countries protect themselves by imposing restrictions on trade and capital movements. The social dimension of globalization reflects the flow of ideas and information, while the political dimension examines the degree of political cooperation between countries.

1.1.3 Sustainable international business

Sustainable international business

The globalisation has placed pressures on the global environment and natural resources and exposing human dependence on our environment. Hence, this book focuses on sustainable international business, which makes companies conscious of the way in which they do business and the consequences, not only for mankind and the environment, but also for society.

The core of sustainable international business is the stakeholder. A stakeholder is a group or individual who influences or is influenced by an organisation or company. Figure 1.2 gives an overview of the types of stakeholder in a company. **Stakeholder**

FIGURE 1.2 Overview of Stakeholders

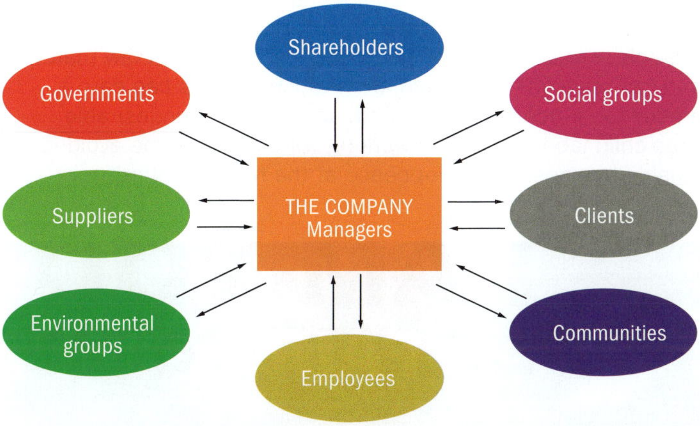

Source: derived from Donaldson & Preston, 1995

Shareholders often focus only on economic results. Not all stakeholders have the same priority. Hence, as well as profit, business should embrase sustainability for innovation and business growth. Therefore, sustainable international business consists of three pillars, namely:
1 People
2 Planet
3 Profit

Ad 1 People
'People' relates to the human side of sustainable international business. It covers people inside and outside the companies, and aspects such as health and safety in the workplace, employment laws, human rights, wages, training and child labour. This is an important pillar, especially when production takes place in low-wage countries, where working conditions are often poor. **People**

Ad 2 Planet
'Planet' means care for the environment. Because our natural resources are becoming exhausted, we shall have to look for alternatives. Aspects such as the efficient use of raw materials and waste management are part of this pillar. A lot of attention has recently been paid to recycling, where products are made from components that can be re-used after the lifetime of the original product. **Planet**

Ad 3 Profit
Of course, profit is a condition for the continuation of an enterprise, but a number of other important aspects contribute towards its prosperity. 'Profit' therefore includes aspects such as location policy, profitability, profit appropriation, dividend distribution, sponsoring and charity policy. **Profit**

For companies, the challenge is to find a good balance among these three pillars, referred to as the triple bottom line.

Due to increasing globalisation, more and more products are produced abroad, and it is not always clear where the raw materials for these products come from. We also do not always know under what circumstances they have been produced. More and more companies accept responsibility for the whole production chain, and therefore more and more companies are participating in 'fair trade' – in the coffee and clothing sector, for example. These 'fair trade' products are made from raw materials for which a fair price has been paid, from which farmers can earn a living. The production process is monitored, and therefore undesirable factors such as child labour and poor working conditions can be avoided. In short, sustainable business does not cease at the home frontier!

Source: http://fairtradelifestyle.files.wordpress.com/2009/05/world-fair-trade-day-logo.jpg

1.2 Why do companies cross borders?

If companies do business abroad, they internationalise. Why do companies make this choice? We will discuss this in this section. First, the basis for international business, international trade, will be explained. Next we will look at another aspect of internationalisation, namely foreign investment. In conclusion, the motives for companies to do business internationally will be explained.

1.2.1 International trade

As indicated previously, the basis for internationalisation is often the trade of goods or services, called international trade. Europe has been familiar with this throughout history, for example through the trade in spices. European countries have had good trade relations with some countries for centuries.

International trade

ECONOMIST, 17 DECEMBER 1998

The history of spices is the history of trade

SOON after dawn on May 21st 1498, Vasco da Gama and his crew arrived at Calicut after the first direct sea voyage from Europe to Asia. If history's modern age has a beginning, this is it. Europe's ignorance of, and isolation from, the cosmopolitan intellectual and commercial life of Asia were ended forever. With ships, weaponry and a willingness to use them both, the countries of Europe were about to colonize the rest of the world. To support this expansion, its merchant classes would invent new forms of commercial credit and the first great corporations, vital parts of capitalism's operating system, and spread their trading networks across the seven seas. And what did the men shout as they came ashore? "For Christ and spices!" Today spices are chiefly flavourings for food, but a hundred other uses have contributed to the demand through history. In ancient Egypt cassia and cinnamon fetched a high price because they were essential for embalming; so too were anise, marjoram and cumin, used to rinse out the innards of the worthy dead. Hammurabi's legal code, which called for severe punishment of sloppy or unsuccessful surgeons, did much to encourage the use of medicinal spices in Sumeria.

1

Why does international trade arise?

International trade has existed since time immemorial, but only in the last 250 years have theories about it arisen. In the past, people attempted to explain the origin of international trade from an economic viewpoint.
The classic economists soon came to the conclusion that macro-economic conditions in the home market – such as national income, the employment situation, national consumption, investment and general price levels – could partly determine international competitive strength.

The viewpoint of (neo-)classical economists was that the origin of international trade can best be explained in terms of differences in (cost) prices and productivity between countries. The country that can manufacture products at the lowest cost will sell them to other countries. After theories of absolute and comparative costs (Ricardo 1817) came Heckscher and Ohlin (1933) with the viewpoint that the availability and cost of production facilities determined the extent of international trade. In this way, India, which in comparison to Switzerland has a large amount of labour available, must concentrate on the production of labour-intensive goods. Switzerland, with more capital than labour, must specialise in capital-intensive products. Modern trade theories, which have been introduced in the past 40 years, emphasize factors other than price elements, such as quality, economies of scale, knowledge, technological development and product differentiation.

The traditional theories, according to Kol and Mennes (1989), are most successful at explaining why there is international trade but they can only partly explain the differences in competitive strength between countries. In 1990, in his book *The Competitive Advantage of Nations*, Porter tried to build a bridge between the viewpoints of the neo-classicists and modern trade theories. In his explanation of national competitive strength, Porter does not concentrate on any one factor at macro level but on several factors at meso level (industrial branch level). The following factors are involved in distinguishing among sectors:

- the extent and nature of domestic competition
- the presence of an adequate supply industry
- the conditions in the home market (infrastructure, capital, labour)
- the demand level (responding to the diversity in customer demand)

Because of these factors, it is possible that some industrial branches remain largely confined to their home country while others internationalise at an early stage. Ilustrations include computers (Silicon Valley in the United States), logistics (Rotterdam in the Netherlands), software outsourcing (Bangalore in India) and fashion (Paris in France).

There are different types of international trade, which are explained below:

- import
- export

These terms often appear in this book.

Import

Import

Importing is buying foreign products, which are shipped into the home country. A company buys goods or services from an exporting company with the objective of selling them at a profit. Because the world is becoming ever smaller, there are products or components on the shelves that have been manufactured thousands of kilometres away. This can happen for two reasons:

- The production of goods or components is cheaper in other countries, as a result of which products are often developed in Europe and produced in that particular country. This occurs for various reasons:
  - In the country of origin, labour costs are lower than in Europe.
  - The raw materials are easily available in the country of origin. The processing of the raw materials in the country of origin not only produce time benefits, it also has the advantage that the knowledge that is necessary for the production of the product is available on site.
- The product or service has not been supplied in Europe.

VOLKSKRANT, 23 FEBRUARY 2010

Cadillac will try again in Europe

ZURICH - The American car manufacturer General Motors will make a fresh attempt to establish the Cadillac brand in Europe. To this end, the subsidiary company Cadillac Europe has been established, the company reported on Monday.

The 2011 Cadillac CTS Coupé (Reuters)

The new business unit will import and sell models that have been designed specifically for the European market. A network of dealers and service companies will also be set up.
Several years ago, Cadillac attempted to storm the European market.
Cadillac is presenting its CTS Coupé next month at the Autosalon in Geneva. This will be its European premiere.

Export

Exporting is the selling of domestic products or services to foreign importers. Exporting is thus the opposite of importing. The most significant motives for entering a foreign market are the following: **Export**

- New technologies and new products constitute a challenge. In a less-developed market, demand for such products will be greater than in an already developed market.
- The domestic market is too small for the product; there is too little demand or too much supply of a similar type of product.
- To assure the continuity of the company, there must be a constant search for new markets.
- The cost price of the product that the company supplies makes it competitive in the foreign market.
- If the company is suffering from overcapacity, it is attractive to sell products in a foreign market.

1

www.ft.com

Songwriters enjoy royalties to tune of £166m

Robust international demand and tighter licensing laws helped British and Irish songwriters more than double their royalties from music exports in the past decade. According to PRS for Music, the royalties collection society representing songwriters and composers, British and Irish musical talent earned £166.6m from overseas markets in 2009, up from £66m in 1999.
The figures strike an unusually positive note amid the travails of the wider music industry, which has seen revenues from recorded music sales collapse and is still struggling to find a sustainable digital revenue model.

Britain is one of only three net exporters of music in the world, second after the US and ahead of Sweden. The largest segment of international royalty in-come in 2009 was derived from music used in television programmes and ad-vertising, which generated more than £50m in revenue, up from £15m in 2000, while radio play yielded over £35m, compared with £23m at the start of the decade.

Karen Buse, international director at PRS for Music, said the successful export of British television formats such as X Factor, Who Wants To Be a Millionaire and The Weakest Link – which use music written by British composers – had bolstered royalties from broadcast. Meanwhile global tours by bands including Take That and U2 helped lift royalties income from live performances in 2009 to £18m, from under £14m in the previous year and less than £2m in 2000.

The most significant demand for British and Irish music came from the US, France, Germany and Japan. But growing appetite from emerging markets, including central and eastern Europe and South America, has also boosted royalties.

22 January 2011

1.2.2 Foreign investment

Besides engaging in international trade, companies can invest abroad, so-called foreign direct investment. This takes place when there is direct investment in production in another country, by building a factory, for example. It can also occur by starting up a company in another country, by taking over a local company or by merging with another company.

Foreign direct investment

● www.fdiintelligence.com

Proceeding with caution: the post-crisis world of FDI

According to data from Greenfield investment monitor fDi Markets, the most active foreign investor since the figures started being collected in 2003 has been the German trading and retail company Metro. In the past seven years, this firm has made 406 investments on a truly global basis. But in the past year, the firm appears to have slowed down the scale of its investments and expansion strategy. This year fDi Markets shows Metro has remained largely in the European market. Perhaps an indication of risk aversion. Apart from investments in Russia, Turkey and a few in Eastern Europe, the data suggests that Metro has greater interest in more developed economies. However, Metro's CFO, Olaf Koch, told fDi Magazine that Eastern Europe and Asia will figure largely in its expansion plans for 2011, specifically mentioning China, Russia and Turkey. He says: "Our international activities account for more than 60% of our sales volume. We want to accelerate our international growth with a focus on Eastern Europe and Asia. In particular, the fast-growing countries in Asia will play an increasingly important role in our expansion programme." Mr Koch cites new developments in China that will take place near Beijing, the Yangtze River Delta, Shanghai and the Pearl River Delta with Guangzhou.

25 January 2011

1.2.3 Motives

There are many reasons why a company may decide to do business abroad. In some cases, it just happens. The company stumbles across an interesting product abroad and decides to bring this product to Europe. Or one of its representatives accidentally meets a Turkish entrepreneur while on holiday in Turkey. They start talking and decide to collaborate, with the result that a truckload of ceramics comes from Turkey to Europe every month. Naturally, the most important reason is to earn money, but that is often not the case. Table 1.2 lists the principal motives. These can be divided into proactive and reactive motives. Proactive motives are derived from the policy that a company establishes to do business internationally, while reactive motives derive from a threat in the home market or the nature of the product.

Proactive motives

Reactive motives

1

TABLE 1.2 Motives for internationalisation

Proactive motives	Reactive motives
Profit and growth goals	Competitive pressure
Managerial urge	Small and/or saturated home market
Distinctiveness of the product	Utilisation of overproduction/excess capacity
Anticipating foreign market opportunities	Reduction of dependence on customers/ suppliers
Economies of scale	Stabilisation of seasonal factors
Integration of the supply chain	Proximity of customers/suppliers
Tax benefits	Perishable products

Source: Albaum et al., 2008, p. 76

An explanation of these motives follows at present.

Proactive motives
As stated above, proactive motives are derived from the company policy, i.e. with no external influence or threats. Seven proactive motives can be identified.

1 Profit and growth goals
Companies can come to the conclusion that their growth goals are no longer feasible in the domestic market because that market is fully covered. To be able to meet the formulated growth targets, management can decide to enter foreign markets.
Especially in the current economic environment, cost saving is an important factor. By moving production to low-wage countries, companies can make savings on production costs, and achieve more profit.

2 Managerial urge
The management board of the company has decided to internationalise. Management and staff are ready to accept this new challenge; travelling may be involved. This decision is sometimes strengthened because the management board consists of people from different cultures who see opportunities in their country of birth.

3 Distinctiveness of the product
A company can profile itself abroad with a product that positively distinguishes itself from other products.
Examples of distinguishing features are low price, superiority of the product quality, speed of delivery, design and good service. A company may supply goods or services that are not yet available worldwide. A product with high distinctiveness is difficult for competitors to copy. Some products have technological advantages in a certain area. It is, however, open to question how long these technological advantages will continue to exist because, of course, competitors will not just stand still.

4 Anticipating foreign market opportunities
International businesses often see more opportunities for growth in rapidly expanding countries than in countries where growth has clearly lagged

behind the rest of the world. For this reason, their investment policy is often focused on rapidly growing markets.
Sometimes it is cheaper to produce in one country than another. This depends on the costs of labour, raw materials, capital and infrastructure. The total of these costs determines where the product can be produced at the lowest price. The company will be interested in countries where its products can be made most cheaply, while maintaining good quality.

5 Economies of scale
Economists have shown that it is in some cases possible to reduce the cost price per unit by 10–30 % with every doubling of production quantity. This occurs above all if the production process can be standardised. A company can increase production by entering the international market. This can lead to a reduction in production costs, through which the company's competitive strength in the domestic market also increases.

6 Integration of the supply chain
Some companies practise forward or backward integration to gain more control over the whole chain, from the producer to the customer. The supply chain (see figure 1.3) can consist of: production of raw materials, production of components, production of finished product, wholesaling, retailing and after-sales service. Backward integration, for instance, may involve takeovers of production locations abroad. Forward integration can consist

FIGURE 1.3 Example of a supply chain

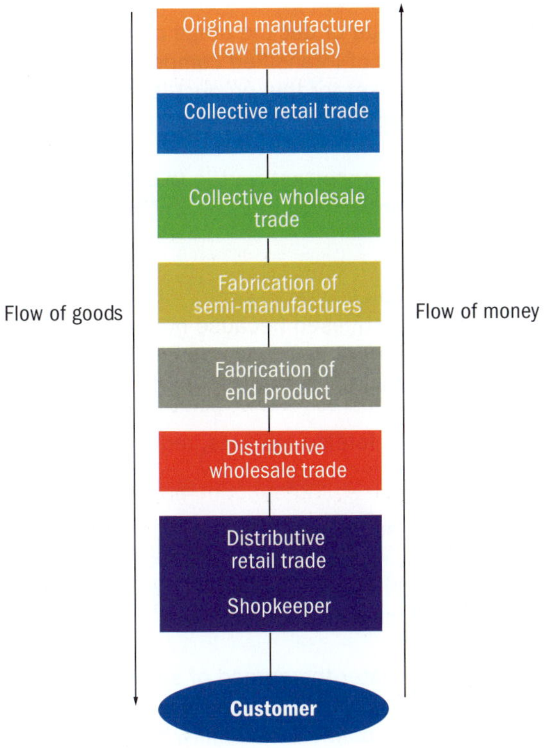

Source: http://www.businessmodellen.com

of taking over a chain of shops abroad. Various benefits arise from integration of the supply chain, such as savings on transaction costs, more power to negotiate with suppliers and purchasers about prices, less chance of products being out of stock and a reduction in overhead costs.

7 Tax benefits
Doing business abroad can also produce tax benefits, as in the case of withholding tax (tax that is deducted when interest, royalties or dividends are received from another country), which for certain countries can lead to exemption or restitution in Europe. Furthermore, no VAT has to be paid on foreign sales.

Reactive motives
Reactive motives arise from external influences or threats and not from the company policy.
Here, too, seven motives can be identified.

1 Competitive pressure
Some companies perceive the competition for a certain product on the domestic market as too intense, as a result of which profit margins can come under pressure, for example. A certain foreign market where the competition is less intense can offer an opportunity to make a reasonable profit. Increasing competition from foreign companies in the home market may also force the company, for financial or human reasons, to compensate for the loss of turnover by exporting products.

2 Small and/or saturated home market
When a product reaches the maturity stage or decline stage of its lifecycle, pressure on the price increases because of intensified competition. Suppose that in another country the market for this product is still in a growth stage. This can result in a decision of the company to enter the other, more lucrative, foreign market.
The size of the market naturally plays an important part in this decision. The market in Europe is small in comparison with markets in China, India and the US.

3 Utilisation of overproduction/excess capacity
If the production capacity is insufficiently utilised because no more products can be sold in the domestic market, entering a foreign market is an ideal way to utilise that capacity. By doing so, the total profit of an enterprise can finally increase.
Surplus stock can sometimes be sold to foreign markets, reducing stock costs to an acceptable level.

4 Reduced dependence on customers/suppliers
In general, the more suppliers a company has, the less chance there is of stock shortages. By doing business with suppliers in several countries, as soon as trade with a certain country declines, a company can switch over to suppliers in other countries.
The more clients a company has, the greater the spread of sales and the lower the risk of loss of turnover if a client is lost. Companies that do business with countries characterised by political instability, high inflation, a balance of payments deficit or sluggish economic growth are especially wise to spread their risk.

5 Stabilisation of seasonal factors
Some companies are troubled by seasonal factors, due to which their turnover in certain months is higher than in other months. For example, a European company sells more golf carts in the spring and summer than in the winter. By supplying golf carts to customers in countries where it is summer when it is winter in Europe (such as Australia and South Africa), seasonal fluctuations in turnover can be reduced.

6 Proximity of customers/suppliers
Because the distances within Europe are relatively small, it is fairly easy to enter these markets. That is why countries within Europe are the main business partners for European enterprises.

7 Perishable products
With perishable products (such as vegetables and flowers) and products that deteriorate in quality over time (such as washing powder), it would be a good idea to sell them abroad before it loses its quality.

Reactive motive: perishable product

1.3 European Union and international business

In this section we look at the performance of the European Union on the international stage. International trade as well as foreign direct investment are discussed. The prospects for world trade are also discussed. In the last section, a summary is given of agencies that assist entrepreneurs in international business.

1.3.1 European Union and international trade

According to data from Eurostat, import as well as export from all 27 EU member states increased compared to 2009. Especially Bulgaria, Latvia and Estonia show an increase in export. Sweden, Lithuania and Czech Republic illustrate the greatest growth when it comes to import.

The main business partners for the member states are the other member states. The main business partners outside the EU are the United States, China and Russia. Exports to Brazil even rose with 53%, but more has been exported also to China (+39%) and Turkey (+36%). Imports from Russia (+37%), China (+30%) and India (+28%) have also increased since 2009.

It seems that the European member states (see table 1.3) mostly import primary goods (food&beverages, raw materials and energy). Otherwise the member states have exported more processed goods (chemicals, machines & transportation) and services.

TABLE 1.3 Member States total trade (intra-EU + extra-EU)

	Total exports			**Total imports**			**Trade balance**	
	Jan–Sep 2009	**Jan–Sep 2010**	**Growth**	**Jan–Sep 2009**	**Jan–Sep 2010**	**Growth**	**Jan–Sep 2009**	**Jan–Sep 2010**
Belgium	195.6	230.5	18%	185.7	216.4	16%	9.8	14.1
Bulgaria	8.5	11.3	33%	12.5	13.5	9%	-4.0	-2.3
Czech Republic	59.4	72	21%	55.0	68.2	24%	4.4	3.7
Denmark	49.9	54.3	9%	44.1	46.8	6%	5.7	7.5
Germany	590.8	701.5	19%	492.9	588.0	19%	97.9	113.5
Estonia	4.8	6.1	28%	5.3	6.6	23%	-0.6	-0.5
Ireland	63.8	65.3	2%	33.8	33.4	-1%	30.0	31.8
Greece	10.7	11.0	3%	32.6	28.8	-12%	-21,8	-17,7
Spain	119.3	135.0	13%	153.3	174.0	13%	-34.0	-39.0
France	257.4	289.3	12%	295.1	335.7	14%	-37.7	-46.3
Italy	215.4	246.2	14%	219.5	265.4	21%	-4.1	-19.2
Cyprus	0.7	0.8	13%	4.2	4.5	8%	-3.5	-3.7
Latvia	4.0	5.1	29%	5.2	6.1	18%	-1.2	-1.0
Lithuania	8.6	11.0	28%	9.6	12.4	29%	-1.1	-1.4
Luxembourg	11.3	10.8	-4%	13.1	13.3	2%	-1.8	-2.5
Hungary	43.2	52.4	21%	40.7	48.4	19%	2.5	4.0
Malta	1.2	1.4	15%	2.3	2.3	3%	-1.1	-1.0
Netherlands	260.3	314.9	21%	231.8	284.3	23%	28.5	30.6
Austria	72.4	83.8	16%	75.7	87.0	15%	-3.3	-3.2
Poland	71.3	88.8	25%	78.3	95.9	22%	-7.1	-7.0
Portugal	23.4	27.0	16%	37.7	41.6	10%	-14.3	-14.6
Romania	21.2	26.8	26%	28.4	33.8	19%	-7.1	-7.0

	Total exports			Total imports			Trade balance	
	Jan–Sep 2009	Jan–Sep 2010	Growth	Jan–Sep 2009	Jan–Sep 2010	Growth	Jan–Sep 2009	Jan–Sep 2010
Slovenia	13.9	16.2	17%	13.9	16.3	17%	-0.1	-0.1
Slovakia	28.9	35.2	22%	28.7	35.6	24%	0.1	-0.4
Finland	32.6	37.0	14%	32.2	37.2	15%	0.4	-0.1
Sweden	69.0	86.2	25%	62.3	81.2	30%	6.7	5.0
United Kingdom	184.8	222.8	21%	255.3	307.6	20%	-70.5	-84.8

Source: http://epp.eurostat.ec.europa.eu/portal/page/portal/eurostat/home/

As shown by table 1.3, the 27 member states of the EU export more than they import. This is called an active trade balance; there is a trade surplus. This is often perceived as positive for a country, because more money comes into the country (money is paid for the products and services are exported) than is spent on imports. The opposite of this is a trade deficit, also called a passive trade balance. Because more money goes out of the country than comes in, this is often perceived as negative. Many developing countries have a passive trade balance. They are dependent on foreign countries for many goods and/or services.

Active trade balance
Trade surplus

Trade deficit
Passive trade balance

1.3.2 Europe and foreign direct investment

According to Eurostat, EU Foreign Direct Investment (FDI) flows have been severely affected by the global economic and financial crisis. They hit a record peak in 2007, but dropped sharply in 2008, for both inward and outward FDI flows (34 % for outflows, 52 % for inflows). While incoming FDI flows recovered slightly in 2009, EU investments abroad continued to decline (by 24%).

TABLE 1.4 EU-27 outward and inward FDI flows in 2006-2009 (EUR bn)

	Outward FDI flows					Inward FDI flows				
	2006	2007	2008	2009p	Share (%) in 2008	2006	2007	2008	2009p	Share (%) in 2008
Extra EU-27	313.0	530.7	347.7	263.3	100.0%	229.0	411.4	198.7	221.7	100.0%
Europe (non-EU, including EFTA) of which	74.1	130.6	103.7		29.8%	66.4	64.0	45.8		23.0%
Switzerland	21.9	39.9	34.0	44.8	9.8%	24.8	29.5	10.6	31.7	5.4%
Russia	11.3	17.2	25.6	-1.0	7.4%	1.5	9.9	2.3	3.1	1.2%
Croatia	4.5	2.7	2.0		0.6%	0.0	0.0	-0.2		-0.1%
Turkey	12.3	15.4	6.3		1.8%	-0.3	0.6	-0.2		-0.1%
Ukraine	2.1	3.0	4.8		1.4%	-0.1	0.4	0.5		0.2%

	Outward FDI flows					Inward FDI flows				
	2006	**2007**	**2008**	**2009p**	**Share (%) in 2008**	**2006**	**2007**	**2008**	**2009p**	**Share (%) in 2008**
Africa of which	11.7	17.9	18.5		5.3%	1.8	4.8	6.0		3.0%
Egypt	2.8	2.0	9.8		2.8%	0.1	-0.1	3.4		1.7%
South Africa	5.1	5.1	2.7		0.8%	0.9	1.8	0.5		0.2%
North America of which	135.8	198.7	129.3		37.2%	85.4	190.5	65.8		33.1%
Canada	31.0	29.8	7.8	2.8	2.3%	11.3	6.9	15.3	11.4	7.7%
United States	104.7	168.9	121.4	69.0	34.9%	74.1	183.5	50.5	96.8	25.4%
Central America of which	38.5	101.5	2.1		0.6%	33.0	75.6	-13.6		
Mexico	1.7	6.5	5.7		1.6%	0.3	0.4	0.9		0.5%
South America of which	13.0	17.6	9.6		2.7%	2.3	27.0	13.4		6.7%
Argentina	3.4	2.4	4.4		1.3%	0.0	0.1	-0.3		-0.1%
Brazil	5.4	14.3	-1.1	6.9	-0.3%	1.5	24.7	10.7	2.8	5.4%
Asia of which	28.5	53.9	70.1		20.2%	34.5	39.0	83.5		42.0%
Gulf Arabian Countries	2.3	4.6	18.9		5.4%	10.1	2.3	63.2		31.8%
China (excl. Hong Kong)	6.7	6.6	4.7	5.3	1.4%	2.2	0.8	-0.1	0.3	0.0%
Hong Kong	3.5	7.3	6.2	3.4	1.8%	-0.2	6.7	2.0	-0.2	1.0%
Japan	-1.6	10.3	5.9	0.1	1.7%	16.0	17.8	7.2	-2.3	3.6%
India	2.4	4.0	3.3	3.2	0.9%	0.5	1.0	3.7	0.4	1.9%
Singapore	9.5	8.5	15.2		4.4%	6.0	10.4	2.6		1.3%
Oceania of which	7.2	9.1	14.2		4.1%	7.0	6.7	-1.3		
Australia	6.7	8.6	12.8		3.7%	6.2	6.7	-0.9		-0.5%
Offshore Financial centers	58.9	150.8	39.4	60.3	11.3%	74.2	106.5	19.6	39.8	9.9%

2006–2008 annual FDI data. Preliminary figures for 2009 are based on annualised quarterly data.
Source: Eurostat

As can be concluded from table 1.4, the other EU member states are the main partners in the area of foreign direct investment in the EU. However the United States and the Arabic Gulf countries play a more important role in direct investments in the EU. It seems that FDI from Russia, China and India has increased substantially in the past few years. Especially the service sector in the EU is a prime sector for foreign investors.

1.3.3 Prospects for international business

The future of international as well as European trade is being influenced by the economic crisis. As can be seen from the article below, after a fierce year, slight growth in world trade is predicted for 2010.

Nevertheless, this slight recovery is fragile. According to the Central Plan Bureau in the Netherlands, this is above all due to the powerful recovery of the economy in Asia. Growth in Gross National Product (GNP) in the euro area is estimated at 1.25 per cent in 2010 and 1.75 per cent in 2011. That is very low in comparison with the pace that is usually achieved after a recession. The European Union is the world's biggest trader, accounting for 20% of global imports and exports. By 2015, 90 % of world growth will be generated outside Europe, with a third from China alone. So in the years to come, the EU needs to seize the opportunity of higher levels of growth abroad, especially in East and South Asia. Developing and emerging countries are likely to account for nearly 60 % of world GDP by 2030. This is compared to less than 50 % today.
China, now the EU's second biggest trade partner, is a source of both major opportunities and challenges. Given its tremendous growth potential, China is a major attraction for exports and investments. But there is no denying that some of China's industrial and macro-economic policies imply an approach based on state capitalism. There are similar issues in relation to Russia; the EU's biggest near neighbour.

Figure 1.4 shows that the biggest growth from GDP will be in Asia and South America. In these regions are the opportunities for the future.

FIGURE 1.4 Average Projected Real GDP Growth during 2010–2011 in percentage

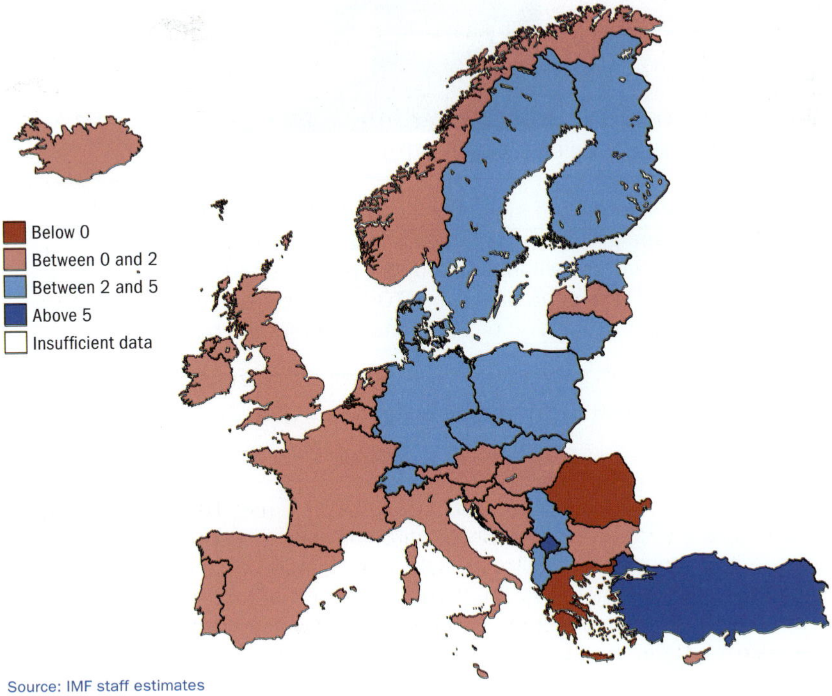

Source: IMF staff estimates

1

According to the World Trade Organization (WTO) extra-EU trade (external trade between the EU and the rest of the world) rose considerably faster than trade within the EU, which remained constrained by low economic activity. Asian exports rose by about 30% in the third quarter of 2010, as compared to the corresponding period of 2009. Exports from Africa and the Middle East were 22% higher than in the corresponding period of 2009 mainly due to the rebound of commodity prices after the crisis.

● www.parool.nl

WTO foresees 9.5 per cent growth in world trade

GENEVA – World trade is expected to grow by 9.5 per cent this year. This expectation was expressed by Pascal Lamy, Director of the World Trade Organization (WTO).

Pascal Lamy, Director of the World Trade Organization (WTO)

'After the biggest economic contraction since the Second World War, in 2009, our economists foresee growth in trade again in 2010,' says Lamy. Trade in developing countries will increase by 11 per cent and in industrialised countries by 7.5 per cent, said the WTO Director. 'This means that there is again light at the end of the tunnel and that is good news for the world economy.'

World trade shrank by 12 per cent in 2009 as a result of the worldwide economic crisis.

6 April 2010

1.4 International business organisations

There are many organisations that support and help companies to collect the right data. Advice that is given can relate to all aspects of international business. Table 1.5 lists these organisations by subject with relevant website addresses.

TABLE 1.5 Organisations that help with international business

Subject	Organisation	Internet address
International business	International Trade Centre	www.intracen.org
Exports	Market Acces Database	www.madb.europa.eu
Imports	Centre for the Promotion of Imports from Developing Countries	www.cbi.eu
Globalisation	Swiss Economic Institute (KOF)	www.globalization.kof.ethz.ch
		www.globalisation.com
	United Nations	www.unsystem.org
	United Nations Conference on Trade and Development	www. unctad.org
	G20	www.g20.org
International competitive strength	IMD	www.imd.ch
	World Economic Forum	www.weforum.org

1

Summary

- International business: economic activities across borders or actions that are necessary to do business abroad.
- Globalisation: the worldwide coalescence of economies, politics and cultures.
- Causes of globalisation:
  - opening of international borders
  - advent of the internet
  - development of low-wage countries
- Advantages of globalisation:
  - contributes to higher economic growth and prosperity
  - spreads technological knowledge
  - leads to widespread cultural integration
- Disadvantages of globalisation:
  - greater chance of wages in developed countries being undermined
  - increased exploitation of workers in less developed countries
  - gives multinationals a great deal of power
- Due to the disadvantages of globalisation, more and more attention is being paid to sustainable international business. Sustainable international business is based on three pillars:
  1 people
  2 planet
  3 profit
- The basis for international business is formed by international trade and foreign direct investment. International trade consists of import and export.
- Import is buying foreign products or services. The reasons for this are:
  - production in other countries is cheaper
  - the product/service is not yet available on the domestic market
- Export is selling foreign products or services. The motives for this are:
  - too small domestic market
  - new markets
  - continuity of the enterprise
  - price is competitive
  - overcapacity
- Foreign direct investments are investments made abroad by domestic companies.
- The principal motives for internationalisation can be divided into proactive and reactive motives (table 1.2).
- The most important trading partners for the European Union are United States, China and Russia.

Questions and assignments

Questions about the opening case

1.1 What form of international trade is carried out by Amazon?

1.2 What was Amazon's motive for starting international business?

● www.fd.nl

Eurobag: globalisation in a nutshell

'The wages are three to four times higher here than over the border on the Chinese mainland', says Alexander Kraima. 'Until recently we had 22 people here; now there are 14 and soon we shall have even fewer. It is simply cheaper in China,' he says.
Kraima is the Director of Eurobag in Hong Kong, a company that manufactures around 4 million bags annually. Eurobag supplies retailers like C&A and Scapino and brands like Reebok, Diadora and Lotto in Europe, Australia and Latin America. Furthermore, it carries out quality control for its parent company Pare, which under own management puts brands like Brunotti and Daniel-Ray on the European market.
The story that Kraima tells is a story of division of labour , specialisation and cost savings. It begins with the parent company in Drenthe (Pare), which started importing canvas bags from Asia at the beginning of the 1970s. At the beginning of the 90s, the company decided to open a branch in Hong Kong to organise the purchasing and quality control on site: Eurobag. That company developed into a connection between designers in the Netherlands, sample makers and manufacturers in China and clients all over the world.

4 June 2010, edited

1.3 Why is the article headed 'globalisation in a nutshell'?

1.4 What disadvantage of globalisation emerges strongly from this article?

1.5 Play the game Trade Ruler at http://nobelprize.org/educational_games/economics/trade/game/ruler.html.

1.6 Find the most recent import and export figures for the 27 European member states.

PERU PER

2 Political & economic environment

International business in a political and economic environment means that every type of business anywhere in the world has to take note of worldwide trade policies. Trade policy is the sum of all the measures a government can take to control foreign trade. Trade policy therefore affects companies operating internationally.
In this chapter we discuss international and European trade policy. Finally, we look at international organisations that wish to promote free world trade and the OECD guidelines with regard to corporate social responsibility. They offer a basic outline for corporate codes of conduct or how to deal with social issues like child labour, environmental impact and corruption.

Apple admits to using child labour

Apple has admitted that child labour was used at the factories that build its computers, iPods and mobile phones. At least eleven 15-year-old children were discovered to be working in three factories that supply Apple last year.

The company did not name the offending factories, or say where they were based, but the majority of its goods are assembled in China. Apple also has factories in Taiwan, Singapore, the Philippines, Malaysia, Thailand, the Czech Republic and the United States.

Apple said the child workers are now no longer being used, or are no longer underage. "In each of the three facilities, we required a review of all employment records for the year as well as a complete analysis of the hiring process to clarify how underage people had been able to gain employment," Apple said, in an annual report on its suppliers.

Apple has been repeatedly criticized for using factories that abuse workers and where conditions are poor. Last year, an employee at Foxconn, the Taiwanese company that is one of Apple's biggest suppliers, committed suicide after being accused of stealing a prototype for the iPhone.

China Labor Watch, a New York-based NGO, accused Foxconn of having an "inhumane and militant" management, which neglects basic human rights. Apple admitted that at least 55 of the 102 factories that produce its goods were ignoring Apple's rule that staff cannot work more than 60 hours a week.

The technology companies own guidelines are already in breach of China's widely ignored labour law, which sets out a maximum 49-hour week for workers. Apple also said that one of its factories had repeatedly falsified its records. "When we investigated, we uncovered records and conducted worker interviews that revealed excessive working hours and seven days of continuous work." Only 65 per cent of the factories were paying their staff the correct wages and benefits, and Apple found 24 factories where workers had not even been paid China's minimum wage of around 800 Yuan a month.

Edited source: The Telegraph, 27 February 2010

2.1 Free trade

Free international business benefits from the free movement of goods and services. Due to this, the consumer has a wider choice of products. Competition between imported and local products pushes prices down and quality up.

The European Union (EU) is the world's biggest trader, accounting for 20% of global imports and exports. The trade policy of EU-members is primarily determined by the Common Trade Policy of the European Union. The EU strives for the harmonious development of fair and sustainable world trade. This resulted in trade barriers disappearing within the EU. The EU removed the obstacles of imports and exports and businesses are now free to transport and sell goods throughout the EU. Through liberalised trade, the most efficient producers in the EU will be able to compete with producers in other countries in a fair manner.

European Union
Common Trade Policy

To help developing countries, the EU is prepared to open its market to exports from those countries.

Furthermore, within the EU, a single import tariff is applied. Thus the same tariff is paid for imported products regardless of whether they are imported into the EU via the port of Rotterdam or from Hamburg. A Korean car for which import duty has been paid on arrival in Germany can be shipped to Belgium without the need to pay extra import duty or VAT.

Free trade is restricted in two ways:

1 by **regional trading arrangements** between a number of countries
2 by limiting trade to protect the economy (**protectionism** – see section 2.4)

2.2 Regional trading arrangements

There are various forms of economic cooperation. The objective of regional trading arrangement is to reduce trade barriers between the member countries. They merely remove tariffs on intrabloc trade in goods. Sometimes it also covers nontariff barriers and extend liberalization to trade and investment. The most common forms of cooperation are:

Economic cooperation

- free-trade bloc
- customs union
- common market

An Economic and Monetary Union is another type of trade bloc.

2.2.1 Free-trade bloc

In this intrabloc trades area there are no trade restrictions among the participating countries. For trade with other (non-participating) countries, each participant operates its own customs policy.

Countries strive for free trade because this form of trade has advantages:

- an efficient use of factors of production
- stimulation of competition
- prevention of trade wars
- promotion of trade and investment
- promotion of welfare

Examples of Regional Integration Agreements are the European Free Trade Association (EFTA) and The North American Free Trade Agreement (NAFTA).

EFTA comprises Norway, Switzerland, Iceland and Liechtenstein. Their goal is the promotion of free movement of people, goods, services and capital among these countries. There is also economic collaboration.
EFTA countries, with the exception of Switzerland, have an agreement with the EU: together, they form the European Economic Area (EEA). The following countries therefore belong to the EEA:

- The European Union countries
- Liechtenstein
- Norway
- Iceland

NAFTA comprises Canada, the USA and Mexico. This agreement strives to abolish impediments to trade and investment between the United States, Canada and Mexico. For example, it has lifted trade barriers on agricultural products between the United States and Mexico.

2.2.2 Customs union

A customs union exists when two or more countries abolish all mutual import tariffs. Besides mutual free trade, the participating countries have a joint external tariff; that is to say, with respect to non-member countries the same import duties are levied.

Joint external tariff

A customs union is therefore a comprehensive free-trade association. The problem of the final destination of imported goods is irrelevant here because the participating countries levy the same tariff for non-member countries.
A customs union is necessary because otherwise importers would import goods into the country with the lowest import duties and subsequently transport them to a country with high import duties.
Examples of customs unions are Mercosur and the (partial) union between the EU and Turkey.

Mercosur

Mercosur was established in 1991 and comprises the following countries: Argentina, Brazil, Paraguay and Uruguay. The goal of the organisation is to promote free trade and the free traffic of goods, people and capital. Bolivia, Chile, Colombia, Ecuador, Peru and Venezuela are associate members.
Mercosur is now the fourth-largest economic power in the world after the EU, the USA and Japan.

Turkey and the EU

The customs union between the EU and Turkey means that no import duties are levied on Turkish trade with the EU. An exception is made for olive oil and certain agricultural products. These remain outside the provisions of the customs union for the present.

DAILY NEWS, 19 NOVEMBER 2010 (EDITED SOURCE)

Turkey and the EU: Time for a new dynamic

It is EU accession that we are talking about when it comes to EU-Turkey relations, and nothing short of it.
Thanks to Turkey's commitment to its strategic goal of EU accession, its reforms have a clear European footprint. Democracy, fundamental rights and the rule of law are being steadily strengthened. Legislation is aligned more and more with EU standards. The economy, already highly integrated with the EU through the customs union, is thriving. More and more Turkish citizens come to know and work together with their EU fellows, be it in educational exchange programs, civil society initiatives or business joint ventures. Our knowledge of each other goes well beyond diplomatic and official contacts.
Turkey's transformation is still work in progress. As EU-Turkey relations deepen, we will come across issues that require hard work to resolve. Time has come for Turkey to normalize relations with all EU member states it negotiates accession with. It is now urgent that Turkey fully implements its obligations under the customs union. By doing so, Turkey would take the moral high ground of a country that delivers on its commitments, and which expects others to do so too. This would be the biggest impetus that Turkey could give right now to its accession process.

2.2.3 Common market

A common market is a customs union supplemented by provisions concerning the stimulation of mutual trade. The EU is a common market. There is free traffic of goods, factors of production and services within the 27 EU countries. On all products originating in the EU, no import duties are levied. If goods are imported from outside the EU, there is an EU-standard import duty for and every member state. In this way, the community strives for, among other things:

- the harmonious, balanced and sustainable development of economic activity
- a high level of protection and improvement of standards of living and quality of life
- solidarity among the member states

The EU also fully supports the fight against trademark pirates, the recognition of technical standards and the effort to improve the position of third-world countries in the world market.
Although the EU constitutes only 7 per cent of the world's population, its

trade with the rest of the world accounts for around 20 per cent of world trade. The mutual trade among the EU member states accounts for two-thirds of all EU trading.

TABLE 2.1 EU countries listed alphabetically

No	Country	Inhabitants (× 1,000)	Area (km² × 1,000)	GNP ($, billions)
	Total	491,820	4,425.2	14,868.0
1	Austria	8,210	83.9	323.1
2	Belgium	10,414	30.5	381.0
3	Bulgaria	7,205	110.9	90.5
4	Cyprus	1,085	9.3	23.0
5	Czech Republic	10,212	78.9	256.6
6	Denmark	5,549	44.5	200.2
7	Estonia	1,299	45.2	24.4
8	Finland	5,250	338.1	182.6
9	France	64,058	643.4	2.110.0
10	Germany	82,330	357.0	2,811.0
11	Greece	10,737	132.0	341.0
12	Hungary	9,906	93.0	184.9
13	Ireland	4,203	70.3	176.9
14	Italy	58,126	301.3	1.760.0
15	Latvia	2,232	64.6	32.4
16	Lithuania	3,555	65.3	54.8
17	Luxembourg	492	2.6	38.4
18	Malta	405	0.3	9.8
19	The Netherlands	16,716	41.5	654.9
20	Poland	38,483	312.7	690.1
21	Portugal	10,708	92.1	233.4
22	Romania	22,215	238.4	255.4
23	Slovakia	5,463	49.0	115.7
24	Slovenia	2,006	20.3	55.8
25	Spain	40,525	505.4	1.368.0
26	Sweden	9,060	450.3	333.5
27	United Kingdom	61,376	244.4	2.160.6
	Total	491,820	4,425.2	14.868.0

GNP: Gross National Product

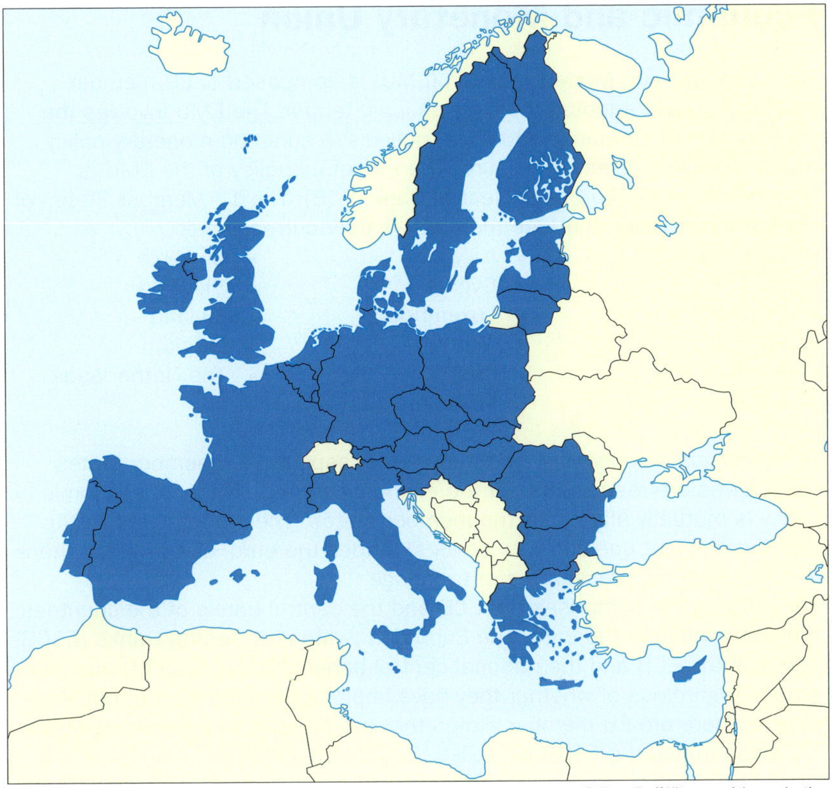

The European Union

SOLVIT

The internal market offers citizens and businesses many opportunities. While the Internal Market generally works well, mistakes are sometimes made. For example, a business could be faced with administrative obstacles, unjustified refusal of access to a national market or problems in getting reimbursement of VAT. Sometimes these problems arise because of a lack of information about the rights in Europe and about how procedures work in other EU member states. SOLVIT is an on-line problem-solving network in which EU member states work together to solve, without legal proceedings, problems caused by the misapplication of Internal Market law by public authorities. There is a SOLVIT centre in every European Union Member State (as well as in Norway, Iceland and Liechtenstein). SOLVIT Centres may assist with handling complaints from both citizens and businesses. They are part of the national administration and are committed to providing real solutions to problems within ten weeks. The main objective has been to promote convergence of competition policy instruments and practices across countries, and to facilitate cooperation with competing authorities in other countries.

SOLVIT

2.3 Economic and Monetary Union

The Economic and Monetary Union (EMU) is composed of EU member states that have adopted the euro as legal tender. The EMU involves the coordination of economic and fiscal policies, a common monetary policy, and a common currency, the euro. The monetary policy of the EMU is determined by the European Central Bank (ECB). The 17 Member States of the European Union that use the euro as their currency are:

- Germany
- Estonia
- Ireland
- Greece
- Spain
- France
- Italy
- Cyprus
- Luxembourg
- Malta
- Austria
- Portugal
- Slovenia
- Slovakia
- Finland
- Belgium
- The Netherlands

The EMU has an economic and a monetary aspect. The member states themselves are responsible for the economic aspect. National economic policy is mutually aligned by the member states. The monetary aspect is that there is just one currency as legal tender, the euro, due to which there are no longer reciprocal rates of exchange.

Eurosystem

The Eurosystem comprises the ECB and the central banks of the countries that have adopted the euro. The European System of Central Banks (ESCB) contains the ECB and the national central banks (NCBs) of all EU member states, regardless of whether they have implemented the euro or not. As long as there are EU member states that are not part of the euro zone, the Eurosystem and the ESCB will exist alongside each other.

2.4 Protectionism

Protectionism is defined as the measures that the government of a country takes to protect its own economy against international competition. The World Trade Organization (WTO) combats protectionism in a number of ways. One way is by making sure that member countries abide by the WTO rules governing protectionist trading.

Measures to restrict the import of goods from other countries are taken, for example, to:

- advance employment in the home country
- counteract dumping (very cheap sales)
- keep the balance of payments in equilibrium (see chapter 5)
- improve the terms of trade (see chapter 5)
- provide the government with more revenue
- boycott particular countries for political reasons

THE BUSINESS DAILY AFRICA, 11 NOVEMBER 2010 (EDITED SOURCE)

Protectionism hinders merger of regional blocs

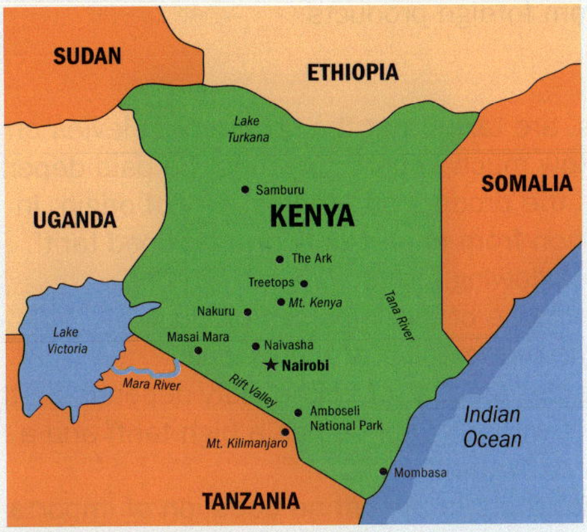

Some countries' reluctance to liberalise their economies could derail the planned merger of three regional market blocs, warned trade ministry permanent secretary of Kenya while calling for a common approach in the elimination of barriers to trade.

"While it is true that there may be justifiable reasons for seeking short term protection due to revenue, health, environment and other reasons, our respective treaties have clearly outlined how such time-bound protection measures can be justified and made available to our member states," he said in a statement.

Reluctance by countries to fully open up their markets under the arrangement, however, remains controversial amidst concern that some are imposing non-tariff barriers (NTB) which frustrate merger efforts.

There are two ways to protect one's own economy, including by means of:

1 measures that cost money (tariff) and
2 measures that set requirements for trade (non-tariff). These are also called 'new protectionism'.

Tariff
Non-tariff

The flow of goods between the EU and non-EU countries can be restricted by these measures. Non-tariff measures are based on European and/or international legislation. In most cases, these measures result in goods being subject to an extra control or to qualitative or other restrictions. In some cases, there is prohibition.

The most important tariff measures are:
- import duties
- turnover tax
- excise duties
- preferential tariff measures

These measures are discussed in sub-section 2.4.1.

The most important non-tariff measures are:
- customs formalities
- technical requirements
- administrative procedures
- quality requirements

- export restrictions
- subsidies

These measures are discussed in sub-section 2.4.2.

2.4.1 Tariff measures

Tariff measures are all measures that cost money. They protect a country's products against competition from foreign products.

Import duties

Import duties, also called tariffs, are taxes that the government levies on imported goods and services. How much import duty must be paid depends on a number of factors, such as the product and the country of origin. In some cases, there is an exemption from import duty or a reduced tariff. Import duties can appear in the following forms:

- specific: a fixed amount per volume of the imported product
- ad valorem: a fixed percentage of the value of the product
- sliding or variable scale: here the amount of import duty depends on the price of the product. A product with a low price has a high tariff and a product with a high price has a low tariff
- prohibitive: a tariff so high that there is almost no question of importation
- implicit: the tariffs are structured such that raw materials are taxed at a low rate and end products are taxed highly

The amount of import duty payable depends on the CN code and the country of origin of the goods.
What is the CN code?
In accordance with internationally agreed classification rules, goods that can be traded freely are assigned a code. This code is based on an international standard, the Harmonised System. The Harmonised System (HS) has been developed into a European standard, the Combined Nomenclature (CN) – see the diagram on the following page. Because of this, all EU countries apply the same codes, comprising eight digits, for the declaration of goods. Based on this code, the application of tariff and non-tariff measures on the goods can be checked. The List of Goods for International Trade can be retrieved from the website of the European Union: www.hscode.org and http://eurlex.europa.eu.

Import into the EU

Import duties are the same in the entire EU. In terms of import duties, it makes therefore no difference via which country goods are imported into the EU. The online customs tariff database, also called the TARIC (http://ec.europa.eu/taxation_customs/common/databases/index_en.htm), is a database in which all measures relating to tariff, commercial and agricultural legislation are integrated. The TARIC ensures uniform application of the rules by all Member States, and gives a clear view of all measures to be undertaken when importing goods.

Export from the EU

The European Commission makes sure that trade opportunities are translated into real market access for European exporters. The Market

CN code	Description	Conventional rate of duty (%)	Supplementary unit
1	2	3	4
6401	**Waterproof footwear with outer soles and uppers of rubber or of plastics, the uppers of which are neither fixed to the sole nor assembled by stitching, riveting, nailing, screwing, plugging or similar processes:**		
6401 10 00	**– Footwear incorporating a protective metal toecap**	17	pa
	– Other footwear:		
6401 92	**– – Covering the ankle but not covering the knee:**		
6401 92 10	– – – With uppers of rubber	17	pa
6401 92 90	– – – With uppers of plastics	17	pa
6401 99 00	**– – Other**	17	pa
6402	**Other footwear with outer soles and uppers of rubber or plastics:**		
	– Sports footwear:		
6402 12	**– – Ski-boots, cross-country ski footwear and snowboard boots:**		
6402 12 10	– – – Ski-boots and cross-country ski footwear	17	pa
6402 12 90	– – – Snowboard boots	17	pa
6402 19 00	**– – Other**	16,9	pa
6402 20 00	**– Footwear with upper straps or thongs assembled to the sole by means of plugs** ...	17	pa
	– Other footwear:		
6402 91	**– – Covering the ankle:**		
6402 91 10	– – – Incorporating a protective metal toecap	17	pa
6402 91 90	– – – Other	16,9	pa

Access Strategy pays particular attention to the needs of EU exporters that want to export to or invest in non-EU countries.
The *Market Access Database* (http://madb.europa.eu/mkaccdb2/indexPubli.htm), an interactive free online service, provides information for EU exporters about more than 100 countries on:

- the import tariff and internal taxes
- the import formalities (e.g. customs procedures and requirements) with samples of all the necessary forms, and
- the most important trade barriers faced by EU exporters abroad.

Turnover taxes (VAT)

Turnover tax

For the supply of goods and services, companies must pay turnover tax. This turnover tax is better known as VAT (value added tax). The VAT in the European Union is a general, broadly based consumption tax assessed on the value added to goods and services. It applies more or less to all goods and services that are bought and sold for use or consumption in the Community. Thus, goods that are sold for export or services that are sold to customers abroad are normally not subject to VAT. Imports are taxed to keep the system fair for EU producers so that they can compete on equal terms on the European market with suppliers situated outside the Union.

Value added tax is:

1 a general tax that applies, in principle, to all commercial activities involving the production and distribution of goods and the provision of services.
2 consumption tax because it is not a charge on businesses but the final consumer.

3 charged as a percentage of price, which means that the actual tax burden is visible at each stage in the production and distribution chain.
4 collected via a system of partial payments whereby taxable persons (i.e., VAT-registered businesses) deduct the amount of tax they have paid to other taxable persons on purchases for their business activities from the VAT they have collected.
5 paid to the revenue authorities by the seller of the goods, who is the "taxable person", but it is actually paid by the buyer to the seller as part of the price. It is thus an indirect tax.

Excise duties

Excise duty is a consumer (indirect) tax on the consumption or the use of certain products. In contrast to Value Added Tax (VAT), it is mainly a specific tax, i.e. expressed as a monetary amount per quantity of the product. Excise duties are commonly applied on

a alcoholic beverages
b manufactured tobacco products and cenergy products (motor fuels and heating fuels, such as petrol and gasoline, electricity, natural gas, coal and coke).

All EU Member States apply excise duties to these three product categories. The revenue from excise duties accrues entirely to the Member States.

● www.ec.europa.eu

EU and US launch joint website against counterfeiting and piracy

International trade in counterfeit and pirated goods is estimated at $250 billion a year. With a view to encourage SMEs to break into foreign markets and avoid risks in terms of the violation of their intellectual property rights (IPR), the US and Europe are joining forces. On the occasion of the Transatlantic Economic Council in Washington a new website is launched, the TransAtlantic IPR Portal, offering guidance to enterprises in the EU and the US that wish to successfully do business in other countries. The portal is part of the mission to strengthen cooperation between the EU and the USA.

17 December 2010

Preferential tariff measures

Preferential tariff measures are measures that result in certain products being wholly or partially exempted from import duties. These measures can apply:

- to a certain product
- to products originating from a certain country
- for a certain period

Preferential tariff measures can be divided into four types:
a tariff preferences
b quotas
c special destinations
d anti-dumping duty

Ad a Tariff preferences
A tariff preference is a commercial policy measure, whereby it is possible to import certain goods from a developing country at a reduced or zero tax rate. These import duties can be divided into autonomous and conventional duties. Autonomous import duties are established unilaterally by a country and applied to all other countries. Conventional import duties are established in a trade treaty after negotiations with a counter party. This is called the preferential system.

Autonomous import duty
Conventional import duty

Whether a tariff preference means zero tax rate or a reduced tariff can differ from year to year. A large supply of imported products can be a reason to end or adjust preferences for a certain product. Tariff preferences on the EU market enable developing countries to participate more fully in international trade. The objectives of these developing countries are:
- increased export income
- promotion of industrialisation
- accelerated economic growth

The EU has concluded preferential trade agreements with the following countries or groups of countries:
- Group A: Developing countries General System of Preferences (GSP). The list of countries that belong to the GSP ranges from Afghanistan to Zambia. The complete list can be found in EC Council Regulation No 732/2008 on: http://eurlex.europe.eu.
- Group B: EUR-1 and EUR-MED countries.
  The EU has trade agreements with a number of countries and groups of countries. In order to profit from the preferential rate during a customs clearance, a EUR-1 certificate, in short EUR-1, must be handed over to the competent authority (usually a customs administration). The treaties and corresponding areas/countries are:
  – Pan-Euro-Mediterranean agreement (EUR-MED)
  – EEA (Norway, Iceland, Liechtenstein and the EU)
  – Europe agreements (Turkey Agricultural, Turkey EGKS, Switzerland and the EU)
  – Magreb (Morocco, Tunisia, Algeria)
  – Mashrek (Egypt, Lebanon, Jordan, Syria)
  – Faroes, Ceuta, Mellila, Israel, Palestinian Authority
  – Countries in Africa, the Caribbean region and South Pacific (ACS)
  – Countries Areas Overseas (LGO), South Africa
  – Croatia, Bosnia-Herzegovina, Serbia, Kosovo, Macedonia, Montenegro (all with separate agreements), Albania, Moldavia
  – Mexico, Chile

To benefit from these agreements, the goods must originate in one of these ‘agreement areas’.

EXAMPLE

For a Norwegian exporter shipping a product from Norway to Belgium, either the Agreement establishing the European Economic Area or the EC-Norway Agreement applies.

Source: http://ec.europa.eu/taxation_customs/resources/documents

EXAMPLE

The EFTA/Egypt Agreement would apply to goods exported by an Icelandic exporter to Egypt. (Iceland signed the Agreement with Egypt not in its own right but as a Member State of EFTA).

Source: http://ec.europa.eu/taxation_customs/resources/documents

EXAMPLE

A Jordanian producer who wishes to export goods to the West Bank and Gaza Strip will refer to the agreement between Jordan and the West Bank and Gaza Strip.

Source: http://ec.europa.eu/taxation_customs/resources/documents

- Group C: Turkey
  The EU has a customs union with Turkey. With an ATR certificate, most goods can be mutually imported free of duty. This is further discussed in chapter 10.

EXAMPLE

A Turkish exporter who wishes to ship a product from Turkey to the United Kingdom will operate within the provisions of the agreement between Turkey and the European Community. In this case as the United Kingdom is a Member State of the European Community it is the agreement between the exporter's country and the EC that applies.

EXAMPLE

Turkish goods exported to Morocco will be subject to the terms of the agreement between Turkey and Morocco.

Source: http://ec.europa.eu/taxation_customs/resources/documents

Ad b Quotas

Quantitative restrictions

It is possible that the preferential tariff measures described above are connected with quantities. This means that imports at a reduced or zero tax rate are subject to quantitative restrictions, otherwise known as quotas or ceilings. The allocation of quotas takes place in Brussels. There are also quantitative restrictions for textiles and agricultural products. Once the quota has been reached, it is still possible to import the product in question but at the general, higher tariff.

Quotas are managed by the application of one of the following methods or a combination thereof:

1 According to traditional trade flows: part of the quota is reserved for importers or exporters who can demonstrate that they have imported or exported the product or the products covered by the quota during a preceding period.
2 According to the principle of 'first come, first served'.
3 In relation to the quantities requested. The EU commission proceeds with an investigation of the data supplied by the member states and establishes the size of quota for which agencies must issue import or export licenses.

EXAMPLE

A company imports 20,000 sweaters from Peru. For these sweaters, 10 per cent import duty is paid because Peru is a GSP country. However, there is a tariff quota for sweaters. An application is made to the CSIE. After investigation in Brussels, the company is allocated a tariff reduction for 10,000 sweaters. This means that 10 per cent import duty can be claimed only for this number. For the remaining 10,000 sweaters, a higher import duty must be paid, for example 13.5 per cent.

Ad c Special destinations
A destination right means that the import tariff is reduced provided that the goods are going to a certain destination and/or will undergo certain treatment. It therefore applies to goods for which lower import duties apply than to the same goods without this special destination.
Examples of special destinations are materials destined for the seats of aeroplanes, live horses destined for breeding and raw sugar cane for refining.

Ad d Anti-dumping duty
If foreign companies offer goods at a price that is lower than the cost price in the recipient country or the price in the producing country, it is referred to as dumping.

● www.bike-eu.com

China's Bike Industry Campaigns for Drop of Anti-Dumping Duties

BRUSSELS, Belgium – After first issuing statements on the cumulated losses the bike industry in China endured during the 17 years of European anti-dumping duties, the country is now knocking on doors in Brussels to avoid another 5 year term of extra levies on its exported bikes. Jiang said the EU industry actually enjoyed higher profitability and a larger market share despite the economic crisis and rising competition. "The European manufacturers managed to sell at a price of 20% higher in 2009, as compared to what they did five years ago. And despite the strong competition with Asian imports the European bicycle industry is still strong, producing more than 60% of the EU market consumption. At the hearing the delegation from the Chinese industry also brought forward that the lack of competition results in European consumers having to pay an unjustifiable higher price and that they are deprived of better choice. Further, said the delegation, the anti-dumping measures are interfering with EU's 'green transport' campaign.

17 December 2010

Dumping is used to get rid of production surpluses, acquire market share or eliminate the competition and thereby obtain a monopoly position, for example. Dumping results in price decay in the importing country.

Monopoly position

Once it has been established that dumping has occurred and that other suppliers have suffered losses, the government can impose a dumping tax in addition to the import tariff on the importing country or the EU: an anti-dumping duty. This increases the selling price so much that the advantage of dumping is eliminated.

An anti-dumping duty is not imposed randomly. Worldwide, in the context of the WTO, agreements have been made about the imposition of anti-dumping duties. Based on a complaint about dumping to the European Commission, a thorough investigation is performed. The Commission examines the complaint on four criteria:

1 Is this a case of dumping?
2 Have losses been incurred?
3 Is there a causal relationship between the losses and the dumping?
4 Are the anti-dumping measures in the interests of the European Community?

2.4.2 Non-tariff measures

Non-tariff measures include all measures taken by the government to restrict imports of foreign goods, such as:

- customs formalities
- administrative procedures
- technical requirements
- quality requirements
- subsidies
- export restrictions

Customs formalities and administrative procedures

Customs formalities are related to the import, export and transit of goods to and from non-EU countries. A declaration must be made to customs before the goods can be delivered. The customs service can require additional documents for certain goods and/or demand an inspection. This can be time-consuming and therefore obstructive.

EXAMPLE

With imports of chemical substances from outside the EU, such as tins of paint, tubes of glue, clothing, batteries, car components or office articles, the importer is responsible for any legally required (pre-) registration of the imported substances with the European Agency for Chemical Substances (ECHA) in Helsinki (REACH).

There can also be a trade embargo. This means that there is a ban on trading with a certain country for socio-political reasons, for example. There is currently a partial trade embargo with Iraq.

Trade embargo

Technical requirements

If a great many technical requirements and regulations are imposed on products that are imported into the Europe, it is less attractive for foreign companies to export to Europe.

For trade within the EU member states, there is the principle of mutual recognition. This means that if a product has been lawfully manufactured in a member state, this product may not be banned in another member state, even if the product differs from the prescribed technical or quality regulations of that other member state. Exceptions are only made if there is a danger to public safety, health or the environment. But there is also a local content requirement. This requirement means that imported products can be exempted from trade barriers only if a large part of the added value of the end product is achieved in the home market.

EXAMPLE

Imports of fresh meat and meat products into the European Union are subject to veterinary certification, which is based on the recognition of the competent authority of the non-EU country by the Directorate-General for Health and Consumer Protection. This formal recognition of the reliability of the competent authority is a pre-requisite for the country to be eligible and authorized for export to the European Union. Legally and adequately empowered authorities in the exporting country must ensure credible inspection and controls throughout the production.

CE mark

Conformité Européenne (CE) is a European standard that indicates that a product complies with certain minimum requirements. It is therefore not a mark of quality but an indication that the product complies with requirements in the fields of safety, health, environment and consumer protection. Manufacturers and importers trading outside the EEA must apply the CE mark to all products covered by the New Approach Guidelines. When imports come from countries outside the EEA, the importer is regarded as a manufacturer. It is the responsibility of the importer to affix the CE mark.

Origin marking

For export to countries outside the EU, for example the USA, origin marking is not mandatory. Within the EU, origin marking ('Made in ...') is not mandatory either. It is, however, mandatory to specify the manufacturer or importer on the packaging of a product. National legislation can impose additional requirements. The manufacturer can apply origin marking if the product has been wholly obtained in the marked country or the product has undergone sufficient modification or processing there.

EXAMPLE

A clothing manufacturer imports textiles from the USA and makes coats in Italy. The processing of the textiles is sufficient to apply the origin marking 'Made in Italy'. The manufacturer could equally apply 'Made in the EU'.

Indication of the country of origin is mandatory if the trademark contains a geographic image, flag, drawing or person, for example, which could suggest a different origin.

EXAMPLE

A perfume manufacturer has a drawing of the Eiffel Tower on its label. The brand has been registered with the trademark office and the raw materials are entirely obtained in Germany. From the draw of the Eiffel Tower on the label, however, consumers get the impression that it is a French perfume. In this case, the design of the label is associated with a country or region where the goods have not been produced. To avoid such confusion, the manufacturer must apply an origin marking.

Regarding the label 'Made in the EU' there are two main rules:

1 The goods must have been obtained in the EU.
  Example: minerals that are mined in the various countries of the EU.
2 If the accumulation of economic operations in two or more EU countries on a product or raw materials from a third country results in a new product, the product fulfils the origin criterion. The last manufacturer may then add 'Made in the EU' to the label.

Subsidies and export restrictions

An alternative policy is to provide a subsidy (a direct payment) to domestic producers to improve their competitiveness in both the home and world market. Most commonly governments provide other types of assistance to firms to make it cheaper or more profitable for them to sell overseas. For example, the countries offer their potential exporters an array of services, including the provision of information, sponsorship of trade expositions, and establishment of contacts for businesses overseas.
Export restrictions are limitations on the quantity of goods exported to a specific country or countries by a government in a given year. The most common type of import or export restriction from a quantity basis is the quota. From the standpoint of imports, a quota limits the quantitative amount of a product allowing to be imported in a given year.

● www.engineeringnews.co.za

Export restrictions play major role in food price increases

As global food prices once again increase sharply, World Trade Organisation director-general Pascal Lamy reiterated that trade could play an important role in addressing the rise in food prices, and tackling food insecurity.
Export restrictions play a major role in food crises, he stated. Lamy said that the 2010/11 price rise for cereals had much to do with the export

restrictions of Russia and Ukraine, which were imposed after both countries were hit by severe drought.
"These restrictions hurt net-food-importing countries; and could actually starve them. Export restrictions were just one element of the trade barriers preventing efficient agricultural markets from emerging, and Lamy said that the Doha Round of trade negotiations could contribute to the medium-to-long term response to food price crises, by removing many of the restrictions and distortions that have harmed the supply-side picture.

24 January 2011

2.5 International organisations

Liberalisation

International trade is growing by 6% annually. The United Nations (UN), the World Trade Organization (WTO), the World Bank and the International Monetary Fund (IMF), among others, are international organisations that wish to promote the liberalisation of world trade. Furthermore, the OECD has developed guidelines as to what governments expect of companies. They constitute a model for the codes of conduct of companies with regard to social issues in international business.

2.5.1 United Nations

The UN is an international organisation founded in 1945, just after the Second World War. It is a worldwide organisation of governments that collaborate in the fields of international law, global security, the preservation of human rights, the development of the world economy and research into socio-cultural developments. The principles of the UN are established in the *United Nations Charter*.

The principles and objectives described in the charter are, among others:
- the maintenance of international peace and security
- the development of amicable relations on the basis of respect for equal rights and the self-determination of nations
- attaining international collaboration in the resolution of global issues of an economic, social, cultural and humanitarian nature
- the promotion of respect for human rights and fundamental freedoms

Within the UN there are also specialist organisations. In the context of international business, the following specialist financial organisations are of interest:
- International Monetary Fund (IMF)
- International Labour Organisation (ILO)
- World Intellectual Property Organisation (WIPO)

These will be discussed in an other section. In addition, the UN has established UNCTAD for trade and development.
UNCTAD stands for United Nations Conference on Trade and Development and it has the important task of ensuring that all countries are involved in global trade. UNCTAD promotes the development-friendly integration of

THE GUARDIAN UK, 01 JANUARY 2011

Do UN Women need to make a difference?

UN Women become operational today, but will it have the clout and the funds to end gender discrimination around the world?

January 1st marks an important day in these women's lives, and in the life of every woman around the world. UN Women, the UN entity for gender equality and the empowerment of women, becomes operational today. Gender inequality remains deeply entrenched in every society. Women everywhere suffer violence and discrimination, and are under-represented in political and economic decision-making processes. There are millions of women and girls in developing countries who could and should play a part in their countries' economic development, but are not. Gender inequality means poverty passes from generation to generation. In rural Bangladesh, poor families who do not have enough food for their children prioritise feeding their sons, because it is they who will provide for their parents in their old age. As a result, daughters are underfed and malnourished. When they reach 12 or 13 they are forced to marry and have their own children, thereby bringing another sick child into the world, because they themselves are undernourished. And so the cycle continues. It must be broken.

developing countries into the world economy. It aims to maximise trade, investment and development opportunities in developing countries.

UNCTAD is engaged in the following tasks, among others:
- Research into trends in the world economy and assessing their consequences for development.
- Assistance to developing countries in the maximisation of the positive effects of globalisation and liberalisation.
- Research into global trends in foreign investment and their effects on trade, technology and development.
- Assistance for developing countries in attracting investment and the development of enterprises.

Regional projects

It does this by means of regional projects. Examples of these regional projects are:
- The Automatic System for Customs Data (ASCD), whereby governments are supported in the modernisation of customs procedures and policy by the latest technological innovations.
- The Anticipatory Cargo Information System (ACIS), which helps African countries to develop their transport sector and uses computer technology to track goods shipped by land and sea routes.

2.5.2 The World Trade Organization (WTO)

The WTO is one of the three major international organisations that strive to promote the liberalisation of world trade.

The World Trade Organization is better known as the WTO. The WTO is based in Geneva and was established in 1994 to monitor the new world trade treaties. Over 150 states are currently members. The WTO is an intergovernmental organisation that monitors compliance with agreements between countries on trade.

In an intergovernmental organisation, the member states are bound by the treaty of the international organisation because they have formally agreed to it.

The WTO is focused on boosting trade. It does this by allowing countries to negotiate the lowering of import tariffs, abolishing rules that restrict trade and by applying the same rules for trade to all countries. The WTO cannot make rules itself: decisions can be taken only if all the member countries agree.

Not all types of products are covered by WTO rules. Agriculture, textiles and some services are in all cases covered, but goods produced by industry (for example, televisions or cars) are an exception to WTO-rules.

The basic rules of the WTO are:

- If one member country obtains favourable trade conditions, these conditions also apply to all the other countries.
- No distinction may be made between foreign and 'domestic' products.
- Tariffs must be fixed; this gives dependability and cultivates trust.
- Unfair trade practices such as export subsidies and dumping are not allowed.

Countries can submit complaints to the WTO if other member countries do not abide by the rules. If unfair practices are involved, the WTO can allow a country to take 'retaliatory measures' to compensate for losses.

The EU operates as one entity within the WTO. The European Commissioner for Trade is responsible for negotiations on behalf of the member states and for dealing with trade conflicts. The EU is a proponent of the liberalisation of trade (lower tariffs, fewer quotas).

2.5.3 The International Monetary Fund (IMF)

International monetary and financial system

The IMF is an association of 186 countries that encourages worldwide monetary collaboration. The Fund's most important objective is to ensure the stability of the international monetary and financial system. Further, it strives for free international trade, high employment, sustainable economic development and the reduction of world poverty.

The supervision of the IMF relates to:

- controlling economic and financial developments
- the provision of policy advice that is primarily aimed at avoiding an economic crisis

The IMF also lends to countries with balance of payments problems and provides them with temporary funding. Policy is further focused on combating poverty by the provision of loans to developing countries.

BUSINESS INSIDER, 9 JANUARY 2011

Recapitalizing Europe

The implications of the economic crash of 2008 have made one thing very clear: China has emerged as the engine of growth in the world. The US became the land of sub-prime loans, and Europe is the land of finely dressed paupers. The Europe of today is not the Europe of old. If you look at the bail out of Ireland, so far the only money that has been disbursed is to the Irish Retirement funds. In fact, Europe is trying to get everyone, including the IMF, involved. It's quite simple. Europe is not properly capitalized to keep up the lifestyle it demands. There is no quick solution to a shortage of an estimated 5 trillion or more of new real capital.

2.5.4 The World Bank

The World Bank provides financial and technical aid to developing countries all over the world. The World Bank is composed of two institutions, which are in the hands of 186 countries – the International Bank for Reconstruction and Development (IBRD) and the International Development Association (IDA).

The IBRD focuses on middle-income and creditworthy poor countries, while the IDA focuses on the poorest countries in the world. They offer low-interest loans, interest-free credits and subsidies to developing countries that invest in education, healthcare, public administration, infrastructure and the financial and private sectors.

HLN ECONOMIE, 17 MARCH 2010

Women disadvantaged at work worldwide

Women worldwide have to contend with many restrictions imposed by governments, which limit their opportunities to work or start a company. The World Bank confirmed this. The World Bank established in its annual report on this subject that in only 20 of the 128 economies investigated did the same employment laws apply to women and men and

warned that this is inhibiting growth in many developing countries.
The vast majority of the 20 countries with equal employment laws are the industrialised countries. None of them are in Eastern Europe, Southern Asia or the Middle East. Only one country in Africa, Botswana, scores well in this regard.

Pay gap of 17 per cent
Worldwide only a third of companies are owned or co-owned by women. The pay gap between men and women was 17 per cent on average in 2008.

2

2.5.5 The Organisation for Economic Cooperation and Development (OECD)

The OECD has 30 member states – see table 2.2.

The OECD's guidelines are endorsed by 10 non-OECD states: Argentina, Brazil, Chile, Estonia, Israel, Latvia, Lithuania, Romania, Slovakia and Slovenia. China, India, Indonesia and South Africa have been invited to open discussion rounds for OECD membership.

TABLE 2.2 The 30 member states of the OECD

Australia	Finland	Iceland	Mexico	Slovakia
Austria	France	Ireland	Netherlands	Spain
Belgium	Germany	Italy	New Zealand	Sweden
Canada	Great Britain	Japan	Norway	Switzerland
Czech Republic	Greece	Korea	Poland	Turkey
Denmark	Hungary	Luxembourg	Portugal	USA

The OECD's guidelines are in fact a code of conduct for international trade and industry, and are based on the UN Declaration on Human Rights, ILO conventions and the UN Rio Declaration on the Environment and Development. They are the most wide-ranging guidelines in the field of sustainable business practice, and important because the European Union is a proponent of the further liberalisation of international trade and international investment (globalisation). The European business community benefits from this, but, in return, companies must also recognise their social responsibility. In the opening case we read that Apple has been criticised over a breach of OECD guidelines.
What are the OECD guidelines on corporate social responsibility?
The guidelines encourage international companies to organise their activities in a socially responsible manner. Important recommendations are made in the following areas:

- *Human rights*: To respect human rights, as established in the Universal Declaration of Human Rights.
- *Provision of information*: To publish regular, reliable and relevant information about their activities.

- *Labour*: To respect the rights of employees to representation, to not discriminate among employees and contribute to the abolishment of child labour and any form of forced or hard labour.
- *Environment*: To take account of the need to protect the environment, and public health and safety.
- *Fighting corruption*: Neither directly nor indirectly to offer, promise, provide or demand bribes or any other unfair advantages, to acquire or retain assignments or other illicit advantages.
- *Consumer interests*: To ensure that the goods and services supplied comply with all agreed or prescribed standards with respect to the health and safety of consumers.
- *Science and technology*: To make the transfer and rapid dissemination of technology and knowledge possible, taking into account the protection of intellectual property rights.
- *Competition*: To refrain from entering into or implementing certain anti-competitive agreements.
- *Taxes*: A fee charged ("levied") by a government on a product, income, or activity. The purpose of taxation is to finance government expenditure.

Summary

- Doing business in a political and economic environment means that the company must take account of trade policy around the world.

- Trade policy: measures that governments may take to influence the international specialisation.

- Free trade:
  - Free trade of goods and services
    - Competition between imported and local products lowers prices and increases quality.
  - Free trade is restricted in two ways:
    1. by regional trading arrangements between a number of countries
    2. by limiting trade to protect the economy, protectionism

- Regional trading arrangements
  The objective of regional trading arrangement is reducing barriers to trade between the member countries. They merely remove tariffs on intrabloc trade in goods.
  Forms of cooperation are:
  - free-trade bloc
  - customs union
  - common market
  - economic and monetary union

- Protectionism: measures a country takes to protect its own economy against international competition.
  - Anti-protectionism: WTO
  - Tariff measures:
    - import duties
    - turnover tax
    - excise duties
    - preferential tariff measure
  - Non-tariff measures:
    - customs formalities
    - technical requirements
    - administrative procedures
    - quality requirements
    - export restrictions
    - subsidies

- International organisations:
  - United Nations
    - International Monetary Fund (IMF)
    - International Labour Organisation (ILO)
    - World Intellectual Property Organisation (WIPO)
    - United Nations Conference on Trade and Development (UNCTAD)
  - World Trade Organization (WTO)
  - Organisation for Economic Cooperation and Development (OECD)
    - OECD guidelines
  - World Bank
    - financial and technical assistance to developing countries

Questions and assignments

Questions about the opening case

2.1 What are the OECD guidelines?

2.2 Why are the OECD guidelines important?

2.3 Companies that do international business according to the OECD guidelines not only benefit humanity and the environment but also are more profitable. Explain this.

● www.texpress.nl

European Court rejects Chinese objection

The European Court of Justice has rejected the objection submitted by China to the 15-month extension of the anti-dumping taxes (10 per cent for Vietnam and 9.7 to 16.5 per cent for China) that were imposed by the EU on imports of Chinese and Vietnamese shoes.
According to the Court, the acceptance of anti-dumping measures is not a penalty for previous actions but a preventive measure to protect one's own markets against unfair competition due to Asian dumping practices. The measure naturally creates tension between the EU and China. To alleviate these tensions, international markets are calling for revaluation of the Chinese yuan. This would put the European, American and Chinese markets on a comparable level. It would also allow foreign investors a better return on Chinese developments, which is currently viewed as insufficient.

27 March 2010

2.4 What form of trade policy do the so-called anti-dumping taxes in the article constitute?

2.5 Explain what an anti-dumping tax is and why China objected to it. Substantiate your answer.

3 Culture

Like politics, culture is an important area in which international business substantially differs from national business. In this chapter, we first explain what culture is and clarify the cultural aspects of language, religion and social structure. Furthermore, a number of theories according to which cultures can be classified are described. In the last section, we focus attention on ethics and international business. Concepts such as corruption and codes of conduct are discussed.

In global airline marketing, idioms must be handled carefully

3

In 1987, Braniff Airlines (red. former American airline) ran ads on television, on radio and in newspapers flaunting the fact that its jets were equipped with all-leather seats. Spanish-language radio ads in the Florida market were the first to reveal an unintended double entendre. Braniff had translated its "fly in leather" slogan as fly "en cuero," which sounds like Spanish slang for "fly naked."

Some speculated the gaffe was an intentional move by marketing to attract attention, but the executive who developed the ad confirmed that the double meaning was accidental.

The airline industry is international by nature, and airlines must adapt their business and language to thrive in other countries. Companies like Braniff have seen many successes, but they have also occasionally failed to anticipate the connotations of a foreign idiom or figurative regional expression in marketing.

A billboard advertisement for Uzbekistan Airways in Tashkent International Airport evokes wariness in its English-speaking travelers by featuring a jet buried in the clouds with only the tail visible and the phrase "good luck" appearing below it in large letters.

This phrase is usually very positive and was almost certainly intended to express well wishes such as "have a nice flight" or "bon voyage," but the end result in context is a far cry from those more reassuring and positive phrases. Instead, the message passengers receive is "good luck – you'll need it!"

As another example, Wings Air, an Indonesian airline (the official language in Indonesia is Bahasa Indonesia), has used the short, grammatically incorrect slogan "Fly is Cheap" on signs, aircraft, airsickness bags and more. Instead of emphasizing affordability and helping customers to feel good about saving a few dollars while experiencing high-quality service, this awkward English emphasizes low-quality connotations of the word "cheap."

Wings Air has apparently noticed the error and has since updated some of its airsickness bags and meal boxes to more appropriately read, "Flying is Cheap." A slightly more delicate marketing touch in English might have resulted in using an even more positive word like "affordable."

Airlines hope that customers will overlook translation blunders as innocent mistakes that do not reflect the quality of service offered. With a little luck and a large market share, the "cheap" blunders of Wings Air and Uzbekistan Airways will not drastically affect their bottom line, but allusions to illicit on-board activities or "flying naked" will certainly leave someone feeling embarrassed.

Edited source: www.desertnews.com, 10 January 2011

3.1 What is culture?

International business implies doing business with people from other countries who have different standards norms and customs. Why do Chinese people accept a business card with both hands? Because we European do not do this, we think it is strange gesture. This is due to cultural differences between the European and Chinese. If you assume that the other person thinks and acts in the same way you do, this is your first underestimation. So it is essential to know what culture is if you wish to operate succesfully in an international business setting. Culture affects: **Culture**

- the way in which we live
- the way in which we think
- the way in which we organise ourselves
- the way in which we communicate
- the way in which we observe

● www.reuters.com

How will Chinese culture influence Africa?

So far, media coverage of China's involvement in Africa has mostly been about investment. Stories of Chinese engineers in hard hats standing by roads up mountains in Ethiopia. Stories of Chinese farmers moving to Zambia.

But, in a push to extent its economic reach, China is now making a very real effort to export its culture to the world's poorest continent. Last year the Asian giant overtook the U.S. as Africa's top trading partner, confirming to the West that it has a real battle on its hands to maintain its influence over African nations.

But, while China's economic influence is now mighty and its cheap goods can be bought everywhere from Lagos to tiny tribal villages in

remotest Ethiopia, Africans, especially young ones, still admire and try to copy U.S. culture.
Middle class teenagers in Nairobi dress like suburban kids from Atlanta, posters of Obama adorn minibus windows in Kinshasa, American hip-hop is everywhere.
China now seems to have realised this.
Here in Addis Ababa this week China and Ethiopia signed an agreement to work on a "cultural exchange program" from 2010 to 2013. Ethiopia's state news agency said the countries will dispatch "art troupes, artists, writers and art exhibitions" to each other. It will be interesting to see how mutual the traffic is.
And it's not just China trying to use culture to secure access to a continent overflowing with mineral resources and a largely untapped consumer market of nearly 1 billion people with more money in their pockets each year.
Addis Ababa is host to Chinese, Indian and even Turkish schools where Ethiopian children must sing the national anthems of those countries every morning, where they learn their languages, their dances, their songs, their particular set of manners. And where they learn a foreign history alongside their own. Similar schools from the European powers have, of course, existed for years, educating and, sometimes indoctrinating, Africa's elite. But the British, the French, the Germans and the Spanish are losing ground to the world's emerging powers.
So how will this all play out? What will the impact of these new cultural imports be on the individual cultures of African countries, arguably still the most unique and preserved in the world? Is this really just imperialism version 2.0?

22 January 2011

Culture is a complex system of norms and values, developed over hundreds of years and passed on from generation to generation. This complex system has, as it were been, programmed into human beings, due to which it is part of the thinking, actions and inactions. See also figure 3.1, in which the three levels of mental programming can be seen. Geert Hofstede, a Dutch sociologist who is internationally famous for his intercultural studies, describes culture as the collective mental programming that separates members of one group or category of people from another.

FIGURE 3.1 Three levels of mental programming

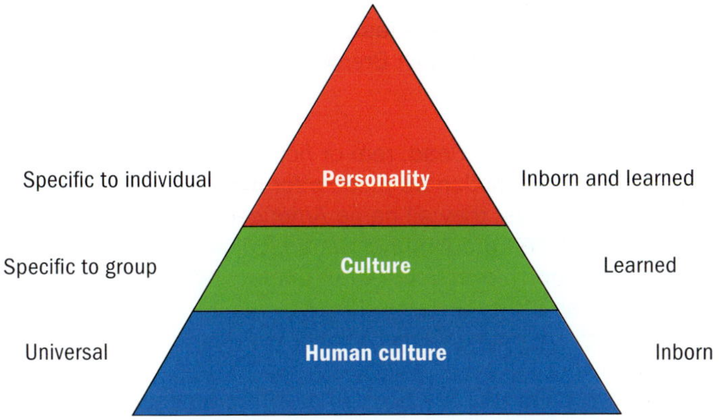

Source: Hofstede, 2005

3.1.1 Layers of culture

According to Hofstede, culture can be looked upon as an onion. The outer layer is visible, the inner layers not. As can be seen in figure 3.2 the onion consists of four layers:

1 symbols
2 heroes
3 rituals
4 values

These four layers together form a culture, the practice.

FIGURE 3.2 Hofstede's onion diagram

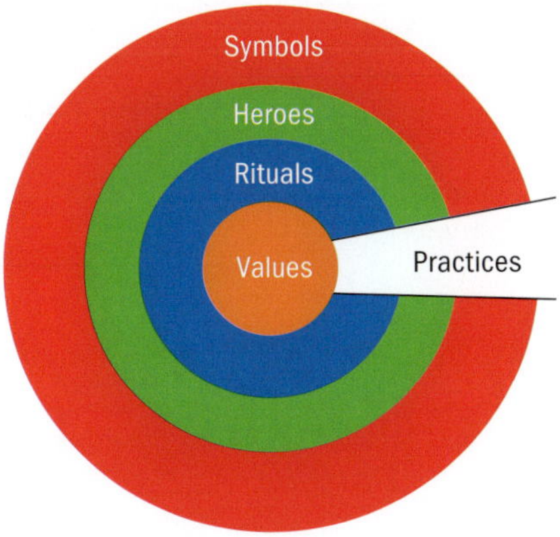

Source: Hofstede, 2005

Ad 1 Symbols

Symbols are the most superficial characteristics of a culture and can be observed by others. They are words, gestures, images or objects with a meaning understood by members of the same culture. In Europe Beethoven's 9th symphony belongs to this category. Every European country has its own manners concerning breakfast. The French have a baquette and the English go for a typical English Breakfast with scrambled eggs.

Ad 2 Heroes

Heroes are the people – alive or dead, real or fictitious – who are highly regarded in a culture. They function as models for behaviour. If you ask Americans about their heroes, they all name American presidents. According to Time Magazine European heroes are U2 singer Bono, Live-8 organizer Bob Geldof, tennisplayer Steffi Graf, opera singer Placido Domingo, Harry Potter and tv cook Jamie Oliver.

3

Ad 3 Rituals

Rituals are symbolic actions that are handed down from generation to generation in the same manner. They are regarded as socially genuine and essential. Examples for rituals are business meetings, church services, morning routine and the way we greet each other.

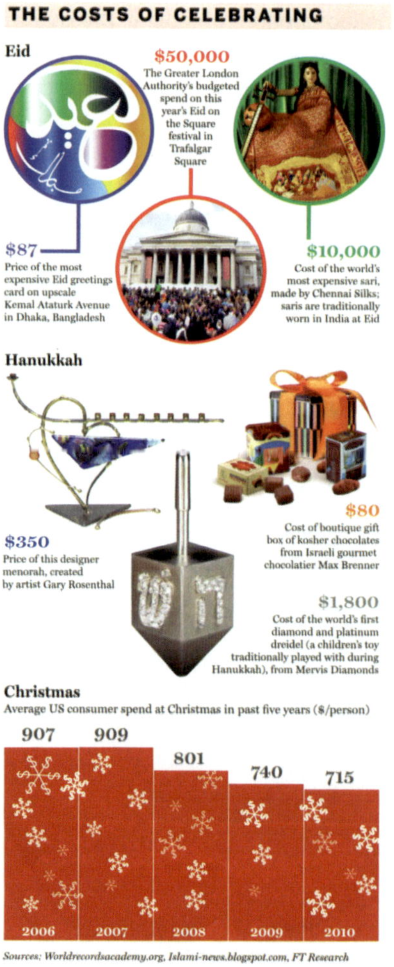

Source: Financial times special report 3-12-2010

Ad 4 Values
At the core of the onion are the values to which we are most deeply attached. Values are closely related to feelings and they engender a collective tendency to favour a certain course of affairs above another. Values are feelings with a direction, which are related to bad as opposed to good, dirty against clean, ugly against beautiful and so forthon. Consensus is a frequently mentioned. There are no values that all European countries have in common. For the Turkish society religion is very important, not for the Czechs. For the Lithuanian people having children is very important for their fulfillment, not for the Germans. There is no set of joint European values.

3.1.2 Cultural levels
Besides the fact that culture can be classified in layers, culture can also be subdivided in different levels. The following four levels of culture can be seen in figure 3.3:
- National culture. The culture of a country or region, which establishes a framework. Compare, for example, the French culture with the English culture.
- Business/industry culture. Every industry or professional field has a different 'code of conduct'. In some professions the code of conduct is very formal – for example in the legal profession. Whereas in other professions, relations are in contrast as highly informal. Think also of the technical jargon that is also different in every sector.
- Corporate culture. This form of culture, within an organisation, is composed of rules and methods and determines the nature of internal

FIGURE 3.3 The different levels of culture

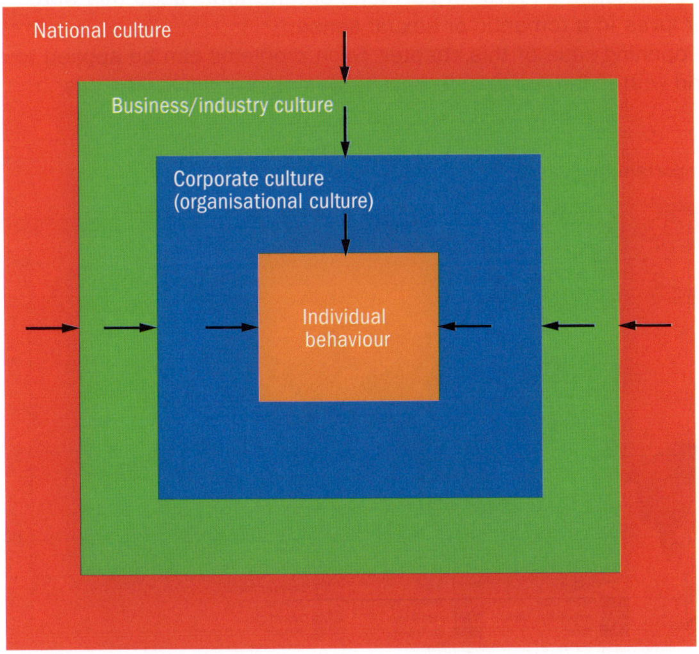

Source: Hollensen, 2010

relations to a large extent. Logica CMG, for example, adheres to norms such as openness, dedication and innovation.
- Individual behaviour. This is influenced not only by the other, higher cultural levels but also by learned behaviour.

It is therefore important to see through these layers and through the layers of the other party, with whom you are doing business. These layers explain why the other party's behaviour differs from yours. Even if you come from the same national culture, you still may behave in a different way. That may be the case for example, because you have a different profession or you work in a different organisation.

3.2 Elements of culture

Culture can be broken down into elements such as social structure, language, religion and education. However, there is no fixed subdivision, and different categories are discussed in various books. In this section the three most important elements are discussed, viz. language, religion and social structure.

3.2.1 Language

Differences in language can constitute a huge barrier to communication. The barrier becomes greater as the difference in language increases. In Russia, for example, hardly anybody masters an other European language and even English may present you with problems there. Even if the same language is spoken, different words can be used for the same thing. For example, the word *love* can refer to a variety of different feelings, states, and attitudes, ranging from generic pleasure ("I loved that meal") to intense interpersonal attraction ("I love my partner") but the Turks used this word just for their loves in a romantic or sexual sense.
Look at the opening case of this chapter. Such problems can be applied to both oral and written language differences. Making oral agreements is

FIGURE 3.4 Overview of most important languages

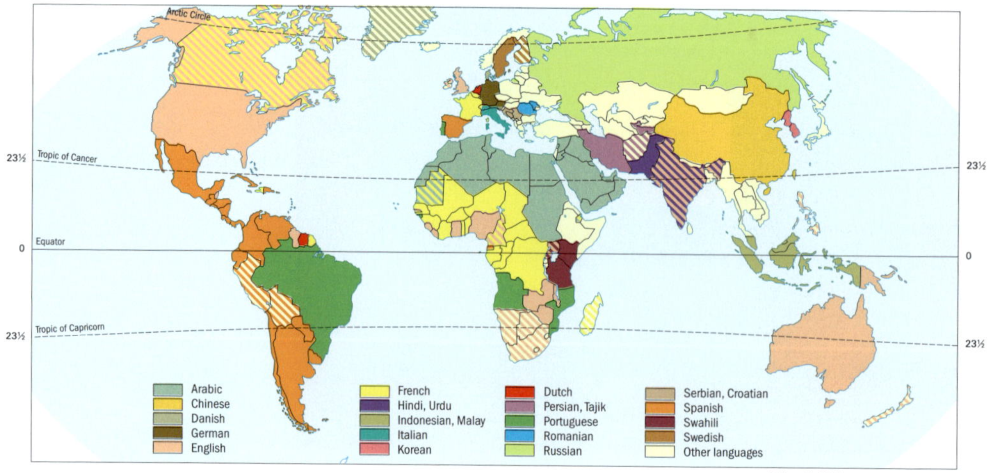

difficult and drafting written contracts is also problematic. The fact that a language is written differently or has different characters from ours, such as Greek, Russian, Arabic and the Asian languages usually constitutes an additional difficulty.

Figure 3.4 is an overview of the most important languages and the countries where they are spoken.

When translating words from one language to the other, information is always lost and when an 'intermediary language' is used, this happens twice. It is therefore important that you speak the language of the country, particularly when doing frequently business there. Literal translations can also lead to hilarity, for example the Rolls Royce "Silver Mist" car, which was rendered into "Silver Dung 'shit" in German. Careful attention must therefore paid when translating brand names and or product names.

3

English or not?
As shown in figure 3.5, after Chinese, English is spoken by the largest number of people. For this reason, English is regarded as a general means language of communication in the business world, but there are countries where the population hardly speaks any English at all. The European should not disqualify people who do not speak English as a second language. Often there was no need for them to speak English in their culture. For example for the Belgium and the Dutch with their small linguistic region and widespread trade, it was very common to speak other languages.

FIGURE 3.5 Top 20 languages based on number of speakers

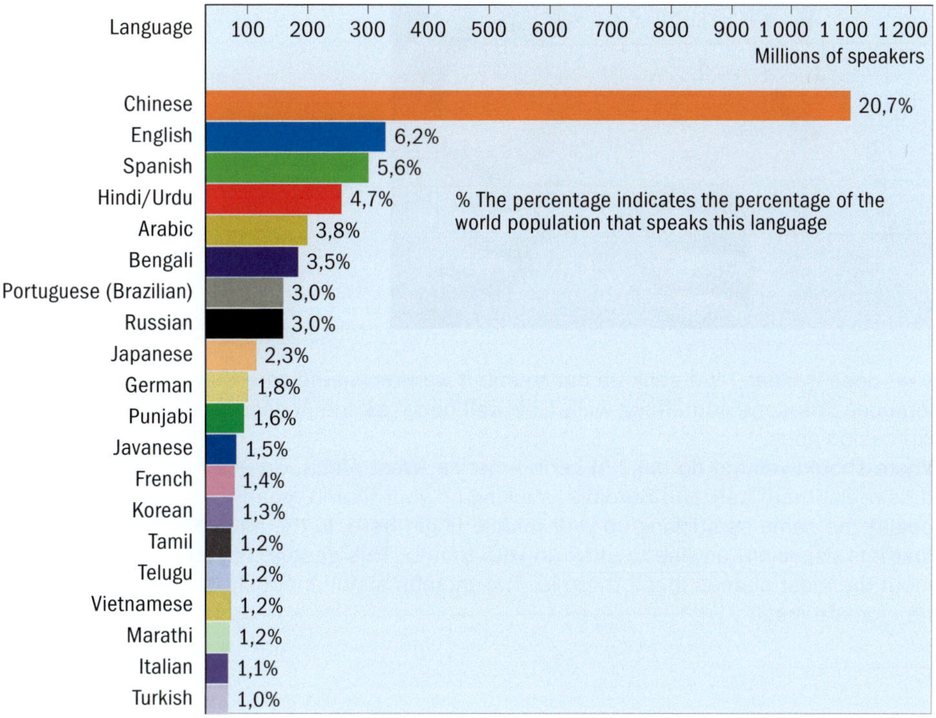

Source: http://www.andaman.org/BOOK/reprints/weber/rep-weber.htm

In the Iberian Peninsula, there is a difference between the Portuguese and the Spanish with regard to communication. Spanish is spoken all over the world and Spaniards therefore find it less important to learn English. Furthermore, Spain has been a strong, independent nation for centuries, and for a long time. The country played a leading role in Europe and in North and South America. Spaniards therefore usually assumed that 'guests' would be able to speak Spanish. For centuries Portugal has been a genuine seafaring, trading nation and is therefore more internationally oriented, so English is commonly understood. The French, as far as their language (and cultural background) is concerned, can be compared to the Spanish. It should also be borne in mind that few Americans or British speak a second language.

Non-verbal communication

Verbal communication

Non-verbal communication

The term language not only refers to verbal communication but also non-verbal communication. Aspects of non-verbal communication include posture, gestures and facial expressions. In some cultures these are more important than the spoken word. It is important to translate the smile in some cultures into European terms: not every smile has a positive meaning. Gestures can have very different meanings in different countries. A friendly gesture from a European can be a serious insult in other countries.

● www.ditwasdag.nl

Thumbs up

What does it mean? We stick up our thumb if we want to indicate that someone has done something well. 'Job well done' as the English expression goes.
Where should you not do this? In Latin America, West Africa, Greece, Russia, Southern Italy and Sardinia, sticking up your thumb means roughly the same as sticking up your middle finger here. In the Middle East it is especially unwise to stick up your thumb. This gesture is just about the most serious insult there is. Two thumbs simultaneously is the ultimate insult.

22 April 2010

Non-verbal communication can be subdivided into a number of aspects, whereby we deal with the most important ones for doing business:

- Time. How important is it to be punctual? In some cultures it is common to arrive late, while this is regarded as inappropriate in other cultures.
- Space, i.e. the physical distance between people. In the West, it is usual to stand a certain distance from the person you are talking to, whereas Arabs and Latin Americans prefer to stand close to the people they are talking to.

- Material possessions (their relevance) and interest in technology. In some cultures, displaying one's material possessions is a status-increasing factor, while in other cultures this is simple 'not done'.
- Friendships. In some cultures it is essential to strike up a friendship before business is done. In some European countries, it is more usual to keep one's private and business lives separate.
- Business agreements. In European culture it is customary to conclude a business agreement with a handshake and subsequently put the deal on paper. In some cultures a business agreement is sometimes concluded by a handshake and sometimes also by expressing mutual thanks. Less value is attached to a confirmation on paper and if one does insist, such a request may result in distrust.

3.2.2 Religion

Language as well as religion plays a crucial part when doing business on an international level. The most followed religions are:

- Christianity, the majority of its followers live in Europe and America, with a growing number in Africa.
- Islam, the majority of its followers live in Africa and Arabia. Indonesia is the country with the largest number of Muslims.
- Hinduism, the majority of its followers live in India.
- Buddhism, the majority of its followers live in Southeast Asia, China, Korea and Japan.

Figure 3.6 gives an overview of religions and how they are distributed across the world.

FIGURE 3.6 Map showing the different religions of the world

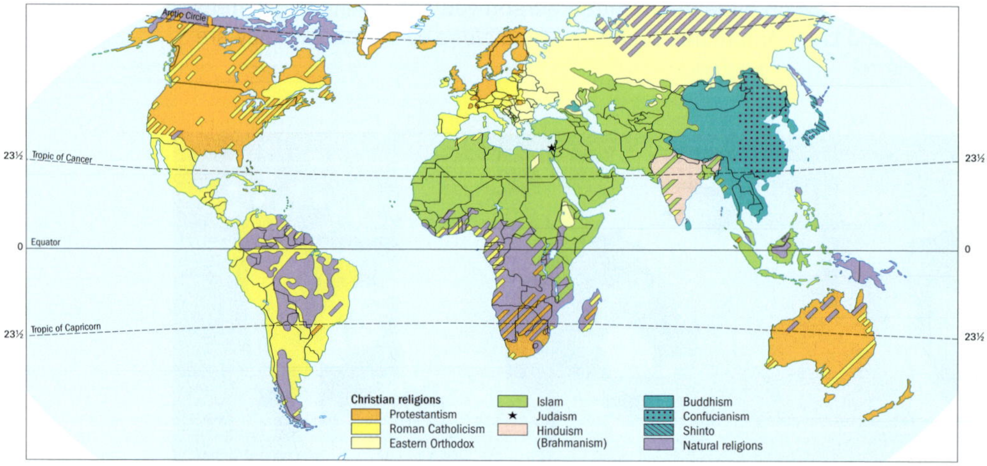

© Noordhoff Uitgevers Atlasproducties

To understand other people and to know why they react to some things in a different way, it is important to know about their religion. This is, for example, an important aspect in personal contact and also in negotiations. This knowledge is also very important to be able to assess whether certain products will be succesfull in certain markets. For example, products made from pigs are forbidden in Muslim countries. Consumption patterns may also differ. Christians do not usually work on Sundays, whereas in Jewish communities Sunday is seen as our Saturday. There are certain days on which normal life is suspended and of which account must be taken: For example on the Chinese New Year's Day factories are closed and workers go home to their families, and the same holds good for Christians on Christmas.

3.2.3 Social structure

Social structure

At the basis of every community is a social structure. This structure is the framework for the role of the individual and the subdivision of the community into groups. These two aspects of social structure are explained below.

The role of the individual highly depends on the degree of connection within a culture. In some cultures, family relations are very important and everything is done in the interest of the family and not out of self-interest. This applies to Arabs and Asians, for example. They think it is perfectly normal for adult children to live with their parents. Care for the elderly is not an individual issue as in the West, but it is considered a family matter. It is therefore in the interest of these people to have as many children as possible because this is their provision for old age. In the Western culture there is a belief that people are masters of their own destiny and that themselves are responsible for the development of their talents. It is, for example, common to enter a negotiation individually, whereas in cultures

where a larger social structure prevails, entire teams will sit around the negotiating table.
To a certain degree, every community divides its people on the basis of family background, profession and income. Membership of a particular group is usually determined by one's parents; people become members of the same group as their parents. An example of this is the caste system in India: once born into a certain caste, it is not possible for an individual to change to another caste, and to a certain extent, his caste also determines his profession. This means that there are perhaps people who have not been able to make a free choice as for their profession; their family or the social system regard their profession as a fact of life. Moving from one group to another is called social mobility. In Western culture there is great social mobility and, by means of education, an individual may move to a higher social class. This makes the role of the individual stronger, whereas in the caste system, family ties play a much more important role and the role of the individual is subordinate.

3.2.4 Cultural diagrams

Cultural differences are the principal cause of failure in international business. The previous sections explain why this is so. There are so many aspects that differ from one culture to another: how can these differences be bridged? A start is often made with a cultural diagram.

Cultural diagram

A cultural diagram is intended as an introduction to the culture of a country. It is general and will not contain all the regional variations but it gives an overview of the culture of a country. A diagram is often made on the basis of desk research before actually visiting a country. Sometimes, it is made by students as a training assignment. Table 3.1 shows what aspects a cultural diagram should contain.

TABLE 3.1 Aspects of a cultural diagram

Customs and Courtesies	People	Lifestyle	Society
Salutations/Greetings	General attitudes	Family	Country and climate
Visiting	Personal appearance	Relationships	History
Eating	Population	Diet	Government
Gestures	Language	Work	Economy
	Religion	Recreation	Education
		Leisure time	Transport and communication
			Health
			Travel tips

Source: Albaum, Strandskov, Duerr 2002

These reports can also be purchased via www.culturegrams.com. An example of a cultural diagram can be found on the website.

3.3 Classification of cultural differences

In order to understand in what way business partners respond and why certain products do or do not take off in a certain market, attention must be paid to cultural differences. Various theories have been developed to classify countries in cultural differences. The following three methodological theories are discussed in this section:
- Hall's background context approach
- Hofstede's five dimensions
- Trompenaars' seven dimensions

3.3.1 Hall's background context approach

Context approach

In his 'background context approach', Edward Hall (1914–2009) analysed the context in which differences arise. The context, according to him, is the underlying background from which interaction with other people takes place. He classifies cultures as high-context or low-context.
High-context cultures have the following characteristics:
- There is little verbally explicit communication.
- There is little in written/formal information.
- Little explanation of what is communicated is needed.
- More personalized understandings of what is being communicated.
- There are long-term relationships.
- There are strict strong divisions between 'insiders' and 'outsiders'.
- The focus is on face-to-face decisions. Decisions focus around personal, face to face relationships, often centered around one person with authority.

Examples of high-context cultures are found in the Arab and Asian countries, where communication consists not only of words but also of body language, which plays a very important part. Besides the words themselves, there are different 'layers' of meaning that the recipient of the message receives and interprets. 'No' in most European cultures means that something will not happen. In Asian cultures it is very impolite to say 'no' and a denial can be expressed by the phrase 'we will come back to it' or 'we will investigate it'. In high-context cultures it is not common practice to immediately produce contracts and to refer to lawyers, because the initial negotiations are used to build up mutual trust and friendship. Figure 3.7 shows which cultures are high and low context. Unfortunately not all Western-European countries were included in Hall's study.

FIGURE 3.7 High- and low-context cultures

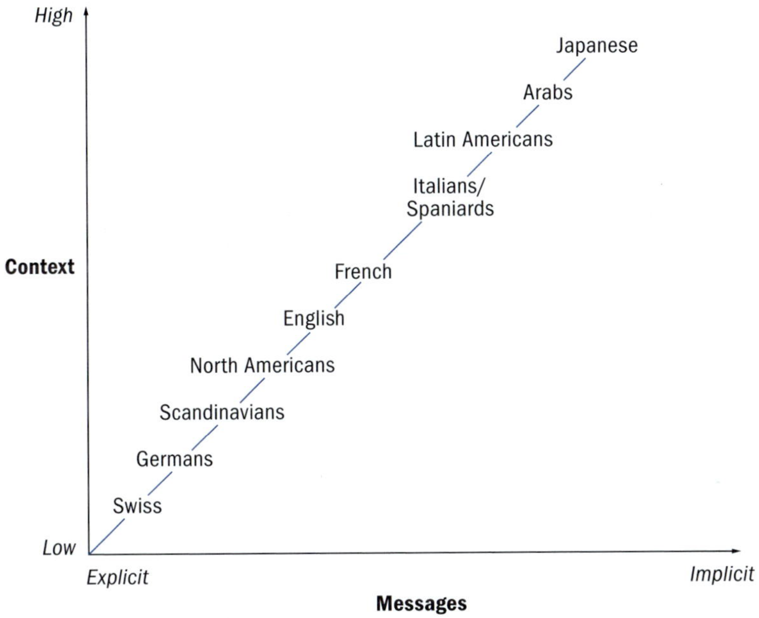

Source: Hollensen, 2010

Low-context cultures are distinguished by means of the following characteristics:

- People act on the basis of external rules.
- Knowledge is defined in codes and is publicly accessible and external.
- Relationships are of shorter duration.
- Knowledge is transferable.
- The task is the central issue; decisions are focused on upholding a sense of responsibility.

European countries have low-context cultures. In this type of culture there is explicit communication: words are more important than body language. It is easier for outsiders to enter low-context cultures because the environment has far more information to enable participation and relationships can be quickly formed on the basis of task performance. It is typical to conduct negotiations on paper, including all the details, to avoid misunderstandings.

3

● www.communicaid.com

Japanese culture – Key concepts and values

- Wa - The most valued principle still alive in Japanese society today is the concept of 'wa', or 'harmony'. The preservation of social harmony dates back to the first constitution in 604 AD and the teamwork needed when living and working on collective farms. In business terms, 'wa' is reflected in the avoidance of self-assertion and individualism and the preservation of good relationships despite differences in opinion. When doing business with the Japanese it is also important to remember the affect of 'wa' on many patterns of Japanese behaviour, in particular their indirect expression of 'no'.
- Kao - One of the fundamental factors of the Japanese social system is the notion of 'face'. Face is a mark of personal pride and forms the basis of an individual's reputation and social status. Preservation of face comes through avoiding confrontations and direct criticism wherever possible. In Japan, causing someone to lose face can be disastrous for business relationships.
- Omoiyari - Closely linked to the concepts of 'wa' and 'kao', 'omoiyari' relates to the sense of empathy and loyalty encouraged in Japanese society and practiced in Japanese business culture. In literal terms it means "to imagine another's feelings", therefore building a strong relationship based on trust and mutual feeling is vital for business success in Japan.

10 January 2011

3.3.2 Hofstede's five dimensions

Geert Hofstede is best known for the culture model he developed. This model makes use of a number of dimensions he identified and which serve as indicators of variation in culture. Hofstede devised his culture model on the basis of a study within IBM in the 1960s. National and regional differences that influence the functioning of institutional organisations (such as governments, families, companies and schools) are made visible and measurable through this model. The models aims to improve an insight into variations in cultures, making them more easily bridgeable. The model covers five dimensions:

1 power distance
2 individualism versus collectivism
3 masculinity versus femininity
4 uncertainty avoidance
5 perception of time

These five dimensions are discussed below.

Ad 1 Power distance

Power distance

Power distance is the extent to which less powerful members of institutions or organisations in a country expect and accept that power is unequally distributed. If expectation and acceptance are low, the culture is called a low-hierarchy culture. For instance, people in the Netherlands have grown up with the ideal of equality and thus they score low on power distance (see also the scores in table 3.5). Scandinavian countries score extremely low. If expectation and acceptance are high, the culture is classified as a high-hierarchy culture. High-hierarchy cultures include those of Asian, African and Arab countries. Countries in Latin America are also high-hierarchy; in Brazil, for example, 10 per cent of the population earns 50 per cent of the national income.
Table 3.2 lists characteristics of low- and high-hierarchy cultures.

TABLE 3.2 Characteristics of high- and low-hierarchy cultures

Low-hierarchy culture	High-hierarchy culture
independent	dependent
functional hierarchy	existential hierarchy
equality of rights	privileges
accessible to outsiders	inaccessible to outsiders

Ad 2 Individualism versus collectivism

Individualism
Collectivism

Individualism versus collectivism is an indicator for the extent to which individuals are integrated in groups. Most people live in groups in which the 'we orientation' is more important than the 'I orientation'. In the West, however, we live in an 'I-oriented' society (see also the scores in table 3.5). We think it is normal to make agreements independently when doing business, without our manager consent. In some other cultures it is very important to have the consent or permission of the manager or even the CEO for agreements. In table 3.3 a number of characteristics of the 'we' and 'I' orientations are listed.

TABLE 3.3 Characteristics of 'we' and 'I' orientations

'We' orientation	'I' orientation
the group: 'We'	the individual: 'Self'
group opinion	individual opinion
implicit communication	explicit communication
shame, loss of face	blame, loss of self-respect
relationship-oriented	task-oriented

Ad 3 Masculinity versus femininity

Masculinity
Femininity

The degree of masculinity or femininity of a culture indicates the extent to which value is attached to traditional male and female characteristics. Male characteristics are, among other things, competitiveness, assertiveness, ambition and the acquisition of wealth and affluence. Female values are modesty, servitude and solidarity. Negotiations in masculine countries mainly concern the details of the agreement and there is little interest in the relationship with the other party. Negotiators in feminine countries attach more value to long-term relationships, and the details of the agreement can be worked out later. Hofstede labelled Japan as the most masculine society and Sweden as the most feminine (see also table 3.5).

● www.businessweek.com

Will France say "qui" to Sunday shopping?

Most U.S. states long ago repealed their blue laws, holdovers from Puritan times, that forbade many stores and other businesses to open on Sundays. But such laws are still widespread in Europe – and nowhere more so than in France, where most shops remain locked up tight on Sundays.
Could that finally change? On July 7, the National Assembly began considering a proposal backed by President Nicolas Sarkozy that would ease some restrictions on Sunday openings, especially in tourist areas and along the country's borders. Seems like that would be a big relief to tourists and locals alike, who often are out of luck if they need to buy essentials such as medicine or lightbulbs on a Sunday.
But the proposal is stirring fierce debate, even though it was considerably watered down before being presented to lawmakers. A poll by survey group Viavoice, published on July 6 in the left-wing newspaper Libération, found that 55% of French opposed relaxing the law, and that 57% would refuse to work on Sunday if asked. Fully 85% said Sunday "should remain a day of rest" for most people.
This isn't about religion. Although most French are nominally Catholic, very few attend church. But many regard Sunday as sacred family time. On Sunday afternoons, parks and woods teem with children, parents, and grandparents strolling or biking together after having enjoyed a leisurely lunch "en famille."

15 February 2011

Ad 4 Uncertainty avoidance

Uncertainty avoidance

Uncertainty avoidance is the extent to which people feel comfortable in an uncertain, risky situation. Cultures which score high on uncertainty avoidance score often have formal, bureaucratic rules, are dependent on rituals and standards and people only trust family and friends. They often need structure and guidelines, while people in a low uncertainty avoidance culture prefer to work informally and flexibly. According to Hofstede, Mediterranean countries, such as Greece and Portugal, score high and Scandinavian countries such as Denmark and Sweden score low (see table 3.5).
In table 3.4 characteristics of low and high uncertainty avoidance are listed.

TABLE 3.4 Characteristics of low and high uncertainty avoidance

Low uncertainty avoidance	High uncertainty avoidance
little need of structure and rules	great need of structure and rules
taking risks	certainty
not showing emotions	showing emotions
relaxation	stress

EXAMPLE

Coping with uncertainly

- In Germany nothing is allowed, unless it is allowed.
- In England everything is allowed, unless it is not allowed.
- In France everything is allowed, even if it is not allowed.
- In the Netherlands …

Ad 5 Perception of time

Perception of time **Long-term orientation** **Short-term orientation**

Perception of time is the extent to which people in a certain culture tend towards a long-term or a short-term outlook. A long-term tendency orientation means striving for a reward in the future, primarily via perseverance and economy.
A short-term tendency means striving for integrity, respect for tradition, preventing loss of face and fulfilling one's social obligations. Cultures with a short-term outlook are focused on immediate results and an urge for truth, whereas cultures with a long-term outlook work on improvements for the future through perseverance and they make frugal use of resources. China scores high on long-term outlook while Pakistan, in contrast, scores very low (table 3.5).

Table 3.5 gives an overview of a number of countries and their scores on these five dimensions.

TABLE 3.5 Indexed scores of countries on the basis of Hofstede's five dimensions

Country	Power distance	Individualism versus collectivism	Masculinity versus femininity	Uncertainty avoidance	Perception of time
Argentina	49	46	56	86	
Australia	36	90	61	51	31
Belgium	65	75	54	94	
Brazil	69	38	49	76	65
China	80	20	66	30	118
Denmark	18	74	16	23	

Country	Power distance	Individualism versus collectivism	Masculinity versus femininity	Uncertainty avoidance	Perception of time
France	68	71	43	86	
Germany	35	67	66	65	31
Greece	60	35	57	112	
India	77	48	56	40	61
Iran	58	41	43	59	
Italy	50	76	70	75	
Japan	54	46	95	92	80
The Netherlands	38	80	14	53	44
Pakistan	55	14	50	70	0
Peru	64	16	42	87	
Portugal	63	27	31	104	
Russia	93	39	36	95	
Spain	57	51	42	86	
Sweden	31	71	5	29	33
United Kingdom	35	89	66	35	25

Source: http://www.geert-hofstede.com/hofstede_dimensions.php?culture1=18&culture2=62

3.3.3 Trompenaars' seven dimensions

The Dutchman Fons Trompenaars, together with Charles Hampden-Turner, developed a seven-dimension model to measure variation differences in culture. The idea behind this model was not only to identify variations in culture but also to reconcile them. The seven dimensions are:

1 universalism versus particularism
2 individualism versus collectivism
3 neutral versus emotional
4 specific versus diffuse
5 achievement versus ascription
6 sequential versus synchronic
7 internal versus external control

Ad 1 Universalism versus particularism

Universalist
Particularist

Universalism roughly means that there is always a definition of what is good and right. Contractual agreements, rational analytical thinking and professionalism are important when doing business in universalist cultures, especially in Western cultures such as the Swiss. For a particularist, friendship, for example, implies certain obligations, which can weigh more heavily than abstract social codes. Loss of face plays an important role here. Countries such as Venezuela, Russia and China have a highly particularist character. To illustrate this phenomenon the following example is given: A friend of yours driving too fast causes an accident. You are sitting next to him in the car. Afterwards, you are subpoenaed. When asked as a universalist, you would admit that your friend was driving too fast. However, as a particularist, you would deny that your friend was driving too fast.

Ad 2 Individualism versus collectivism
Is individual performance valued or is there more emphasis put on an individual's role in the group? In individualistic cultures, the individual is the most important agent, and individual improvements are assumed to lead to improvements in collective matters. Israel, after Canada and the United States, has a very individualistic culture. In these cultures, 'employee of the month' awards are common. In collectivistic cultures, the group is the most important agent, and individual actions are undertaken expressly to maintain and improve the group's position. Countries such as Egypt, Mexico and India are more collectivistic.

Ad 3 Neutral versus emotional
To what extent are emotions shown? In an affective culture, emotions are shown and communication is based on them. In African and Latin American countries, emotions are part of a working relationship: bursting out laughing, being angry, quarrelling. In a neutral culture the emotions are there, but people do not show them. In countries such as Japan and China, it is not usual to show one's emotions and communication is more restrained. In most countries in Europe, too, it is not usual to show one's emotions when doing business.

Ad 4 Specific versus diffuse
To what extent is energy invested in personal relationships? In the Western world we have become accustomed to dividing everything into separate elements, whereas people in some parts of the world prefer a holistic approach. This holistic approach is seen, for example, in the service given by airlines in Asia, in contrast to the Spartan service rendered on flights within the USA. All this has to do with how much of our personality is integrated in the relationship. A typical feature in a specific culture such as

The Netherlands professional and private relationships are kept separate. However, in some countries, the diverse relations of one person run through all others, these relationships overlap. Arab, African, Asian and South American cultures generally have a high overlap.

Ad 5 Achievement versus ascription
Are status and power based on performance achievement or on lineage and class? In cultures in which status is ascribed, a person is not only assessed on how he has performed recently but the person in question also derives a certain status from his lineage, gender, age or education. Graduating from Tokyo university gives high status in Japan. In cultures that are oriented towards achievement, products are recommended on the basis of their output. This aspect is thus highly dependent on the social structure (see subsection 3.2.3) in the country.

Ad 6 Sequential versus synchronic
People from a sequential culture do one thing at a time and view time in parts or pieces. They like planning and applying structure and think it important that people turn up on time. People from a synchronous culture do several things at once and view time as flexible. In Europe, we live in a sequential culture and it is very unusual to turn up late. If you are doing business in a synchronous culture, do not plan too many appointments in one day. Your counterpart will take time for you and is not accustomed to the idea of a person having several appointments one and the same day.

Ad 7 Internal versus external control
What significance do people ascribe to their natural environment? In some cultures (such as that of the United States) people think in terms of managing the environment. In other cultures (such as in Japan) they think more in terms of being in harmony with the environment because it harbours forces that cannot be controlled by man.

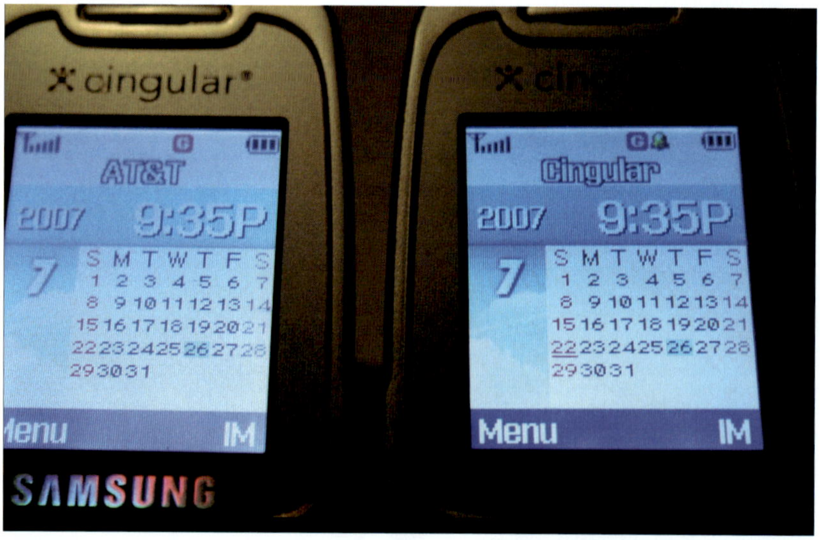

3.4 Ethics

Many scandals have recently taken place in trade and industry – for example, the Probo Koala affair, in which a vessel of that name allegedly dumped toxic chemicals off the Ivory Coast. The subject of child labour, which regularly crops up in the news (see opening case, chapter 2), usually creates quite a scandal. Another example is the current economic crisis, which began with affairs in the banking business caused by a lack of transparency in their dealings. When doing business on an international scale, there is every chance that different norms and values are encountered. The fact that these norms and values are different from those at home can cause distress. Scandals can seriously damage a company's reputation; that is the reason why attention is paid to them in this section.

3.4.1 What are ethics?

Ethics

Ethics can be defined as the principles, standards and norms of individual or corporate behaviour. In this section emphasis is placed on the latter issue mentioned. Naturally, the laws enacted in a country form a basis for ethics. Nevertheless, there is always a grey area – see figure 3.8. Corporate ethics begin where law ends.

Of course, the culture of a country plays a large role in determining its major ethics. Every culture has a set of moral standards for corporate behaviour. These standards influence the decisions and actions of a company in the context of the following relationships:

- Organisational relationships: for example, not just in terms of competition between companies but also in terms of collaboration with other companies (see chapter 6).
- Economic relationships: for example, financing, taxes and local reinvestment policy.
- Employee relations: for example, rewards, safety, human rights and training.

FIGURE 3.8 The relationship between ethics and the law

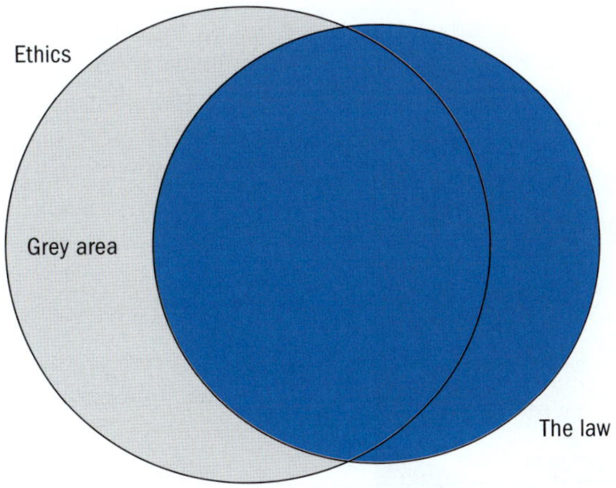

Source: Crane & Matten, 2007

- Customer relationships: for example, in terms of pricing, quality and advertising.
- Industrial relationships: for example, research and development, and infrastructural development.
- Political relationships: for example, not just in terms of complying with the law but also with regard to corruption, subsidies and so forth.

There are two theories for managing ethics in another country:
- **Ethical relativism**, a theory in which every country is considered separately and one takes into account what is acceptable ethically locally, for example, if it is ethically acceptable to work 60 hours a week, then this approach holds good for countries where it is allowed but it is not an acceptable point of view in countries where it is not allowed.
- **Ethical imperialism**, a theory in which the country of origin is taken as a paradigm and these ethics are also enforced in all other countries where business is done. If, for example, in a West-European country a 40-hour working week is permitted, this norm holds good for every country. This can result in enormous difficulties because it is a fairly one-sided vision.

This was the reason why Thomas Donaldson (1996) developed a mixture of these theories. He suggested that at least the following points must be considered if a company wishes to do business in an ethically acceptable way. These elements apply to all actions in all countries worldwide:
- respect for human dignity and human rights
- respect for local traditions
- respect for local institutions which the local population depend on

www.ft.com

Western brands in Bangladesh safety push

Western clothing brands are having to confront the dismal safety record of Bangladesh's garment industry after 26 workers died last week in a factory fire.
The blaze, which injured at least another 100, broke out on the ninth floor of a factory owned by the Hameem Group, which employs thousands of workers making garments for companies such as Gap, JC Penney and Phillips-Van Heusen.

The garment industry accounts for 80 per cent of Bangladesh's exports Survivors complained that locked doors – ostensibly closed to prevent theft – forced panicked workers to jump from the roof, or try unsuccessfully to escape by a rope.
The tragedy follows another fire in February, when 21 workers perished in a factory that produces sweaters for clients including Sweden's Hennes & Mauritz. The fires have exposed the limitations of a decade-long effort by top brands to monitor workplace conditions at their suppliers' factories in Bangladesh. Gap, for example, audited Hameem's factory earlier in the year, and its requirements include clearly marked, unblocked fire exits.
Just one week before the latest fire, western brand representatives, factory owners, government officials and labour activists, had met in Dhaka to discuss the urgent need to reduce fire hazards in the garment industry, which accounts for 80 per cent of Bangladesh's exports.
"The buyers must take responsibility in terms of the prevention of these kinds of incidents," said Korshed Alam, director of the Alternative Movement for Resources and Freedom, a Dhaka-based labour rights group working closely with local unions. "These factories are solely producing for western consumers."
The accident comes at a sensitive time for Bangladesh's garment industry as tensions between workers and factory owners rise over a recent government-mandated wage increase.
Although the wage increase came into effect in November, labour activists say some factories are trying to avoid the increase, with tactics such as reclassifying workers at lower levels that draw lower pay, or by withdrawing other benefits.
In Chittagong, where 70 factories produce clothes for western brands, violent clashes last week between workers and police left three dead, and more than 250 injured.
The labour tensions come as Bangladesh has emerged as a popular low-cost alternative to China for garment production. In the four months from July to October, the country's garment exports jumped almost two-fifths to $6.8bn.

10 January 2011

3.4.2 Corruption

Corruption

Corruption is defined as the abuse of public power to obtain individual benefits. Corruption hinders fair competition, fair pricing and efficiency. It often takes the form of bribery. Recently it was announced that Royal Dutch Shell has paid $48 million for alleged bribery in Nigeria.

There appears to be a link between poverty and corruption. The greater the poverty rate, the more corruption occurs. In figure 3.9 a worldwide overview is given of the extent to which corruption plays a role in business. The darker the colour, the more often corruption occurs.

FIGURE 3.9 Corruption index 2009

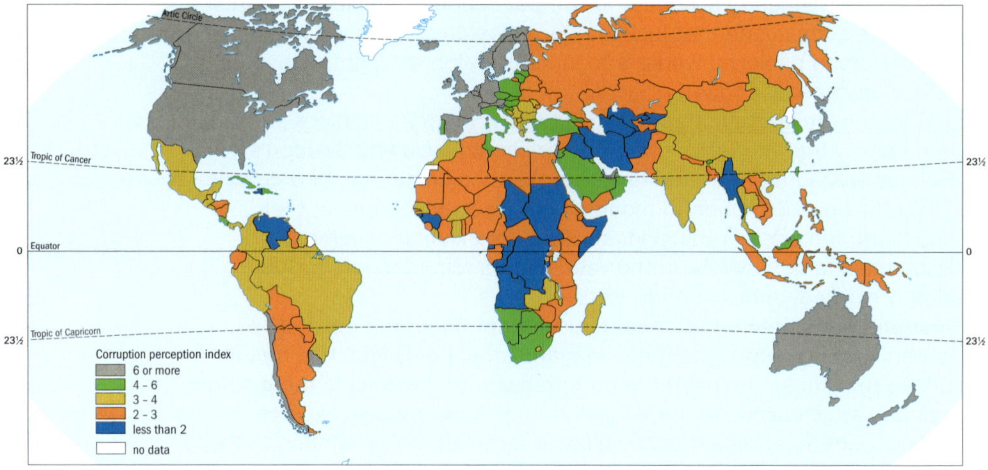

EU companies that attempt to bribe foreign officials and administrators are committing an offence. This is the case both within the European Union and abroad. The idea of the legislation is to combat corruption within and outside national borders. Corruption is ethically reprehensible. Furthermore, the prevention of corruption is one of the focus areas in sustainable international business. In all member countries of the Organisation for Economic Cooperation and Development (OECD) (see chapter 2), the giving and taking of bribes is prohibited, not only in the country involved but also abroad. The agreements on this issue have been established in the OECD Treaty against the Bribery of Foreign Officials in International Business Transactions. The European Union too implements polices to fight corruption, for international and European organisations and for instance under professional activities in the private sector. Each European member state advises companies to refrain from and to prevent corrupt trading. In order to achieve this goal, the GRECO has been established. In addition, Europol is authorized to trace corruption. Some European countries score high on corruption. Albania, Macedonia, Kosovo and Romania but also Lithuania and Greece score relatively high on corruption. Bulgaria and Turkey are doing remarkably well. In South-east Europe especially the healthcare sector is notorious for its briberous activities.

3.4.3 Code of conduct

Code of conduct

As a result of recent scandals, more and more companies have implemented guidelines on ethical decisions. These are also called 'codes of conduct', which can be found on the website of the company concerned. Especially large worldwide operating companies have lately all introduced codes of conduct, as is shown in figure 3.10.

FIGURE 3.10 Increase in percentage of Fortune Global 200 companies with codes of conduct, 1970–2007

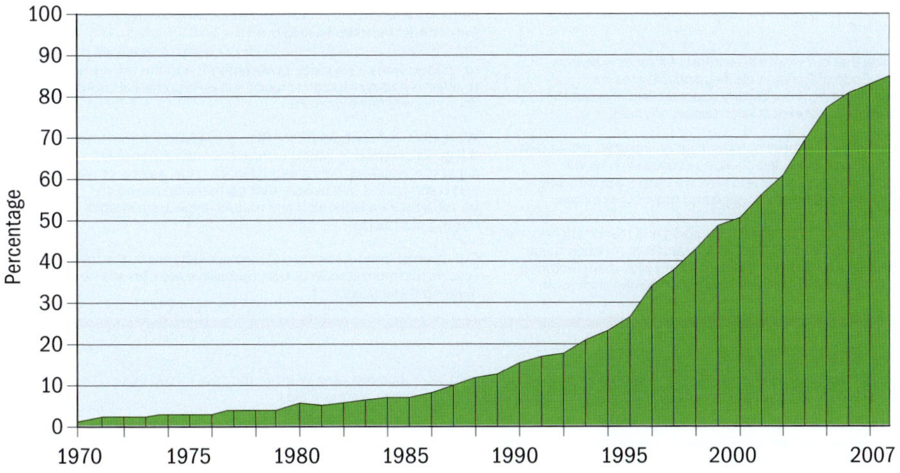

Source: KPMG, 2008

The principal reason for implementing such a code of conduct, according to the *Global Corruption Report* by Transparency International, is the urge to comply with legal obligations. In the United States, the Foreign Corrupt Practices Act (FCPA) has resulted in fundamental changes in business management. Other important reasons for implementing such a code were:

- limitation of liability in case of accidents;
- limitation of government initiatives to create new legislation in this area;
- development of a positive, shared organisational company culture;
- protection and boost of the company's reputation;
- upgrading of the staff's behaviour and corporate social responsibility.

The *Global Corruption Report* by KPMG showed that in 63 per cent of cases, a code of conduct contained passages about corruption and bribery. Issues like conflicts of interest on handling, financial data records and other internal information, on accepting gifts and bribes, on reporting breaches of the rules and regulations, on fair competition and discrimination were frequently mentioned.

The implementation of a code of conduct is very important. The process is more important than the content of the code itself. The success rate is greatest if all stakeholders are involved in the drafting process of the code of conduct. Subsequently, it is important that everyone is informed and understands what is expected. Employees must be inspired and motivated to abide by the code and it must be monitored whether they are indeed acting in accordance with it. The following figure is an example of a code of conduct.

3

NIKE, Inc. CODE of CONDUCT

At Nike, we believe that although there is no finish line, there is a clear starting line.

Understanding that our work with contract factories is always evolving, this Code of Conduct clarifies and elevates the expectations we have of our factory suppliers and lays out the minimum standards we expect each factory to meet.

It is our intention to use these standards as an integral component to how we approach NIKE, Inc. sourcing strategies, how we evaluate factory performance, and how we determine with which factories Nike will continue to engage and grow our business.

As we evolve our business model in sourcing and manufacturing, we intend to work with factories who understand that meeting these minimum standards is a critical baseline from which manufacturing leadership, continuous improvement and self-governance must evolve.

Beyond the Code, Nike is committed to collaborating with our contract factories to help build a leaner, greener, more empowered and equitable supply chain. And we will continue to engage with civil society, governments, and the private sector to affect systemic change to labor and environmental conditions in countries where we operate.

We expect our contract factories to share Nike's commitment to the goals of reducing waste, using resources responsibly, supporting workers' rights, and advancing the welfare of workers and communities. We believe that partnerships based on transparency, collaboration and mutual respect are integral to making this happen.

Our Code of Conduct binds our contract factories to the following specific minimum standards that we believe are essential to meeting these goals.

EMPLOYMENT is VOLUNTARY

The contractor does not use forced labor, including prison labor, indentured labor, bonded labor or other forms of forced labor. The contractor is responsible for employment eligibility fees of foreign workers, including recruitment fees.

EMPLOYEES are AGE 16 or OLDER

Contractor's employees are at least age 16 or over the age for completion of compulsory education or country legal working age, whichever is higher. Employees under 18 are not employed in hazardous conditions.

CONTRACTOR does NOT DISCRIMINATE

Contractor's employees are not subject to discrimination in employment, including hiring, compensation, promotion or discipline, on the basis of gender, race, religion, age, disability, sexual orientation, pregnancy, marital status, nationality, political opinion, trade union affiliation, social or ethnic origin or any other status protected by country law.

FREEDOM of ASSOCIATION and COLLECTIVE BARGAINING are RESPECTED

To the extent permitted by the laws of the manufacturing country, the contractor respects the right of its employees to freedom of association and collective bargaining. This includes the right to form and join trade unions and other worker organizations of their own choosing without harassment, interference or retaliation.

COMPENSATION is TIMELY PAID

Contractor's employees are timely paid at least the minimum wage required by country law and provided legally mandated benefits, including holidays and leaves, and statutory severance when employment ends. There are no disciplinary deductions from pay.

HARASSMENT and ABUSE are NOT TOLERATED

Contractor's employees are treated with respect and dignity. Employees are not subject to physical, sexual, psychological or verbal harassment or abuse.

WORKING HOURS are NOT EXCESSIVE

Contractor's employees do not work in excess of 60 hours per week, or the regular and overtime hours allowed by the laws of the manufacturing country, whichever is less. Any overtime hours are consensual and compensated at a premium rate. Employees are allowed at least 24 consecutive hours rest in every seven-day period.

REGULAR EMPLOYMENT is PROVIDED

Work is performed on the basis of a recognized employment relationship established through country law and practice. The contractor does not use any form of home working arrangement for the production of Nike-branded or affiliate product.

The WORKPLACE is HEALTHY and SAFE

The contractor provides a safe, hygienic and healthy workplace setting and takes necessary steps to prevent accidents and injury arising out of, linked with or occurring in the course of work or as a result of the operation of contractor's facilities. The contractor has systems to detect, avoid and respond to potential risks to the safety and health of all employees.

ENVIRONMENTAL IMPACT is MINIMIZED

The contractor protects human health and the environment by meeting applicable regulatory requirements including air emissions, solid/hazardous waste and water discharge. The contractor adopts reasonable measures to mitigate negative operational impacts on the environmental and strives to continuously improve environmental performance.

The CODE is FULLY IMPLEMENTED

As a condition of doing business with Nike, the contractor shall implement and integrate this Code and accompanying Code Leadership Standards and applicable laws into its business and submit to verification and monitoring. The contractor shall post this Code, in the language(s) of its employees, in all major workspaces, train employees on their rights and obligations as defined by this Code and applicable country law; and ensure the compliance of any sub-contractors producing Nike branded or affiliate products.

August 2010

Source: http://www.nikebiz.com

Summary

- Culture affects the way in which we live, think, organise ourselves, communicate and observe.

- Culture is passed on from generation to generation and a learning process.

- Culture consists of several layers (from outside to inside):
  - symbols
  - heroes
  - rituals
  - values

- Various levels of culture can be identified:
  - national culture
  - business/industry culture
  - corporate culture
  - individual behaviour

- Three elements of culture are:
  - language (verbal and non-verbal)
  - religion
  - social structure

- The background context approach by Hall classifies cultures as high or low context. High-context cultures are characterised by little oral or written communication and are relationship oriented. Low-context cultures are recognisable by knowledge that is transferable (rules) and are task oriented.

- The five dimensions of Hofstede are:
  1 power distance
  2 individualism versus collectivism
  3 masculinity versus femininity
  4 uncertainty avoidance
  5 perception of time

  Each country scores differently on these dimensions. Comparing the scores of the foreign culture with one's own culture makes the differences visible.

- Trompenaars' seven dimensions are:
  1 universalism versus particularism
  2 individualism versus collectivism
  3 neutral versus emotional
  4 specific versus diffuse
  5 achievement versus ascription
  6 sequential versus synchronicous
  7 internal versus external control

  A scoring system is also used here (see Hofstede).

- Ethics are standards and norms for individual or corporate behaviour. To establish them, companies draw up a code of conduct.
  An aspect of ethics is how to cope with corruption. Corruption is common in certain countries and it hinders fair competition.

Questions and assignments

3

Questions about the opening case

3.1 Does Spain have a high- or low-context culture? Substantiate your answer.

3.2 Go through the five dimensions of Hofstede and argue whether Spain scores high or low on these dimensions. Motivate your answer.

3.3 How could this translation problem be avoided?

● www.chinadaily.com.cn

Former deputy director of China's drug watchdog sacked

BEIJING – Zhang Jingli, former deputy director of the State Food and Drug Administration, has been discharged from public employment for serious violations of discipline and law, the discipline watchdog of the Communist Party of China (CPC) said Thursday.
Zhang was also expelled from the CPC, said the Central Commission for Discipline Inspection (CCDI) of the CPC seven months after it announced that Zhang was "under investigation for suspected disciplinary violations."
Zhang, 56, became deputy director of the SFDA in 2003. He was still serving in that position in 2007 when former SFDA director Zheng Xiaoyu was executed for taking 6.49 million yuan (nearly $1 million) in bribes and dereliction of duty.
According to a statement released Thursday by the CCDI of the CPC and the Ministry of Supervision, Zhang abused his office to benefit others and receive "a large amount of money" in return.
Investigations also found that Zhang gained "huge profits" from illegal business operations, fabricated facts to frame others and led a corrupt life.
Zhang's deeds severely violated disciplines and some even broke laws, the statement said, adding that all his illegal gains had been confiscated.
Zhang's alleged lawbreaking deeds will be investigated and handled by judical organs, the statement said.

1 February 2011

3.4 Did China sign the OECD treaty?

3.5 Test your knowledge of the Chinese. Take part in the quiz on http://www.kwintessential.co.uk/resources/quiz/cross-cultural-china.php.

3.6 Compare your home country and China with regard to their scores on the five dimensions of Hofstede. In what respect do they differ most? Can you think of an example?

CHINESE OLYMPIC COMMITTEE
百威成就
皇者
大船
Budweiser
Budweiser
HEINEKEN BEER
Heineken
PREMIUM QUALITY

4

Management & organisation in an international environment

Our world has developed into a global village. Companies that wish to survive must avail themselves of the many worldwide opportunities when these arise. There are far more opportunities than managers to seize the moment when it occurs. Often failures are the result of insufficient knowledge and awareness.
Many companies have taken the international route but there are always stragglers that still have to take their first steps on the international stage. Companies that wish to do business internationally are wise to begin by listing all the advantages and disadvantages of internationalisation for their company before making the choice. This chapter explains what is required to complete the internationalisation process succesfully within a company.

Interview with Jerry Greenfield, Co-Founder of Ben & Jerry's Ice Cream

Find out more behind Jerry Greenfield, an amazing entrepreneur with a taste for good ice cream.

Why did you and your partner, Ben Cohen, decide to start, specifically, an ice cream company?

JG: Ben and I always liked to eat. When we were thinking of starting up, we considered lots of different types of food. We picked ice cream because there was a revival in high-quality, homemade ice cream. Plus, we really like ice cream. Ben remembers his father eating ice cream directly out of a half-gallon container. Ben and a friend sold ice cream for several summers from an ice cream vending truck. I scooped ice cream at the cafeteria in college.

What do you think sets Ben & Jerry's apart from other ice cream companies today?

JG: I think there are three things that set Ben & Jerry's apart. The first is high quality ice cream, with lots of cream, not much air and all-natural ingredients. The second is the unusual flavors, which often have big chunks of cookies and candies, plus swirls as well. The third is the company's commitment to a social mission, where the company measures its success not just by how much money it makes but also by giving back to the community. The company had agreed to be acquired by Unilever, which is based in the Netherlands. Unilever committed 7.5 percent of Ben & Jerry's profits to a foundation and agreed not to reduce jobs or alter the way the ice cream is made.

What are some of the benefits and challenges to starting off as a small business owner?

JG: There are many benefits of having your own business, the best of which is that you can do things any way you want, so the business can be a reflection of who you are as a person. The biggest challenge for us was that it was an incredible amount of really hard work, plus for the first several years, the business did not make any money.

When do you think was the turning point for Ben & Jerry's, from starting off as a small business to becoming a worldwide company? Describe what happened.

JG: I think it was a pretty long process, and there wasn't one particular turning point. What probably set us in the direction was the decision to start packaging our ice cream into pint containers for sale to grocery stores. We began as an ice cream parlor, and we were scooping ice cream to customers in the store. Because the winters in Vermont are so cold, business was really slow for much of the year. We needed to find a way to have the business survive, and so we began to package the ice cream.

Edited source: Amazing Mentor!, April 2010 Issue

4.1 Internationalisation?

Entering a foreign market is a strategic choice because the whole company has to be in support of the process. Quickly acquiring foreign trade often leads to international business blunders. Therefore, proper preparation is half the battle in achieving success in foreign markets. Proper preparation can contribute towards avoiding the many pitfalls in the international market. There are many reasons for the management of a company to decide to enter the international market. It is often an unconscious choice but it can also be a semi-conscious choice, as discussed in chapter 1.

Pitfalls
A company that wishes to enter the international market must be able to overcome a number of new problems on the way. The international environment is more complex than the home environment. Initially, one does not stop to consider the problems because they may not be obvious. New problems that arise in internationalisation, especially at the beginning, require careful attention, knowledge, time, money and means. Companies that perceive the international market as a threat, do not have the knowledge and flexability required to be successful.

A company that starts doing business on the international market may encounter the following problems:

- *Being misled by the self-reference criterion*. One of the most important obstacles when entering foreign markets is known in literature as the *self-reference criterion* (SRC).
  Self-reference criterion
  The self-reference criterion refers to one's own frame of reference in one's own culture. People proceed from the idea: 'That wich is applicable in our own market (own country and culture) also holds good in a different country.' But because it is a completely different environment and people have a different cultural background, attitude and way of thinking, marketing of products and services abroad could require a completely different approach. A successful international company listens to local experts, so that decisions are taken to make the company successful in a foreign environment.
- *Higher costs and risks than on the home market*. International business involves more transport costs, insurance costs, packaging costs, import duties and the costs of money transfers and overhead. Furthermore, the issue of bribes often needs to be considered, even though attempts are being made to reduce bribery in business. Moreover, there are the risks of currency devaluation, non-payment, language problems, poor investments and political instability. All of these topics are discussed in the following chapters.
- *Unsuitable internal organisation and lack of knowledge*. The internal organisation has to be adapted in order to be successful on the foreign market. Staff must be appointed to guide the international trade along the right lines. Furthermore, personnel must have a command of languages and must be trained to work with international documents.
- *Inability to survive a long run-up period*. Usually a considerable period elapses between the moment when a company starts collecting information about a foreign market, selects a foreign buyer and finally makes the first delivery. Moreover, the time over which investments will be paid back must be taken into consideration. It is well known that investments

in China cannot be recouped quickly due to all kinds of government stipulations (trade policy).

- *Flag preference*. The phenomenon of flag preference is encountered in former colonies, which generally prefer suppliers from the former mother country. Price is less important. If flag preference applies, it is more difficult for a foreign company without any connections to the former colony to enter the market.
- *Adaptation of the product*. Sometimes products have to be adapted to the local culture in order to be accepted. Moreover, account has to be taken of adapting production capacity and extra changeover costs. These are the costs incurred when changing the production process of a product.

EXAMPLES

The export of margarine, which contains pork fat, cannot be exported to a Muslim country because Muslims regard pigs as unclean animals.

The French do not like oven-baked chips because they have less flavour than those from a deep-fat fryer.

Just-in-time deliveries

- *Insufficient working capital*. Financial resources are needed, among other things, to finance foreign stocks and debts. In case of 'just-in-time deliveries' (delivery of the goods just when the client needs them) then sea transport may take too long. The company's customer requires stock to be stored in a nearby warehouse, so that deliveries can be made precisely on time. There are different modes of payment for goods supplied. For instance in the Netherlands on average payment takes place after 42 days, but in France it 63 days and in Spain 98 days are common terms of payment.

4.2 Strategic management

Every company is free to determine its own strategic course. Many companies see entering the international market as a good strategic option for growth. For example, it took beer producer Heineken a number of decades to grow into the second-largest beer brewery in the world.

International strategic management

International strategic management is understood as an all-embracing and continuous planning process for the formulation and implementation of strategy, so that the company is able to compete effectively on the international market. Before a feasible international strategy is formulated, the company must first find answers to a number of fundamental questions:

- Does entering foreign markets fit in with the vision and mission of the company?
- What products and services will the company offer its customers?
- How will the company produce and/or purchase the products and services?
- How will the company sell the products and services?

- Which products are suitable for the international market and to what extent must these products be adapted to the foreign buyer's wishes?
- Where and how will the company offer these products and services for sale?
- Does it know which foreign markets are attractive and which are not?
- How will the company distinguish itself in the market, especially with regard to the competition?
- Is the organisation equipped and prepared to enter the international market?
- What would the profile of a future reliable partner look like?
- How can the right foreign partners be selected via a systematic selection method?
- Which risks are acceptable to the enterprise and which are not?
- How much capital is needed to build up and maintain the foreign sales channel and does the company have sufficient capital and manpower?
- What is the chance of profitability and how soon can profit be expected?

Once these questions have been answered by the company, an international strategy can be developed. The development of an international strategy involves formulation and implementation.

Strategic plan

In the formulation phase, goals are set and a strategic plan is made to achieve these goals. In the implementation phase, the emphasis is on the tactics needed to achieve the formulated goals.
In practice, it seems that specifically formulated plans do not always work during the implementation process. Some managers therefore say: "The plan is nothing, the planning is everything." Awareness of a dynamic world which is constantly changing must be created. A good plan must therefore be feasible and effective in the current international market, as in which conditions change rapidly which may make a plan quickly outdated.
In figure 4.1 you can see how an international strategy is formulated in stages.

FIGURE 4.1 Step-by-step process for the formulation of an international strategy

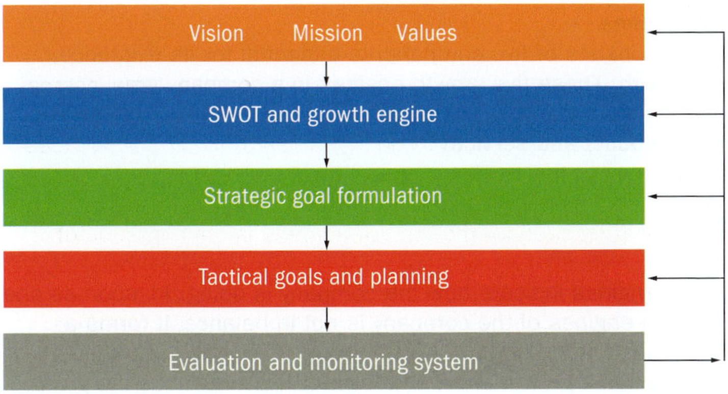

The five steps needed for the formulation of an international strategy will now be discussed.

4.2.1 Vision, mission and values

Companies begin with the formulation of a vision, mission and values.
- The *vision* reflects the future of the company, for instance to become eventually number 1 or 2 in a certain market.
- The *mission* defines the long-term outlook of the company. What kind of organisation do we want and who is our target group; in other words, the answer to the question: What business are we in? The mission is usually formulated as briefly and concisely as possible and distinguishes the company from competing companies. For example, Avis's mission is: 'Our business is renting cars.'
- *Values* can be described as the manner in which the mission can be achieved.
  - *Physical values*, such as tidiness, orderliness, punctuality and safety, provide more energy for the staff of a company.
  - *Organisational values*, such as standardisation, systematisation, discipline, communication and freedom, ensure that departments and staff function better and more harmoniously together.
  - *Psychological values*, such as the respect for the individual, integrity, creativity and decisiveness, ensure that emotional and mental energies are released. They ensure pride and dedication. These values are very useful at top management level. These values can motivate employees as well as customers.

4.2.2 SWOT analysis and growth engines

The second step is mapping the environment by making a SWOT analysis and determining the five growth engines.

SWOT

The abbriviation SWOT stands for Strengths, Weaknesses, Opportunities and Threats. By identifying the opportunities and the threats in the environment, an attempt is made to form an image of the way in which the company can best respond to these external influences. In the formulation of the strengths and weaknesses, the company tries to describe what it is good or bad at.

Five Growth Engines

Every business consists of five components essential for its existence, survival and growth. These five growth engines in a company are:
1 market
2 technology (product and service)
3 people
4 organisation
5 capital

The five growth engines indicate how the company is doing. As soon as one of the five growth engines of the company is not in balance, it forms a barrier to the growth of the company. The strongest engine gives the company the strongest growth and the weakest engine reduces the growth of the company the most. It is practical to work with a scale of 0 to 100 and to award each engine a number.

Linking the SWOT analysis to the five growth engines is an interesting activity because this gives the SWOT analysis more structure and order (see figure 4.2) and it makes it is easier to analyse in what way the company can improve its performance.

FIGURE 4.2 Balance in the five growth drivers and link with the SWOT

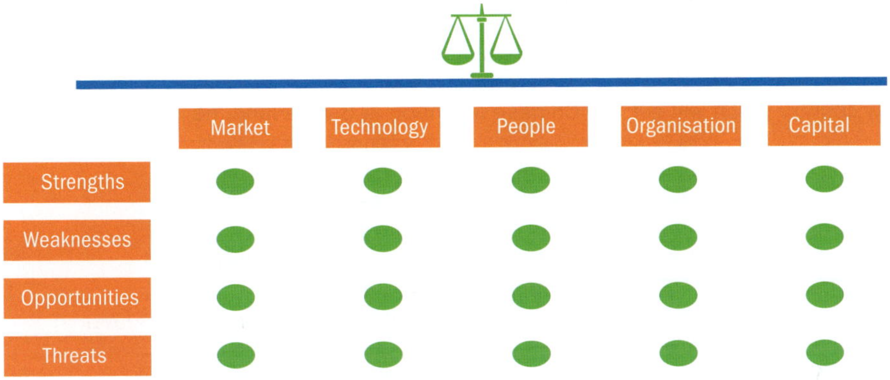

4.2.3 Strategic goal formulation

The third step is the formulation of strategic goals. The goals must be achievable, measurable and realisable within a certain period. The strategies represent the broad outlines of how to achieve these goals and they can be divided into:

- international strategy
- multinational strategy
- worldwide strategy

International strategy

Export strategy

This is in principle an extension of the export strategy. Management strives for foreign expansion with its own national strategy as a reference. An example is the collaboration between AirFrance-KLM and NorthWest Airlines.

Multinational strategy

An international expansion strategy is implemented via local market strategies. The company adapts its products and marketing strategy to a foreign market. McDonald's, for example, adapts its food to the consumer market in different countries. Some McDonald branches in Israel are completely kosher and some McDonald branches also take into account the food regulations in Islamic countries (halal). Another difference among the branches is that in some countries, such as Germany, they sell alcohol.

Worldwide strategy

The company sees the world markets as one global market. It follows the same strategy in each market by selling its same standardized products in the same way in every market. The company thus offers the same products in all foreign markets. This is called a worldwide strategy, as the same marketing strategy is used worldwide. This is the case with Coca-Cola and Dell computers.

- www.citywire.co.uk

Europe is insignificant to China, says Asia expert

Speaking at the Fondsmesse in Zurich on the China expert John Naisbitt said:
'Europe is not going to be one of the main players in the future. What do the Asians say about Europe? Not very much at all.'
The only country which will get any Chinese attention is Switzerland, he thinks.
'Switzerland will go a long way, it is going to get a fine trade negotiation with China as Swiss goods are in very high demand,' said Naisbitt. 'The European Union has two hearts, one for social welfare and one for economics. So it has two hearts, but 27 different mindsets,' Naisbitt said, with China and the US at the centre and Europe and other countries as mere 'sideshows.' He added that the Chinese do not receive Western criticism well.
'What the Chinese can't bear is being lectured to. They will walk their own path.
'Competition in China is amazing. Between cities, provinces, companies and individuals, competition energises the whole country. It's the efficiency of autocracy combined with the participation of democracy that is driving China'.

4

4.2.4 Tactical goals and planning

The fourth step is the formulation of functional strategies to archieve the strategic goals formulated in step 3. This may imply that the structure of the company has to be changed: for example, more representatives are recruited or the company enters into a collaboration with a foreign company. Usually, the various departments, such as Marketing/Sales, Production or R&D, develop the functional strategies. A change of strategy may mean a change in personnel, e.g. in transfers or in recruitment.

4.2.5 Evaluation and monitoring system

The fifth step involves testing. A system is set up to find out whether the strategic goals are achieved within the timescale, and if any interim adjustment is necessary. But before evaluation and monitoring can take place, the planning has to be done.

KOREA TIMES, 17 DECEMBER 2010 (EDITED SOURCE)

Samsung to beef up risk management

In its global strategy meeting between Samsung's headquarters and its international business divisions, the company expressed high hopes to exploit the growth in the markets for 3D televisions and smartphones, which will be critical for sustaining its leadership in its main markets of consumer electronics and mobile phones.
Samsung will also look to strengthen its positions in emerging markets such as Eastern Europe and Africa, and expand to new business areas such as the solar cell industry.
The company expected the global demand for sophisticated products such as 3D and connected "smart" televisions, smartphones and touch-screen computers, dubbed as tablets, to grow significantly in 2011.
Samsung will also improve their risk management abilities at its 200 regional business branches in global markets and plan ahead to deal with the changes in markets and financial situations.
Samsung, one of the planet's biggest technology companies, boasts a dual strength in parts and finished products, being the world's leading maker of flat-screen televisions, liquid crystal displays (LCDs) and computer memory chips, and the runner-up vendor of mobile phones behind Nokia.

4.3 Value chain analysis

On the basis of the SWOT analysis in combination with an assessment of the five growth engines, the situation the company finds itself in, can be established. Thereafter, management opts for a strategy based on the needs of the foreign client. Thus managers should select company strategies based on the company's activities that customers find valuable. The value chain model by Porter shows activities that an enterprise can undertake to obtain competitive advantage. The model provides an insight into ways of operating better or more cheaply than the competition. Furthermore, the entire company does not have to be involved in achieving competitive advantages and profits. It is therefore important that first, an insight is obtained into the primary and secondary activities of the company. The value chain model is illustrated in figure 4.3.

Competitive advantage

FIGURE 4.3 Porter's value chain

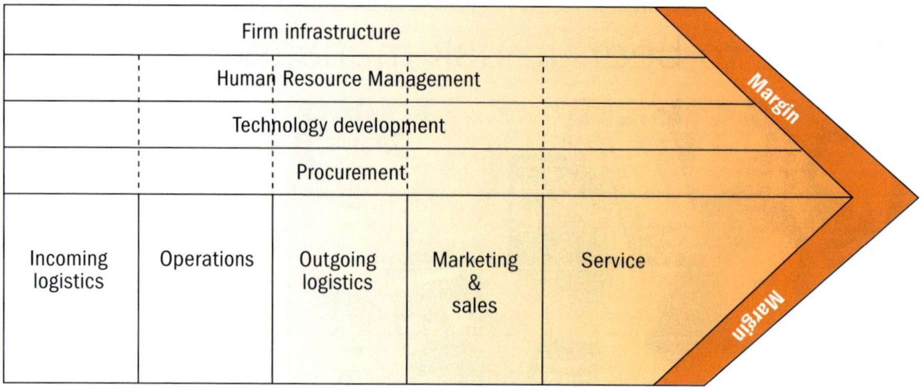

Source: Management models, M. Mulder, Porter's value chain 'Competitive Advantage'

4

Primary activities

The lower half of the value chain consists of primary activities. These are activities that directly add value to the product. They include:

1 incoming logistics: the receipt, storage and internal distribution of raw materials
2 operations: transforming the raw materials into the finished product (production)
3 outgoing logistics: packaging, storage and distribution of the finished product
4 marketing and sales: offering, recommending and selling the finished product
5 service: support, repairs and training for clients

Support activities

The upper half of the value chain consists of the support activities. These are activities that make the primary activities possible, i.e.:

1 firm infrastructure: management activities such as general management, financial management, planning and logistics.
2 human resource management: the recruitment, selection and development of staff
3 technology development: includes research and development, process automation and other development used to support the value chain activities.
4 procurement: purchasing of raw materials and the necessary products and services

Porter uses the word "margin" for the difference between:

- the total cost of all primary and support activities and
- the total value of the organisation.

System of values

The different chains of the company are part of a so-called system of values. The system of values represents all the value chains, from the supply of raw materials to the consumption of products by consumers. Instead of a 'product' the term may refer of course to a 'service'. Companies sometimes try to control several value chains (of the industrial chain), in order to control the costs and the addition of value. This can be seen in the supermarket business.

Tesco, for example, not only sells products in supermarkets but, in certain cases, also handles the purchase, production and distribution of raw materials. Shops like Zara and Ikea keep down the prices of their goods by means of efficient purchasing process and efficient logistics.

4.3.1 Differential advantage

The analysis of the value chain can help companies determine if they have and where they can create a differential advantage. A company can obtain differential advantages through product differentiation, by differentiation in terms of price and by ensuring the correct positioning of the product.

Product differentiation

- Most companies try to distinguish themselves from the competition through product differentiation. Various factors then play a part, such as the quality of the product, the speed of delivery, the design, and the quality of service.
- There are also companies that compete on price. In price competition the emphasis is on offering a keen price in combination with the lowest costs. Companies like Primark and H&M, for example, have their clothing produced in low-wage countries.
- The unique advantages of the product must be observable, communicable and acceptable to the client.
- For example Nike attracted attention by the simple advertising slogan "Just do it!" .

4.4 Strategic planning

Strategic planning gives the company a broad view of what must be done. In general, strategic planning is a management activity. In large companies, planning departments are set up to do this. Once the strategic planning has been done, operational plans are developed. Operational planning is short-term planning and gives a detailed picture of who, what, how and when. Planning has a number of advantages and disadvantages.

Strategic planning

Operational planning

The advantages of planning

- *It creates sufficient time to acquire knowledge about a foreign market.* The time is taken to conduct research into the market before important decisions are made. If these decisions are taken under time pressure, the best choices may not be made as a result of a knowledge gap. Knowledge and experience acquired in the home country is not always relevant abroad: success at home is no guarantee of success abroad. It is wise to realize that a small mistake can have big consequences for the company's success abroad. The accumulation of know-how about a foreign market increases the chance of success.

MISCALCULATIONS IN INTERNATIONAL MARKETING, ZUURHOUT, HEIJBLOM,WOLTERS-NOORDHOFF, 1988 (EDITED SOURCE)

4

International blunders

A Dutch company exported milk powder in tins (1, 2.5 and 5 kg) to Sudan and Nigeria. Then an Irish exporter came into these markets with milk powder in paper bags. Its product was much cheaper because tins are expensive. The result was that the Dutch exporter lost a large part of its export market in a very short time. The Dutch exporter decided to package the milk powder in laminated bags. The African customs authorities had little experience of small laminated bags of milk powder and were not informed in advance about the new packaging. This meant that whole shiploads were held in quarantine until the material had been thoroughly analysed and certificates could be issued by the authorising bodies. Due to these delays, the Irish exporter was temporarily the only supplier in these markets.

The international blunders of the Dutch exporter were:

- It did not know that the tins had an additional function. They were used to fetch water, to cook in and build walls with.
- It had rested on its laurels. Things were going pretty well, weren't they? There was no marketing information system. Good research into the African markets, in collaboration with local distributors, would have ensured that the developments of the competition were known.
- It failed to inform the African customs authorities in advance about the new packaging.

Better planning and research of the market developments could have prevented a great deal of misery for the Dutch exporter.

- *It can lead to a an awareness boosting process within the company.* Planning is an awareness boosting process. As a result, a collective vision emerges and people are agreed on how the company should approach the foreign market. Furthermore, planning can help ensure that

the established internationalisation strategy is not lost sight of and that staff are made responsible for adhering to the strategy.
- *It can lead to the selection of attractive foreign markets*. In one country the prices for a product are lower than in another country. Competition usually results in lower prices. If there is an import surplus (the volume of imports surpasses that of exports), local competition is usually weak because local companies cannot even meet the local needs.
- *It can lead to the selection of the best local partners*. The selection of a reliable local distributor is a very important success factor in a foreign market. Often, the image of the appointed distributor gradually becomes equated with the exporter's reputation. Good planning as to the choice of distributor is thus of great importance.

The disadvantages of planning
- *It costs time*. The collection and analysis of largely foreign data often takes a great deal of time. The development of plans on the basis of who, what, where, when and how is also time consuming.
- *It prolongs the decision-making process*. Sometimes, decisions have to be taken at short notice. There is no time to organise everything and discuss matters with each other. Richard Branson of The Virgin Group (airlines, cinemas, casinos) is an example of someone who can rapidly identify an opportunity in the market with the aid of experts. If they make a decision, they start implementing it the following day. In multinationals, such analysis and implementation processes usually take months.

Selection and implementation processes

THE ECONOMIST, 6 JANUARY 2011

European Tyremakers Bouncing back

A couple of decades ago two tyremakers, Pirelli of Italy and Continental of Germany, were locked in a takeover battle. A merger would have brought them close to the size of the world's big three tyre firms: Bridgestone, Goodyear and Michelin. It didn't happen. Continental fought off Pirelli and they went their separate ways. Both have had a bumpy ride.

In 2011, for the first time in 20 years, Pirelli will supply Formula 1 racing teams with tyres to burn up at high speed. Mr Tronchetti, its boss, describes this as "the best possible marketing tool".
Pirelli reckons its narrower focus on tyres, especially premium ones, will prove an advantage as it expands in emerging markets. Half of its business is already in the emerging world – "more than any other of the top five tyremakers". Its salvation during the recent crisis was Brazil, where it is the leading brand.
Pirelli was one of the first into China when majority foreign ownership of tyre factories was allowed in 2005. In November it signed joint-venture agreements with Russian Technologies and Sibur Holding of Russia to upgrade a tyre plant (for premium and winter tyres) and to reorganise a truck- and farm-tyre plant which employs 12,000 people. Other tyre companies regard this as "brave", given the difficulty of doing business in Russia.
Pirelli will not yet touch India: the market for premium tyres is tiny, and the wheel sizes of commercial trucks and of the Tata Nano (a super-cheap car) are too small.

Which company is best-positioned for the future? Pirelli has the best brand and is the favourite of many car enthusiasts. Apart from sidelines such as branded clothes, latex mattresses and a calendar featuring unclad women, it is focused on making tyres.

4.5 Internal organisation

After planning, the implementation processes must take place within the company. Organisation is the arrangement of a business in such a way that the employees can do their tasks. Internal specialisation involves grouping of the activities carried out by a unit on the basis of the final result. Four work levels are commonly found in companies that operate in the international market. In the following subsections, the characteristics of each level is described and an indication is given of the corresponding organisational structure.

4.5.1 Level 1 Product-oriented

Management has a sales or product-oriented way of thinking and working. Companies of this type are typically those in which people collectively make products by performing physical activities.
Many small and medium-size companies do little planning. International decisions are usually taken without being systematically checked, carefully considered or planned. They often respond to requests from foreign contacts but they do not approach the foreign market themselves.
Management of a company just starting international activities is usually of the opinion that the activity employed in its own country is more important.

International activities

It usually starts with international activities in countries geographically close to the home market: these are usually countries with a similar or slightly lower level of prosperity. The company sells exactly the same products in the foreign market as it does in the domestic market and does so in more or less the same way.

Sometimes companies accept a lower price for their products in foreign markets than they do in their home market because export is seen as the ultimate means of disposing of one's excess stock. In this case, they are often prepared to sell the products in the foreign market at a lower price. As soon as an exporting company disturbs the balance in the foreign market by selling goods at excessively low prices, it runs the risk of foreign competitors countering this by dumping goods on its home market. Furthermore, management can regard export as the ultimate means to quickly boost production to the desired level. A number of years ago, for example, printers in Italy and Belgium were prepared to produce printed matter for Dutch companies at extremely keen prices to boost their output to a high level. In such cases, the emphasis is on the short-term.
Selling goods in foreign markets is mostly done via agents if the company has collected little knowledge about the foreign market. No market research on the end-users is carried out, as this is left to the distributive trade.

The organisational structure of a product-oriented company is organized by each product or product group (see figure 4.4).

Type of organisation

FIGURE 4.4 Organisational structure for each product/product group

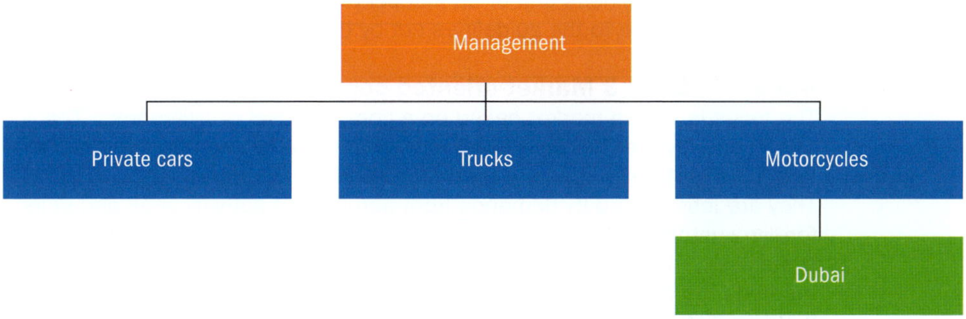

THE FINANCIAL TIMES, 6 MARCH 2010

Gucci eyes Asia as shoppers opt for discreet consumption

Gucci Group is targeting Asia for the lion's share of its investment this year and is also eyeing expansion in Latin America in a further sign of luxury goods companies' dependence on emerging markets for growth.
Robert Polet, chief executive of Gucci Group, part of France's PPR, told the Financial Times that the worst was probably over for the luxury goods industry.
Gucci Group, whose brands include Gucci, Yves St Laurent, Bottega Veneta, and Alexander McQueen, returned to growth. The former Unilever executive said more than 60 per cent of Gucci Group investment was aimed at expansion in Asia, particularly China. Mr Polet said it was clear to him when he joined the group in 2004 that "Asia Pacific was going to be the big prize to be taken".
He has since increased the number of Gucci stores in China from four to 30. "We have more selling square footage in mainland China built in five years than we built up in 30 years in Japan. He added that there were opportunities to expand the group's operations in Latin America, particularly Mexico, Brazil and Chile.

4.5.2 Level 2 Market-oriented simple

The focus is on the market but is based on a simple level of awareness. In this type of company it is understood that for increased turnover growth, it is wiser not to approach the foreign market, with the same products or services in the same way as the home market. The company understands the differences in language, culture, customs, customer behaviour and needs, politics, distribution methods and competition.
A decentralised approach for each international market begins to take shape. The needs and desires of the foreign customers must be satisfied. This process is reinforced if companies decide to establish foreign

branches. Local management of the branch often sees opportunities for the company increase if local demand and supply are anticipated. Furthermore, the need arises for local branches to take their own policy and marketing decisions. A local marketing plan is drawn up. If this is a success, a local business plan usually follows and the branch can be regarded as a business unit or an independent organisation. The branch must often adhere to the guidelines set by the parent company.

Marketing plan

4.5.3 Level 3 Market-oriented complex

The focus is on the market based on a complex level of awareness. The awareness level of the staff is focused on a more systematic approach to find the best foreign markets for the company in the world.
They are less guided by demands from abroad, but actively seek and select foreign customers themselves. In short, they adopt an active, professional, systematic, market-oriented approach to the foreign markets. The working methods are more professional and complex. The type of work that is done is primarily found in companies that employ highly educated specialized employees, and highly trained technicians for the performance of specialist activities. These companies are focused on international strategic planning.

A marketing strategy is developed for each country in order to avail oneself of local market opportunities. Awareness arises that the foreign markets are becoming an increasingly important part of the company's turnover and that these foreign markets must be handled more professionally. For the company it becomes clear that there are both differences and similarities between the various foreign markets. Once the similarities among these markets have been identified, standardised products can be used to meet the needs and wishes of these markets.
The organisational structure of such a company can be seen in figure 4.5.

FIGURE 4.5 Organisational structure for each foreign market

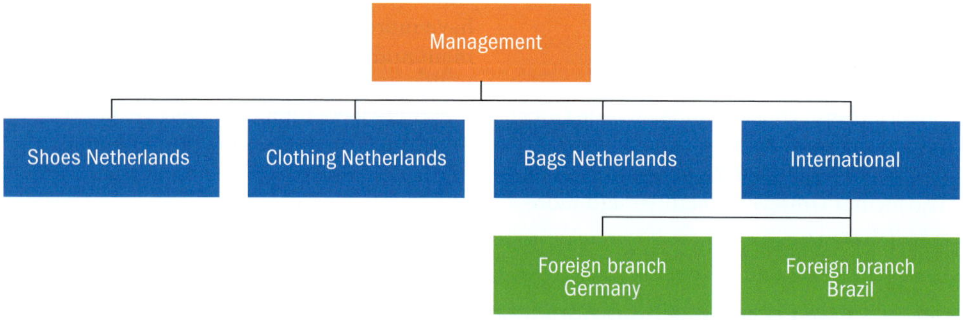

4.5.4 Level 4 Market-oriented absolute

Focus on the markets with the highest level of awareness. A company at this level of awareness shows that emotion, feelings, environmental circumstances have little or no effect on their calculations and all their results. Part of the staff of these companies is deployable worldwide. One characteristic is that they can completely adapt their work to the other foreign culture. Staff of these kind of companies can work anywhere in the world in a professional systematic succesful way. We can say that staff of these companies has reached the highest work level.

EXAMPLE

What happens to a western European manager if, for example, he goes to work in India?

He must try to function without the high demand for punctuality he is used to in Western Europe. The consequence is that he is not as effective as in Western Europe. If, as a precise Westerner, he had tried to impose his super punctuality on his Indian staff, he would have failed.
It is important to remember in this situation that there are always compensating characteristics to be found, which in this case could compensate for the low level of punctuality: for example, low wages and the fact that Indian staff are much more likely than Westerners to carry out an assignment exactly as instructed. What happens if an Indian goes to work in Germany? If the Indian is able to improve his punctuality and skills sufficiently, he will reach the highest level an employee can reach in this world. We call this the absolute level of work.

Multinational companies have grown so much that they have production facilities and sales operations across a large part of the world: they can therefore be called global companies. These companies have 'global managers', who can be deployed anywhere in the world. Companies in this phase, such as Philips, Nestlé, Shell, Microsoft and Intel, pay a great deal of attention to global strategic planning. These companies, with their high-quality products at reasonable prices, strive for market leadership. They want to be in the top five in a certain product category.
At times it may be a wise decision, as done by Unilever, to drastically reduce the number of local brands and concentrate on European or even global brands.
Small and medium-sized companies can become global players if they realise that there is always a market for quality and regard the whole world as their home market. They must distinguish themselves in a unique manner in the foreign market in order not to lose their market. If their

products are almost similar to the products of multinationals, they are in dangerous waters. Being the market leader in a global niche market can also be very attractive. The internal organisation of such a company can be seen in figure 4.6.

FIGURE 4.6 Internal organisation of a multinational

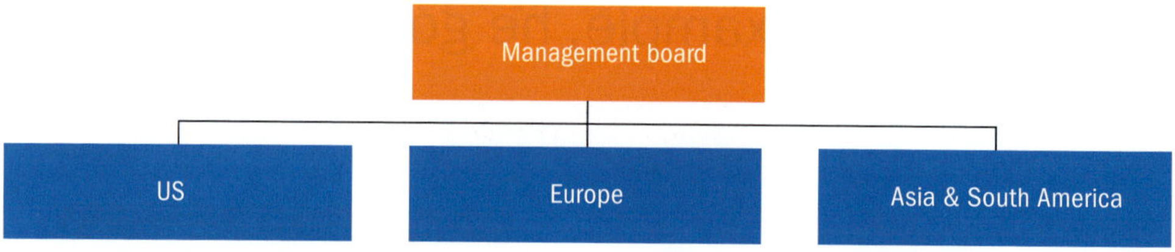

4.6 Human Resource Management

Having discussed the organizational structure of a company, we now turn to the employees. The most important success factor in international business is perhaps personnel. When hiring the right employees and by developing and retaining effective personnel, a company can successfully enter foreign markets. Effective employees are trained and developed. Human resource management can stimulate personnel to function better, as a result of which the organisation can achieve competitive advantage.

4.6.1 Global organisation

Whether and, if so, to what extent a company and its personnel can adapt to a foreign culture depends not only on the differences between the country's culture in question and its own but also on its employees.
There are various ways of setting up an organisation with regard to its international personnel complement. The following variants are discussed:
1 ethnocentric
2 polycentric
3 geocentric

Ad 1 Ethnocentric
If this style of organisation is used, all policy decisions are determined at the highest level. People from the home country manage the offices or the production locations. In this way control is exercised on the foreign locations. The same strategy will be established in every country. The culture of the foreign country is ignored and the culture of the home country is imposed. This style of organisation is often chosen for two major reasons. The first reason is the fact that no qualified personnel can be found abroad. The second is that the new organisation must be identical to the organisation in the home country and it is therefore copied, as it were. As a result, it is possible to transfer the corporate culture from the home country to the foreign country. But it is also very common to opt for this form of organisation if a great deal of knowledge has to be transferred. A disadvantage of this method is the high cost of transferring managers abroad. Another disadvantage is that the foreign branches actually remain foreign branches, even in the eyes of the local clients and employees.

Ad 2 Polycentric

In an organisation styled in this way, a manager from the home country is not sent to the foreign branch, but a local manager is employed. In this way, it is locally determined how the policy must be shaped, this is called decentralisation. The foreign branch is given autonomy in decision-making. In some cases, a regional head office functions as a buffer; the organisation is thus 'regionally-centric'. The great advantage of using local people is that they have a great deal of knowledge about the local business climate. Another advantage, especially for smaller companies, is the lower cost of employing local staff. The great disadvantage of this type of organisation is a possible loss of control over the foreign branch. If a worldwide strategy is implemented, this is the least suitable form of organisation.

Ad 3 Geocentric

In this type of organisation the foreign branch is headed by the manager with the best qualities, regardless of origin. He/she can therefore come from the home country, the host country or from elsewhere. A policy is implemented in dialogue between the home country and the host country. The advantage of this type of organisation is that international managers are developed who can deal with cultural differences worldwide. This is often the method chosen by multinationals. These enterprises can afford to recruit and develop international managers, which is an extremely expensive activity. This style of organisation is also often used if the host country requires a totally different approach from the one in the home country.

The more a company develops its foreign activities, the more the organisation will be adapted. Most companies begin with an ethnocentric approach and switch to a polycentric type of organisation the moment local product adaptations for markets turn out to be very different. To improve the coordination of business activities among the different countries, they then develop a 'regionally-centric' approach. More and more companies want to adopt a global approach and companies therefore often switch to geocentric organisation.
In table 4.1, the advantages and disadvantages of these three types of organisations are summarised.

TABLE 4.1 The effects of three types of organisations on dealing with cultural differences

	Ethnocentric	Polycentric	Geocentric
Culture	• Subordinate	• Problem/threat	• Opportunity • Source of competitive advantage
Expected benefit	• Standardisation • Worldwide integration	• Localisation • Accessibility	• Innovation and learning
Performance criteria	• Efficiency	• Adaptability	• Synergy
Communication	• Top-down	• Top-down • Reporting bottom-up	• All channels
Greatest challenge	• Being accepted	• Creating cohesion	• Utilising differences
Greatest concern	• Inflexibility • Missed opportunities	• Fragmentation • Duplication of effort • Loss of potential synergy	• Confusion • Friction

Source: Schneider & Barsoux, 2003

4.6.2 Levels of working in the company

Having looked at internal organisation, we now turn to the different levels of running a company. In this respect research by Robert van Harten and Natarajan Karmayogi is relevant. They posit that the work we perform can explain the occurrence of international trade, from which international business can result. According to them, four levels of work can be identified (see figure 4.7).

FIGURE 4.7 Four levels of work

1 *Work on a family level*. Work that is done with the support of one's family and circle of acquaintances. Examples include a family that works together in the company, different families of the same ancestry working together to provide a livelihood or a company in which some of the staff is family. Most of them have expanded into leading companies that also operate internationally. Well known international family firms are Porsche, BMW, Danone and LEGO.
A royal family is a good example of a successful family firm. 'Everyone has their role and fulfils it enthusiastically. That's the way it should be.'
2 *Work on a social level*. These companies usually need more employees than family firms. This type of company is primarily seen in industry, where the personnel collectively makes products by performing physical activities and there is a division of labour.

● www.therugcompany.info

The Rug Company

An example of a company that works at a social level is The Rug Company.
Every rug is entirely made by hand. The company is family owned and has operated for years. They are dedicated to personal service and quality workmanship. They continually strive to improve the rug making process both in an environmentally-friendly and ethical way.

3 *Work on a professional level*. Work that is performed within a specific profession or service level. This type of work is found primarily in companies that employ well educated, white-collar people or highly trained technicians to perform specialist activities for the local market, such as banks, insurance companies, accountants' offices, ICT companies and engineering consultancies.
4 *Work on an absolute level*. In these companies the export or import manager, international consultant or global specialist can operate in any country in the world. These people usually work for international companies. In practice, the global manager is able to reduce the work to its essence or work in his own context.The global manager works at the absolute top level if two conditions are fulfilled:
   - He is highly specialized in his job, so he is an expert.
   - He is able to function successfully anywhere in the world, despite differences in culture and language.

Professional profile

A professional profile of the international functions can be drafted on this basis. In a professional profile are described the principles and requirements for a certain profession are described.

Professional profile of the international manager
The global manager is someone who is able to function successfully not only in his country of birth and culture, but also beyond the borders of his country and outside his culture.

Apart from the global manager, the following employees are of importance in an international company:
- buyer
- area manager
- import or export manager
- international adviser or consultant
- assistant

Buyer
The buyer finds and purchases products, services or raw materials for the company or organisation. Purchasing is an important part of business. Buyers can therefore be found in just about all sectors and product divisons, from clothing businesses to hospitals. A buyer is heavily involved in the foreign market because production primarily takes place abroad.

Area manager
The area manager is co-responsible for achieving the target turnover and results for a certain sales area. The focus is on keeping in touch with existing clients and visiting potential clients and agents at home and abroad.

Import or export manager
In this position a manager is responsible for the import or export of products, services or raw materials for the company or organisation. The import or export manager sets the policy with regard to imports or exports and regularly travels to the importing or exporting countries. For this job, the employee should have a pioneering spirit and relish of challenge is required.

Sales Area Manager Responsible for Eastern Europe

You are in charge of developing revenues, margin and market share. Your responsibility covers the following countries: Armenia, Azerbaijan, Bielorussia, Georgia, Kazakhstan, Kirghizstan, Moldavia, Uzbekistan, Russia, Tadjikistan, Turkmenistan, Ukraine.

You enhance sales, optimize our product portfolio, propose improvements to the distribution strategy and manage your network of distributors. You are in charge of a team of local promoters who will assist you in your mission. You define and propose a sales plan and manage customer relations towards customer satisfaction, including orders follow-up, sales contracts and variety registrations. You negotiate internally and comply with a budget, for both Sales Objectives and Operational expenditures.

International adviser or consultant

The adviser or consultant advises organisations on problems or about improvements. It is an all-around professional. An international consultant meets many people at different levels in an organisation. He can look behind the scenes in different departments. It is also a demanding profession. Client expects internal problems to be resolved. The consultant is not expected to know everything, but he must be able to gather the right information quickly and he must be persuasive. This work can also be done by a consultancy bureau.

Assistant

An assistant at an international company deals with international trading on a daily basis. He is expected to regularly consult colleagues within the company or abroad. The language spoken within the company is often English.

Summary

4

- ► Internationalisation?
  - Conscious or unconscious choice
  - Strategic option
  - Pitfalls for companies starting in international business
    - being misled by the self-reference criterion
    - higher costs and risks than on the home market
    - unsuitable internal organisation and gap knowledge
    - inability to survive a long run-up period
    - flag preference
    - adaptation of the product
    - insufficient working capital

- ► Strategic management
  All-embracing and continuous planning process for the formulation and implementation of a strategy
  - Formulation of a strategy
    - vision, mission and values
    - SWOT analysis and growth engines
    - strategic goal formulation
    - tactical goals and planning
    - evaluation and monitoring system
  - Implementation of a strategy (planning)
  - Advantages of planning
    - sufficient time to acquire knowledge about a foreign market
    - awareness boosting process within the company
    - selection of attractive foreign markets
    - selection of the best local partners
  - Disadvantages of planning
    - costs time
    - prolongs the decision time

- ► Internal organisation
  The structure of an organisation enabling people within the organisation can do their tasks.
  Four divisions in companies operate on the international market:
  - 1: product-oriented
  - 2: market-oriented simple
  - 3: market-oriented complex
  - 4: market-oriented absolute

- ► Human resource management
  - When hiring the right employees and by developing and retaining effective personnel, a company can successfully enter foreign markets.
  - An organisation can be set up in three ways:
    - ethnocentric
    - polycentric
    - geocentric
  - Levels of work:
    - family level
    - social level
    - professional level
    - absolute level

Questions and assignments

4

- www.zawya.com

Alshaya takes Cheesecake Factory franchise

Alshaya has entered into a licensing agreement with the US restaurant brand The Cheesecake Factory to build and operate The Cheesecake Factory restaurants in the Middle East.
The first two restaurants are scheduled to open in Dubai and Kuwait in 2012.
The franchise agreement also gives Alshaya the opportunity to expand into other markets, including the rest of the Middle East, North Africa, Central and Eastern Europe, Russia and Turkey.
The new partnership further develops Alshaya's Food Service offer, which has expanded greatly in recent years to reflect the market potential in the region and the strong consumer demand for international brands. Alshaya already partners with a number of leading Food Service brands including Starbucks, Dean & Deluca, PF Chang's, Pinkberry, Le Pain Quotidien, Asha's and Pizza Express. In 2010 it signed agreements with three further US-based food concepts: Shake Shack, Potbelly and Texas Roadhouse, all of which are expected to open their first outlets in 2011.
David Overton, Chairman and CEO of The Cheesecake Factory, said: "With our menu featuring over 200 items that are prepared fresh daily in our restaurants and our focus on quality and hospitality, our restaurants are extremely complex to operate, and we set the bar very high in terms of our standards. We found the premier partner in Alshaya to operate and execute The Cheesecake Factory restaurants in a manner that is consistent with our existing domestic operations. The portfolio of restaurant and retail brands that Alshaya operates is impressive and speaks to its capabilities in successfully bringing leading brands to the Middle East, a highly desirable and growing market for American brands."

26 january 2011

4.1 Suppose Alshaya adopted market penetration as its strategy. What steps should the company then undertake?

4.2 For years Alshaya has been hindered in entering the foreign market. Setting up restaurants abroad is bound by strict regulations. Devise at least two strategies with which Alshaya would be able to conquer the European market.

4.3 After the planning process, the company must be organised. Four work levels can be identified in companies operating on the international market. There are certain characteristics to a certain way of thinking at every level. On which work level is Alshaya operating?

4.4 In the value chain analysis, a distinction is made between primary and secondary activities. For a company engaged in the sale of products to consumers, these activities have an effect on the composition of these primary and secondary activities. What are the primary activities of a retailer who buys from suppliers and who has a central warehouse?

4.5 Talking about the same company, which activities would you class as secondary? Name at least four.

5 External analysis in an international environment

Besides management and organisation described in chapter 4, it is important to analyse the external environment. External analysis is of crucial importance because the possibilities that emerge from the value chain analysis can also be tested. After all, the company is part of the market in which it operates. In practice, a great deal of attention is paid to the external environmental analysis because the company will have to anticipate the demand and needs in the foreign market if it wishes to be successful in a certain market. In this chapter, the external analysis is explained in four steps.

Ikea's New Plan for Japan

After one failed attempt to penetrate the Japanese market, is the second time the charm for the Swedish home-furnishings empire?
Its first attempt to crack the Japanese market was a bust. Now, two decades later, Swedish home-furnishings giant Ikea is giving it another go with a gleaming new mega-store just east of Tokyo. The first time out, Ikea's stores were too small, and few Japanese consumers were willing to assemble Ikea's do-it-yourself kits. Now the chain is striving to blend Swedish design concepts into a much more Japanese shopping experience. And consumers seem willing to check it out. An Apr. 24 opening ceremony, complete with a traditional Swedish log-cutting, lured an estimated 35,000 shoppers to the five-story 40,000-square-foot store.

This time, will they keep coming back? Ikea is leaving nothing to chance. The store's second floor is lined with 70 mini-show-rooms built to the size of a typical Japanese room. Offering design ideas for smaller living spaces, each room is aimed at a different demographic group. There's an entertainment room, for instance, kitted out to appeal to computer-game mad teens. And a compact kitchen filled with space-saving options for families.

To make sure its offerings were in sync with current Japanese tastes, Ikea visited more than 100 homes. Large sofas, beds, and tables, top-sellers in Europe and the U.S., won't be for sale because they wouldn't fit into most Japanese homes. Prices are competitive too. For less than $700, shoppers can pick up an entire living room – including sofa, television stand, and tables.

MODERN AESTHETIC. Hoping to woo Japanese consumers, who are accustomed to lavishly high levels of customer service, Ikea offers home delivery and an assembly service for an extra charge. "The market has changed a lot since Ikea entered Japan the first time," says Ikea spokeswoman Yuki Kusama. "Japanese consumers are more interested in designing the look of their homes by themselves rather than having it done for them."

Analysts agree that recent market shifts bode well for the chain. Ikea's modern aesthetic appeals to Japanese tastes, especially as the retailer has expanded its range to include richer and darker woods. At the same time, consumers are warming to do-it-yourself shops, says David Marra, a consultant at A.T. Kearney in Tokyo.

Edited source: www.businessweek.com
1 February 2011

5.1 What is an external analysis?

External analysis

After a value chain analysis, an external analysis must also be made. In an external analysis, factors that cannot be influenced, but must be taken into account, are inventoried. At a macro-level, these include the economic climate, socio-cultural developments and changes in laws and rules; at a meso-level (the level of the industry), the environment, competitors and suppliers are analysed. In the case of export we look at the product and the market in the potential country. When talking about import we look at the product and the domestic market.

The external analysis can be divided into four steps:
1 initial analysis
2 business environment analysis
3 market research
4 determiniation of market potential

See figure 5.1. These steps are discussed in the following paragraphs.

FIGURE 5.1 Steps in the analysis of international products and markets

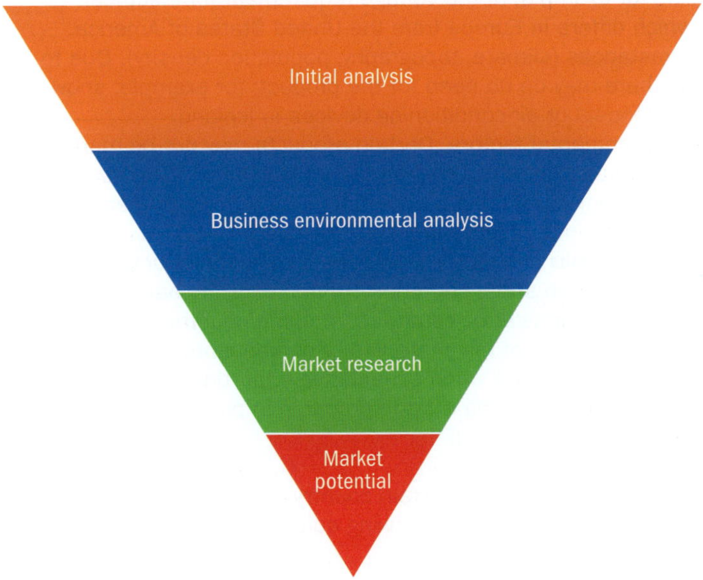

The goal of the external analysis is to provide an insight into opportunities and threats. The external analysis may reveal that it is not profitable to export or import a certain product.

5.2 Initial analysis

Initial analysis

In this section we look at the first step in the analysis. The initial analysis determines whether it is necessary to continue the business environment analysis (see section 5.3). The three components of the initial analysis

– the basic demand analysis, the trade figures analysis and the BERI index – are discussed.

5.2.1 Basic demand analysis

First of all, it is important to find out whether there is actually a demand for the product in another country. This can be done by means of desk research or by means of in-depth interviews with experts from the country. Research into a number of questions shows whether it makes sense to put a product into a foreign market. If you intend to import or export, and the product is not yet available in the domestic or foreign market, you should ask yourself the following question:
Why is the product not yet on the market? This may be due to various reasons:

- Taste/customer preference. Just think of culture differences, due to which a certain product is not attractive and, without some adaptation, has no potential. In Saudi Arabia, for example, orange DAF trucks did not catch on. All such trucks had previously been Mercedes and used to have the colour used by Caterpillar for its earth-moving machines: yellow. Sales were poor until DAF also painted its trucks yellow.
- Legal requirements. There may be completely different regulations in the export country, due to which the product is inadequate in its current state. Think, for example, of the voltage requirement for electrical devices, which differs in Europe from the United States of America.
- Other circumstances (climate, topography, population density). Due to the climate there may be no need for the product; for example, snowboards in Indonesia or air-conditioning devices in Iceland.
- Health or environmental factors. Certain products may not be marketable because of strict health or environmental legislation. Children's clothing in Germany must comply with much stricter environmental requirements than in the Netherlands.
- **Import/export restrictions** or bans. The import of certain products is restricted or banned in some countries. Think about the ban on importing alcoholic drinks in Islamic countries. In some countries it is also common to ban imports of raw materials or components. This aspect must be taken into account when considering importing or outsourcing production. There may also be a trade embargo in place against a certain country (see chapter 2).

If outsourcing the production to a certain country or to invest in a certain country seems a viable option, the following questions should be researched:

- Which countries are the most innovative in the field of production processes? A presence in these countries can be important, not only to gain knowledge and technology know-how, but also because of the competition. These countries attract specific activities; for example, China in low-cost production and India in software development.
- How high are the labour costs? If the labour costs in a certain country are lower than in another country and productivity is almost the same, production will have to be moved to the country offering the lowest costs. Volkswagen moved its car production from Germany to Spain because labour costs were 50% lower over there.

FIGURE 5.2 Minimum wages in the European Union, 2009

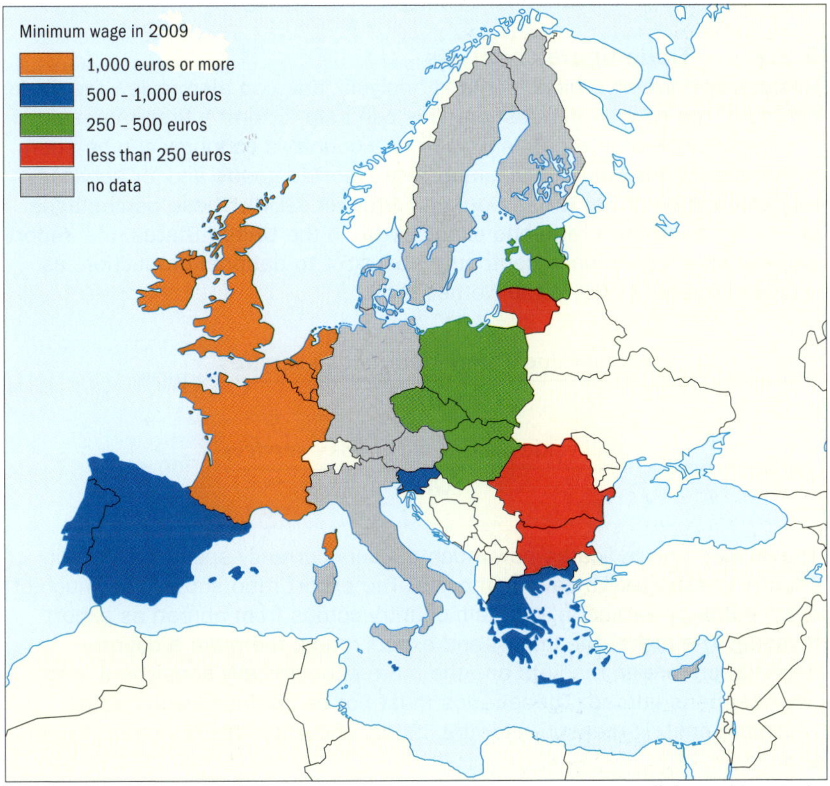

© Noordhoff Uitgevers Atlasproducties

BUITENLANDSE MARKTEN, MARCH/APRIL 2010

Minimum wage increased

For 2010, the Romanian minimum wage was fixed at 705 lei per month (about 170 euros, according to the exchange rate in January 2010). This is an increase of 105 lei (17.5 per cent) with respect to 2009. The minimum wage in Romania has increased substantially in recent years. The legal minimum wage in 2008 was under 540 lei. Nevertheless Romania, together with Bulgaria, has the lowest wages of all the countries in the European Union.

- What is the geographic distance to the current market? If transport costs are a significant proportion of the ultimate price, this is an important factor. If transport costs are a significant factor in the pricing (see chapter 6), it is recommended to locate production closer to the market. If that is not the case, one can opt for production further away. In the example of Volkswagen, the transport costs constitute a relatively insignificant part of the price, due to which production does not need to be done near the home market.

5

If it appears that there is no market for the product from this analysis, research into the foreign country stops after this stage.

5.2.2 Trade figures analysis

Besides performing a basic-demand analysis, one can also review the trade figures of the country in question. This can help to form a first impression. The importance of international trade to a country's economy can be seen by expressing the value of the imported/exported goods and/or services as percentages of the Gross Domestic Product (GDP). These percentages are called the import ratio and export ratio. In the United States, the import and export of goods each contribute about 5% to national production, as opposed to about 50% in the Netherlands.

Gross Domestic Product

$$\text{Import ratio} = \frac{\text{total value of imported goods + services}}{\text{GDP}} \times 100\ \%$$

$$\text{Export ratio} = \frac{\text{total value of exported goods + services}}{\text{GDP}} \times 100\ \%$$

The import ratio indicates how much of every currency spent in a certain country is exported to pay for imports. The export ratio shows how much of every currency earned in a certain country comes from abroad as export revenue. The higher the import and export ratios, the more a country depends on foreign markets and the more economically sensitive it is to what happens abroad. These ratios must not be confused with quotas, which are limiting measures for the import of certain articles (see chapter 2).

Balance of trade

The import and export volumes are stated on a country's balance of trade. The balance of trade gives a systematic overview of income from and payments to foreign countries in a period of one year. If a country imports more than it exports, it will have a trade deficit: this is called a passive trade balance. The European Union has had a passive trade balance for decades. A trade deficit generally leads to a higher inflation rate: this makes European products cheaper abroad due to currency depreciation and more good/services can be exported. The increasing export can result in a more favourable balance of trade, until a new balance is achieved. Unfortunately, more also has to be paid for imports and there are often goods that have to be imported because they are not available in that country (for example, oil). The developments in international trade over the last 20 years show that many third-world countries are becoming increasingly poor compared to the rich, exporting countries, due to the necessity for imports and a growing inflation.

Terms of trade

The European Union tries to keep the relationship between imports and exports stable to retain its balance of trade (figure 5.3). Important in this relationship are the terms of trade: that is, the relationship between the price index for exported and imported goods. If the price of exported products rises faster than the price of imported products, there is said to be an improvement in the terms of trade. Fewer products now need to be exported to pay for the same package of import goods. A terms of trade deterioration is a common phenomenon in third-world countries.

$$\text{Terms of trade} = \frac{\text{price index export}}{\text{price index import}} \times 100\ \%$$

FIGURE 5.3 Development of external trade, EU-27([1]) (EUR 1 000 million)

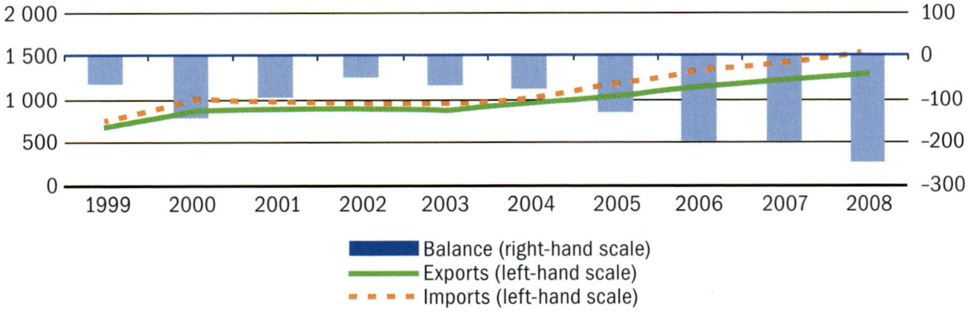

([1]) External trade flows with extra EU-27.
Source: Eurostat (ext_it_intertrd)

5

A figure used to express the relationship between the imports and exports of a country is the import cover, which shows the degree to which the imports can be paid for by the exports revenue. If a country spends more (on imports) than it receives (from exports), the balance of trade is upset. Just as it is the case with a household purse, this situation should not continue too long, or extra money will have to be printed, which will lead to inflation.

Import cover

$$\text{Importcover} = \frac{\text{total value of exports}}{\text{total value of imports}} \times 100\ \%$$

FIGURE 5.4 Trade figures analysis for Pakistan and cars

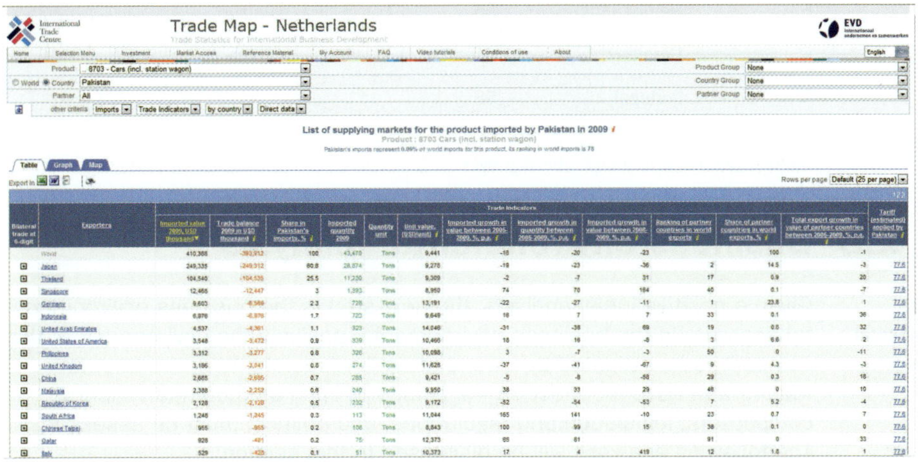
Trade Map - Netherlands
Trade Statistics for International Business Development

Product: .. 8703 - Cars (incl. station wagon)
Country: Pakistan
Partner: All
Product Group: None
Country Group: None
Partner Group: None
other criteria: Imports | Trade Indicators | by country | Direct data

List of supplying markets for the product imported by Pakistan in 2009
Product : 8703 Cars (incl. station wagon)
Pakistan's imports represent 0.09% of world imports for this product, its ranking in world imports is 75

Exporters	Imported value 2009, USD thousand	Trade balance 2009 in USD thousand	Share in Pakistan's imports, %	Imported quantity 2009	Quantity unit	Unit value (USD/unit)	Imported growth in value between 2005-2009, %, p.a.	Imported growth in quantity between 2005-2009, %, p.a.	Imported growth in value between 2008-2009, %, p.a.	Ranking of partner countries in world exports	Share of partner countries in world exports, %	Total export growth in value of partner countries between 2005-2009, %, p.a.	Tariff (estimated) applied by Pakistan
World	410,368	-393,912	100	43,470	Tons	9,441	-18	-20	-23		100	-1	
Japan	249,335	-249,312	60.8	28,874	Tons	9,278	-19	-23	-36	2	14.5	-3	77.6
Thailand	104,540	-104,535	25.5	11,230	Tons	9,309	-2	-7	31	17	0.9	20	77.6
Singapore	12,466	-12,447	3	1,393	Tons	8,950	74	70	184	40	0.1	-7	77.6
Germany	9,603	-8,569	2.3	728	Tons	13,191	-22	-27	-11	1	23.8	1	77.6
Indonesia	6,976	-6,976	1.7	723	Tons	9,649	16	7	7	33	0.1	36	77.6
United Arab Emirates	4,537	-4,361	1.1	323	Tons	14,046	-31	-38	69	19	0.8	32	77.6
United States of America	3,548	-3,472	0.9	339	Tons	10,466	18	16	-6	3	6.6	2	77.6
Philippines	3,312	-3,277	0.8	328	Tons	10,098	3	-7	-3	50	0	-11	77.6
United Kingdom	3,186	-3,041	0.8	274	Tons	11,628	-37	-41	-67	9	4.3	-3	77.6
China	2,685	-2,695	0.7	285	Tons	9,421	-5	-8	-58	29	0.3	18	77.6
Malaysia	2,388	-2,252	0.6	240	Tons	9,950	38	33	29	48	0	10	77.6
Republic of Korea	2,128	-2,128	0.5	232	Tons	9,172	-52	-54	-53	7	5.2	-4	77.6
South Africa	1,248	-1,245	0.3	113	Tons	11,044	165	141	-10	23	0.7	7	77.6
Chinese Taipei	955	-955	0.2	108	Tons	8,843	100	99	15	38	0.1	0	77.6
Qatar	928	-491	0.2	75	Tons	12,373	65	61		91	0	33	77.6
Italy	529	-425	0.1	51	Tons	10,373	17	4	419	12	1.8	1	77.6

Source: www.trademap.org/netherlands/Country_SelProductCountry.aspx

At the product level one can see the trade figures for imports and exports on the basis of the Combined Nomenclature (see chapter 2) via desk research. This will give you an impression of how trade is doing for these concrete products. Figure 5.4 gives an example of the trade figures for a particular country and product.

All these figures give an impression of the economic situation of a country. In order to be able to make decisions about export/import or investments in a certain country, the BERI index must also be used.

5.2.3 BERI index

BERI index

A frequently used country analysis is the Business Environment Risk Index (BERI). The BERI index measures the quality and the risk level of the business climate in the country concerned, and was developed by the University of Delaware. The index comprises 15 criteria, including economic, political and financial factors, which are given certain weightings. This results in a final score between 0 and 100. Scores between 0 and 41 indicate that the investment climate is unfavourable. It is questionable whether long-term investments – such as investments in assembly and production facilities – in these countries can be recouped. These are investments recovery of which takes some years. It is usually too risky to make certain investments in such countries and it is wiser to export to them instead. Scores above 71 indicate a low country risk. This means that the investment climate in these countries is favourable. Table 5.1 shows the scores of a number of countries.

TABLE 5.1 BERI index 2006

Position	Country	Score	Position	Country	Score
1	USA	75	8	Austria	57
2	Switzerland	74	9	Turkey	56
3	Belgium	73	10	Czech Republic	55
4	Japan	72	11	Hungary	55
5	Netherlands	66	12	Poland	52
6	Germany	61	13	China	46
7	Portugal	58			

Source: http://the.wikipedia.org/wiki/BERI index

5.3 Business environmental analysis

Business environmental analysis

Given a positive initial analysis, the next step is the business environmental analysis. In the business environmental analysis the environment of the company is investigated by means of desk research. All environmental factors that have an effect on the company, such as (potential) clients, competitors, legislation and regulations, and politics, must be assessed. The following analyses will be discussed in this section:

- DEPEST analysis

- competition analysis
- supplier analysis
- distribution analysis

DEPEST analysis

The DEPEST analysis takes place at a macro level and the other three analyses at a meso level. The macro level is the level relating to the country and the market. The meso level is the level relating to the industry or market sector in which the company operates. All these analyses must be weighed against the domestic market and the differences investigated. From the conclusions of the business environmental analysis, the type of market entry strategy and the marketing mix are determined, as shown in figure 5.5. This step is elaborately discussed in chapter 6.

FIGURE 5.5 From the business environmental analysis to the marketing mix

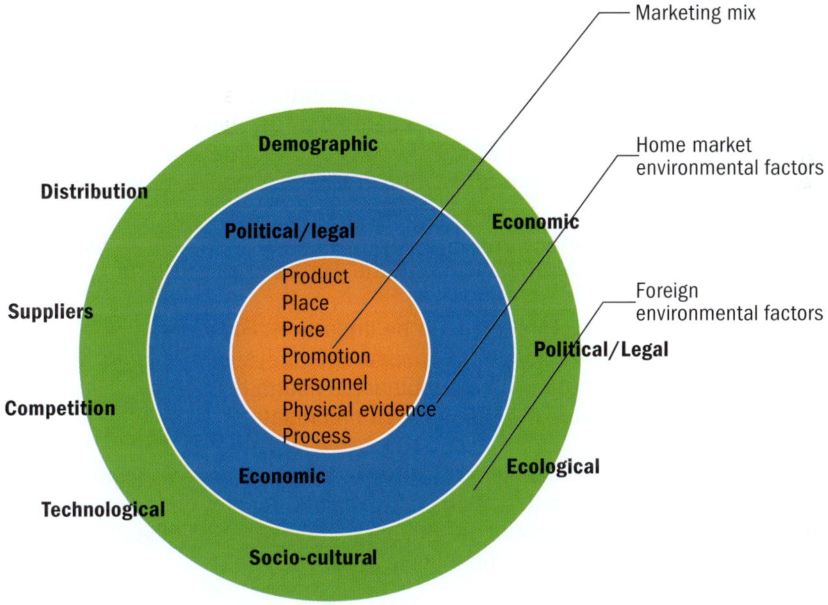

5.3.1 DEPEST analysis

Another model used for an external analysis is the PEST analysis, also extended to DEPEST analysis. Figure 5.6 shows the factors included in this analysis. These factors are discussed below.

FIGURE 5.6 DEPEST analysis

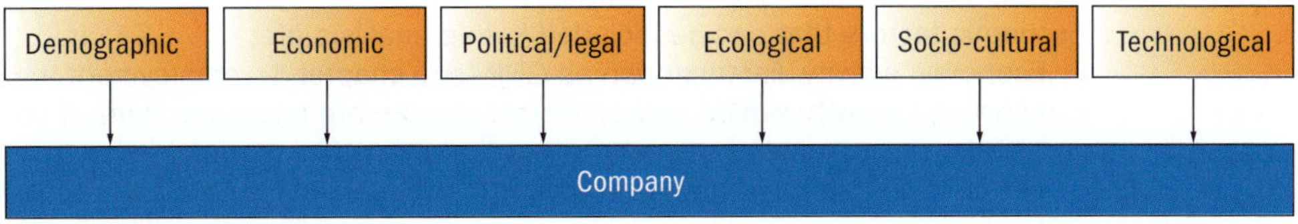

Source: Mulders, 2007

5

Demographic environmental analysis

To estimate the size of the market and determine the distribution pattern, it is important to know the structure and composition of the population, the market. The target group is determined on the basis of demographic factors. Demographic variables that can be included in this analysis are:

- Population structure. It is important to include growth so that the future of the market is incorporated. But ethnic composition must also be taken into account. There is for instance a growing demand for Halal products in European supermarkets because a growing part of the population is Islamic.
- Number of households. If one focuses on the business-to-consumer market, this is a critical factor. The number of households is determined by the type of society. In Asia it is quite normal for three generations to live together: because of this, a household numbers more people on average than in Europe, for example.
- Age distribution. If the target group is composed of older people, it is necessary to know what percentage of the population is found in this target group. Furthermore, it may be necessary to find out where the largest number of this target group is located.
- Educational level. The higher the educational level, the greater the need for high-quality products. Bringing books into the market in a country where the majority of the population is illiterate makes no sense.

These data can be obtained from the Organisation for Economic Cooperation and Development (OECD) through the website www.oecd.org.

Other demographic factors can also be important. For example, in the clothing sector, information about measurement systems is important; in the medical sector, data on the population's health is important. These data are often available from the branch organisation.

The above factors are usually applicable to the business-to-consumer market. In the business-to-business market, the market does not consist of consumers but of companies. In this case, the characteristics of companies and institutions should be investigated, such as:

- number
- size
- type of organisation
- branch
- dispersion

Economic environmental analysis

Economic environmental factors

Economic environmental factors include all those factors that influence the income and purchasing power of the consumer. You may have a certain target group in mind, but if this group has insufficient purchasing power to buy the product, your efforts are wasted.
Economic factors that can be included in this analysis are:

- Economic activity. Factors such as GNP (see chapter 1), employment, economic growth, wages and economic climate are important here. If the GNP is low, it is questionable whether there is sufficient purchasing power to buy the product. What you see is that world citizens can be found in all large cities everywhere: a small group of people with sufficient purchasing power.

- Income distribution. How are incomes spread in a certain country? Some groups have more to spend than others. For example, the wealthiest 10% of a country may earn 80% of total income.
- Purchasing power. How much can people spend? What is the situation regarding price level and inflation? If inflation is high, disposable income drops. Countries with inflation rates of more than 10%, as was the norm in Turkey for many years, are not unusual. To compare purchasing power internationally, use is often made of a measure called the purchasing power parity (PPP). This is a way of comparing the purchasing power of two countries. It represents the relationship between the amount of one's own currency and the amount of a foreign currency that is necessary to buy the same basket of goods and services. Look at table 5.2, in which the prices of a McDonald's 'Big Mac' in different countries are compared.

Purchasing power parity

● www.ft.com

Asia: the rise of the middle class

This year could be the one when talk of Asia's export-led development begins to give way to a realisation that much of the region's future growth will be self-generated. That could even begin to address the global imbalances resulting from Asia's export-led model that have been at the heart of the global financial crisis.

Not only in China but in countries including India, the world's second most populous; Indonesia, a fast-growing nation of 240m; and Vietnam, 85m-strong and following in China's developmental footsteps, the consuming class is beginning to grow. Even in less obviously successful economies such as the Philippines, which has a population of nearly 95m, years of steady if sub-optimal growth are creating pockets of broader affluence.

The emergence of a middle class in Asia beyond the prosperity that already exists in Japan, South Korea, Taiwan, Singapore and Hong Kong will have far-reaching consequences. With growth likely to be anaemic in Europe and possibly America for many years to come, businesses from food to insurance are desperate for new consumers with money to spend. Many may find the opportunity they need in Asia.

1 February 2011

TABLE 5.2 The price of a Big Mac in different countries

Country	**Big Mac price**		**PPP***	**Actual Exchange Rate 1 USD =**	**Over(+) / Under(−) Valuation against the USD, % ****
	in local currency	**in US dollars**			
United States	$ 3.57	3.5700	---	1.0000	---
Australia	A$ 4.34	3.9501	1.22	1.0987	11.0403
Brazil	Real 8.03	4.5778	2.25	1.7541	28.2709
Canada	C$ 3.89	3.6688	1.09	1.0603	2.8011
China	Yuan 12.5	1.8279	3.50	6.8386	−48.8199
Egypt	Pound 13.0	2.3520	3.64	5.5273	−34.1451
Euro Countries	€3.31	4.8293	0.93	0.6854	35.6872
Hong Kong	HK$ 13.3	1.7155	3.73	7.7527	−51.8877
Indonesia	Rupiah 20900	2.1945	5854	9523.81	−38.5330
Israel	Shekel 15.0	3.9600	4.20	3.7879	10.8794
Japan	¥ 320	3.5876	89.6	89.1961	0.4528
Malaysia	Ringgit 6.77	1.9824	1.90	3.4150	−44.3631
Mexico	Peso 33.0	2.5874	9.24	12.7542	−27.5533
New Zealand	NZ$ 4.90	3.5469	1.37	1.3815	−0.8324
Poland	Zloty 7.6	2.6414	2.13	2.8773	−25.9723
Russia	Rouble 67.0	2.2196	18.8	30.1862	−37.7199
Saudi Arabia	Riyal 11.00	2.9321	3.08	3.7516	−17.9017
Singapore	S\$ 4.22	3.0292	1.18	1.3931	−15.2968
Taiwan	NT$ 75.0	2.3220	21.0	32.3000	−34.9845
Thailand	Baht 64.49	1.9422	18.1	33.2043	−45.4890
Turkey	Lire 5.65	3.7417	1.58	1.5100	4.6358
Uruguay	Peso 61.0	3.0409	17.1	20.0600	−14.7557
United Kingdom	£ 2.29	3.7260	0.64	0.6146	4.1328
South Africa	Rand 17.95	2.4106	5.03	7.4462	−32.4488
South Korea	Won 3400	2.9294	952	1160.63	−17.9756
Sweden	SKr 39.0	5.4338	10.9	7.1773	51.8677
Switzerland	SFr 6.50	6.2693	1.82	1.0368	75.5401

* The Purchasing Power Parity (PPP) rate is the local Big Mac price divided by its price in the United States. Prices and their corresponding implied PPP rates are the latest figures available from The Economist.

** The Over/Under valuation against the dollar is calculated as follows using OANDA's latest rates: 100 x (PPP Exchange Rate) / Exchange Rate

Source: http://www.oanda.com

The following factors can also be considered:

- Consumption expenditure. Factors like interest rates, spending, availability of capital and consumer confidence are involved here. When the credit crisis started in the United States in 2007, it turned out that consumers could no longer pay their mortgages and had very little confidence in the economy. This caused spending to decline sharply and some companies got into trouble.
- **Exchange rate**. This factor is very important when doing business internationally if payment is made in a foreign currency. A climbing rate of foreign exchange (a depreciation of domestic currency) means that imported products become more expensive. This can result in the imported product being priced out of the market. If the rate of exchange is stable, more accurate financial planning is possible. The more the rate of exchange fluctuates, the more the risks will have to be covered (see chapter 9).

Economic factors are influenced by the politics practised in these countries. Think, for example, of the implementation of the euro or the accession of countries to the WTO.

Political-legal environmental analysis

This analysis includes all the political measures and legislation that affect the operation of a company abroad. One aspect has already been taken care of in the initial analysis, namely import bans or restrictions. If these apply, it makes no sense to export the product. The following factors should also be investigated:

- Political barriers. These can be sub-divided into:
  - Tariff measures (see chapter 2) such as import duties, turnover taxes, excise duties.
  - Non-tariff measures (see chapter 2) such as customs formalities, administrative procedures, technical requirements, quality requirements and subsidies.
- Legal obstacles, such as:
  - Price legislation. This enables the government to establish minimum or maximum prices, for example, for oil.
  - Prohibition of corruption (see chapter 3).
  - Business establishment requirements, such as work permits.
  - Intellectual property rights (see chapter 8).
  - Product requirements, such as mandatory seals of approval (see chapter 8).
  - Anti-cartel legislation which is in effect or not.
  - Product Liability Act (see chapter 8).
  - Regulations regarding foreign investments.

The legislation in the host country must also be investigated. This may be important for the country of export, investment or import, as certain cooperations rules are relaxed or even identical at times. Think, for example, of the European Union.

Ecological and ethical environmental analysis

Environmental aspects are playing an increasingly important role in international business. Due to emissions of the greenhouse gas CO_2, the Earth is warming up and this will give rise to a change in the climate in the long run. This is why attention is paid to this aspect all over the world. Because of this, new products and services are created, such as alternative sources of energy (solar and wind power) and recyclable products. Aspects that can be included in this analysis are:

Ecological factors

- Ecological factors, such as:
  - Weather/climate. A change in the climate has a significant effect on the sale of winter sports articles, for example.
  - Availability of natural resources and minerals. Some natural resources, such as oil, are not infinite. If you operate in or are dependent on this industry, alternatives will have to be sought. The prices of scarce raw materials will also rise.
  - Environmental pollution. This includes air, water and soil pollution as well as noise pollution. Worldwide, there are increasing numbers of government actions in this area. This means there is an increasing demand for environmentally-friendly products and services.

Ethical factors

- Ethical factors, such as:
  - Child labour. In some Asian countries this is a commonly used form of labour. In Western society, the question of child labour is receiving more and more attention and has been characterised as reprehensible. For sectors like the clothing industry, this has consequences for the production process.
  - Health. In every country there is a different perspective about health consequences having used a certain product. Genetically modified products, for example, cannot be sold in all markets.
  - Corruption. This factor was discussed in chapter 3 but it is also relevant in this analysis. For example, will your customers accept that

you are working with dictatorial regimes or in countries where corruption is a common feature?

After reading about all these factors, you may have the impression that there are only threats. The opposite is true. There is an enormous demand for products and services that address these factors. And here technological developments play a large part.

Socio-cultural environmental analysis

As was seen in chapter 3, culture is an uncontrollable external factor that cannot be influenced. It is, however, one of the most important factors for the success of a product in foreign markets, and therefore the subject deserves a great deal of attention. Naturally, analyses can be performed on the basis of the models developed by Hall, Hofstede and Trompenaars, which were discussed in chapter 3. These are good starting points for discovering the differences between the home culture and the culture of the foreign market. But in order to be able to determine the market entry strategy and the marketing mix in the following step, more specific information is needed.

A socio-cultural analysis can be broken down into the following factors:

- Layers of culture. Desk research can reveal something about the visible layer of a culture (see also 'cultural elements' below), but it is also important to investigate the invisible layers (see chapter 3). This can be done in discussions with people who grew up in the specific country, for example. Factors that must be included in the analysis are:
  - Values and norms. What is desirable and what is seen as justified? When considering the introduction of a product, this is a crucial factor.
  - Manners and customs. Are there any customs that can affect the consumption of the product?
  - Aesthetics. What is perceived as beautiful and what is not? This can be very important in terms of the size and packaging of the product.
- Cultural levels. Depending on the market in which one operates, different levels of a culture must be investigated. For the business-to-consumer market, the national culture and individual behaviour patterns are important. For the business-to-business market, business/industry and corporate culture are important. If you are thinking of setting up a branch abroad, industry and corporate cultures are factors that must certainly be analysed, independently of the market in which you are operating.
- Cultural elements. There are three more factors to which attention must be paid:
  - Language. The spoken language is important for the product name and also for the packaging, for example. Certain brand names evoke the wrong association, such as the Mitsubishi Pajero: a car with a name that means 'bandit' in Spanish. Non-verbal communication is also an important consideration, above all in high-context cultures (see chapter 3), where people attach less value to the written word and more to personal contact. The effects may lead to enormous differences in the promotion of a product.
  - Religion. In certain religions, some products are forbidden, such as alcohol and pork meat in Islam. Religion can also be important in

terms of dress codes. Short trousers are not common in Asian cultures and such a product therefore needs to be adjusted. Certain colours can have a religious meaning, and this must be investigated in advance.
- Social structures. The so-called 'reference groups' must be closely examined. Who influences the people who make the decisions about buying products? In Europe it is usual to consult the recommendations of other consumers when buying on the internet. What is the situation in other countries?

Technological environmental analysis
The technological analysis examines the trends that take place outside one's own sector and over which the company has no influence. Important factors that must be examined are:
- Spending on research and development (R&D). Do many innovations come from the country or are many products copied? The Chinese, for example, are masters at copying products. If you are producing a high-quality technological product, the techniques required to produce it may not be available in the country.
- Speed of technology transfer. If a company plans to develop new technology in the target country, the infrastructure needed to transfer this technology to others is usually present. This is also naturally related to the educational level of the population (see 'demographic environmental analysis'). It is, however, a fact that the transfer of technologies is much faster through the internet. Because of it, information can be shared and obtained worldwide.
- Changes in information technology. What is the state of the infrastructure for information transfer, such as the internet and mobile telephone technology? Does the country have access to these or are these technologies not likely to be available any time soon ? In a developing country like Namibia, national mobile telephone coverage is 50%.

The results of the technological analysis can lead to improvements in a number of areas. In the production process it will be possible to produce more quickly and efficiently, and improvements in logistics can result in greater efficiency. Furthermore, information technology can be used in marketing to attract attention to products in a new way, such as advertising via email or SMS. It can also be used in market research, which is discussed in section 5.4.

To conclude the DEPEST analysis, all the results are put next to each other. The strong and weak points are used to formulate the opportunities and threats for this new market. These can be used as input for the types of market entry and marketing strategy adopted (see chapter 6).

5.3.2 Competition analysis

From the internal analysis (the value chain analysis – see chapter 4), it is already obvious where the company can achieve competitive advantage. In the external analysis the environment or market in which it operates, is researched. That is why it is called a competition analysis. This analysis provides an overview of the strong and weak points of the competitors. This has to be carried out carefully and it should not be based on impressions or suspicions, but on facts instead. At this stage, a visit to an exhibition or participation in a trade mission can provide the necessary information.

Competition analysis

A good competition analysis includes the following characteristics:

- Number, size and financial position of the competitors. This information can be obtained, for example, via commercial organisations such as Dun & Bradstreet or via the financial-economic or sector-specific trade press.
- Turnover and market share. What is the present situation and how will it develop? Are there, for example, competitors who gain a bigger market share every year? Who is the market leader? This information can be obtained via industry and trade associations, research bureaus or chambers of commerce, via the annual auditor's report.
- Marketing mix. What is the effect on the '7 Ps' (see chapter 6)? This can often be investigated by means of desk research.
  - Product. What does the product look like? What is the quality of the product?
  - Place. Where are the customers located?
  - Price. How much does the product cost? How will the price develop?
  - Promotion. What promotion strategy do the competitors use and how effective is it?
  - Personnel. Is an after-sales service necessary? How is this best provided?
  - Physical evidence. What does the website look like? How is the range shown?
  - Process. How good is the after-sales service?

These data can be compared with those relating to your own company to clarify the position of your company and the strengths and weaknesses of the competitors. The results can be reproduced in scores. Table 5.3 gives an example of a strength of competition analysis.

TABLE 5.3 Scores on strong and weak points of the competition and own company

Characteristics	**Competition**			**Own company**
	A	B	C	
Size of company				
Financial position				
Turnover				
Market share				
Marketing mix				
Product				
Place				
Price				
Promotion				
Personnel				
Physical evidence				
Process				

5.3.3 Supplier analysis

Supplier analysis

The supplier analysis looks at the suppliers of the competitors in order to assess the extent to which the competitors have organised their supply chain. Factors covered are:

- Source of the product: is the product imported or is it locally produced? If the product is imported, the following must be investigated:
  - Origin. Where are the producers located?
  - Quantities. Are minimum quantities required? How much capacity does the producer have?
  - Quality of the suppliers. Are they reliable? Is their financial situation stable or are there financial problems that threaten their continuity?
  - When importing. What tariff measures are there in this country? This affects the profit margin.
- Margin. What is the cost price of the product and at what price is it sold for?

To collect these data, a visit to an trade fair may be worthwhile. Conversations with suppliers in this sector can also provide the necessary information. In some industries, there are also investigation reports that can be read after payment. From these, a conclusion can be drawn as to whether it is beneficial to outsource production to or import the products from certain countries.

5

TNS DISOVER BRIC, 1 FEBRUARY 2011

Social media in China great expectations

No other recent phenomenon has generated as much anticipation and excitement among marketers as social media. Fazed by increasing clutter and deteriorating ROI from conventional media, marketers are salivating at the thought of social media providing them with more opportunities to bond with the increasingly elusive consumer. Research conducted by TNS among marketers in China found that social media is viewed as one of the most effective marketing tools available today.

There is a common perception that social media is on its way to carve out a sizeable share for itself at the expense of conventional media.

However marketers are also clear that the potential offered by social media is far from realised – in fact they feel that only a fraction of its potential is being tapped into today. TNS research revealed that:

- very few companies understand social media
- the social media scene changes so fast that it is difficult to keep up

- there are so many options to chose from
- companies are not able to find the right agency partners or vendors to work with.

What has marketing got to do with it? Research indicates that in addition to popular topics, there is a lot of discussion about products and brands online. According to a TNS survey, 86% of social networking users have come across a negative comment about a brand online. Marketers have got to be there to defend themselves, but it is not just about crisis management. 90% of consumers have come across a positive comment online about a brand – pointing to the tremendous opportunity that online media offers to existing and new brands. Marketers have the choice to either ignore this space or they can attempt to monitor, moderate and veer conversation in a positive direction.
China fact: In China, 54% of internet users are highly engaged compared to 48% in Brazil, 43% in Russia and 43% in India.

5.3.4 Distribution analysis

Distribution analysis

The last element in the analysis of the business environment is the distribution analysis. It is important to know how the distribution of the product needs to be organised in the new market. The choice of distribution channel is often determined by the production location, from which the product must be transported to the market. The choice has a number of consequences for the market entry strategy and therefore it is important to look into it. Factors included in the distribution analysis are:
- Kind of product: size, shelf life, packaging and whether there are many links in the distribution chain.
- Way of delivery to the client: in some countries it is not usual, for

FIGURE 5.7 Distribution chain for a certain product

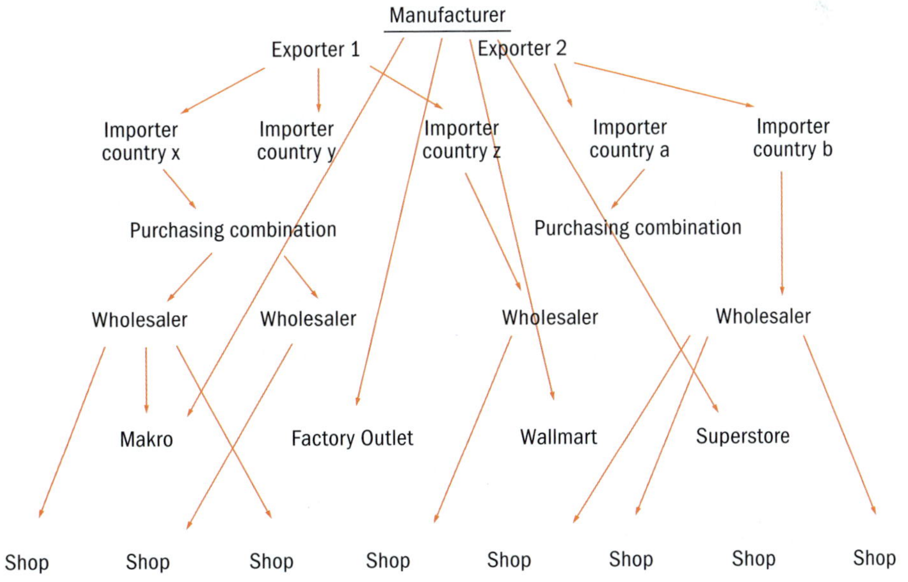

example, for clients to purchase via wholesalers. This can be determined by the culture.
- Margin. When there is a large margin, there will be several links in the distribution chain. As every link has to earn some money on the product, with a small margin there must be as few links as possible.
- Organisation of the distribution chain. Are there the same links used abroad as in the home country? Collect as much data as possible from exporters, wholesalers, agents, et cetera. This is often possible via industry and trade associations in the foreign country.

Since the rise of the internet, it has become common to skip a number of links in the distribution chain. Sometimes, products are sold directly to end users by means of a web shop, instead of via the usual wholesalers. It must be investigated whether this option is applicable abroad or may be a possiblitiy in the future. Figure 5.7 shows a distribution chain for a certain product. For the different names of distribution forms see chapter 6, in which several forms are explained.

5.4 Market research

Market research

If the environmental analysis reveals that further research into the market is needed, the third step, market research, is taken. Market research consists of the collection and analysis of data from which a conclusion must be drawn. It helps export managers to make decisions about entering a new international market. In market research, one can go deeper into developments that can change the size of the market, such as changes in purchasing behaviour, cultural trends, technological developments, but also the competition. Moreover, market research in an international context includes the testing of products in foreign markets. In many cases, a research agency is employed for research in another country.

International market research, however, has three problems in comparison with national market research. These concern:
- Availability of data: detailed information on Western countries can easily be found, but data on developing countries is harder to obtain. Furthermore, you must always look carefully at the data sources. It seems that methods of collecting data are not always reliable.
- Comparability of data: data from other countries must be interpreted with great caution. Terms like 'poverty', 'consumption' and 'literacy' differ from country to country and must therefore be properly defined so that they can be compared. Some countries express their foreign direct investments in terms of their monetary value, others in terms of projects. But an investment in a developed country can be worth much more than an investment in a developing country.
- Cultural differences: first of all, in terms of language, it must be possible to interpret the data correctly. Furthermore, the translation of the data must be done very carefully. In some countries, due to the high degree of illiteracy, questionnaires are out of the question and data must be collected in other ways. If written questionnaires are used, there is the question of postal deliveries. In some countries, postal deliveries are unreliable. Use must be made of local market research bureaus in these

markets. They know what type of research is appropriate and what questions can and cannot be asked.

The data obtained by market research can be divided into two categories:
1 primary data
2 secondary data

These will be discussed in the following subsections.

5.4.1 Primary data

The term primary data refers to information that is specifically collected for the client: customised information. The disadvantage of obtaining primary data is that it is very expensive and time-consuming. So perhaps the necessary information can be obtained from secondary data. If this is not the case, specific research will have to be set up to provide the company with the required data or to collect any missing data. These data can be collected by means of qualitative or quantitative research. In table 5.4, the characteristics of quantitative and qualitative research are summarised. Methods used for the collection of primary data, are:
- Observation: store checks and measurements of TV viewership, for example.
- Experiment: usually used in test marketing, for example to see how consumers respond to new products.
- Survey: by means of questionnaires, for example. This is the most frequently used method.

The collection of primary data can be done in various ways. Recently, email questionnaires have increasingly been used, but telephone and mail surveys are also still common. Sometimes use is made of personal interviews, but this is an expensive method. Furthermore, a visit to a trade fair or participation in a trade mission can produce concrete and useful information.

TABLE 5.4 Characteristics of quantitative versus qualitative research

Comparison dimension	Quantitative research (e.g. a postal questionnaire)	Qualitative research (e.g. group discussion or interview)
Objective	• quantification of data • generalisation of results to the population	• obtaining a initial understanding of underlying reasons and motives
Type of research	• descriptive	• exploratory
Flexibility in research design	• low (as a consequence of standardised/structured questionnaire)	• high (in personal interviews, the interviewer can change the questions during the research)
Sample size	• large	• small
Choice of respondents	• representative sample of population	• persons with knowledge of the problem

Comparison dimension	Quantitative research (e.g. a postal questionnaire)	Qualitative research (e.g. group discussion or interview)
Information per respondent	• low	• high
Analysis of data	• statistical summary	• subjective, interpretative
Ability to replicate	• high	• low
Requirements of interviewer	• no special skills required	• special skills required (good understanding of the interaction between interviewer and respondent)
Time consumption during research	• design phase: high (correct formulation of questions) • analysis phase: low (coded answers)	• design phase: low (no set of exact questions) • analysis phase: high (as a result of many different answers)

Source: Hollensen 2007

5.4.2 Secondary data

Data that already has been collected, independently of the company's specific research, are called secondary data. It is thus wise to seek out availability of secondary data before giving instructions to collect primary data. Secondary data can often be collected by means of desk research and thus the process is much cheaper than the collection of primary data. Below a number of websites of organisations that provide secondary data are listed:

- www.offstats.auckland.ac.nz
- globaledge.msu.edu/resourcedesk
- Europe.eu/index_nl.htm
- www.europages.nl
- www.intracen.org
- www.adb.org
- www.cia.gov
- www.lexisnexis.nl
- www.euromonitor.com

Specific data about the relevant sector are also available from industry and trade organisations at home and abroad.

● www.adage.com

Unilever Puts in Face Time With the Chinese Consumer

SHANGHAI (AdAge.com) – Alan Jope's schedule last week illustrates the importance of the Chinese market for multinationals in almost every industry.

ON-THE-SPOT ADJUSTMENTS: After Alan Jope learned that Zu Quingrong couldn't understand the entire Omo range of laundry products, he told staff to ramp up improved packaging designs.
But the meeting on his agenda most likely to help Unilever achieve its 20% revenue-growth goal this year was not with an elite power broker. It was an afternoon he spent hanging out with Zu Qingrong, a 41-year-old woman from Dalian, a city in northeast China.
An outgoing, curious Scotsman, Mr. Jope pries into their daily lives, asking about hygiene practices, internet-surfing habits, finances and child-care philosophies, along with fears and dreams. And, of course, he asks how and where they consume food and personal-care products. Sometimes the conversation even turns to topics such as political beliefs and extramarital affairs – nothing is off-limits. After these visits, Mr. Jope will tell managers to switch dollars to online advertising, tweak packaging or the like.
Overall, Mr. Jope came away satisfied that the Chinese consumer is steadily moving toward quality multinational brands. "She's proud of where she is and what she has achieved. This was a sharp reminder of how independent Chinese women are in urban markets."

2 February 2011

5

5.5 Determining market potential

Market potential

The last step in the external analysis process is to estimate the size of the potential market. This can be determined from the information collected in all the previous steps. There are various methods, as described in the book *International Marketing Research* by Craig and Douglas. In this section two methods are discussed, namely estimation by analogy and lead-lag analysis, to give you an idea of how it works.

5.5.1 Estimation by analogy

Market estimation

This theory assumes that the market data for a certain country correspond with those of the target country. An example of this is estimating the number of refrigerators sold in Germany correlating the size of the population. The formula is as follows:

$$\text{Xd} = \frac{\text{Xnl} \times \text{Yd}}{\text{Ynl}} = \frac{800\,000 \times 82 \text{ million}}{10{,}4 \text{ million}} = 6.3 \text{ million refrigerators in Germany}$$

Xd is the sales for refrigerators in Germany
Yd is the German population size: 82 million
Xnl is the demand for refrigerators in the Belgium: about 800,000 items per year
Ynl is the Belgian population size (10,4 milion), used to standardize the German refrigerator sales in terms of Belgian sales

This theory assumes that the German market is identical to the Belgian market in terms of culture, purchasing power, taste, prices, consumption patterns and so forth. This theory can be used to make a rough estimate of the market if available data is limited. If you have an idea of the market share you want to achieve, people know from the start how big the turnover of a certain product is.

5.5.2 Lead-lag analysis

Lead-lag analysis

In a lead-lag analysis a series of historical figures on a certain product in a certain country are taken as a basis for the market potential in another country. This is based on projection. Here it is assumed that the factors that influence diffusion are the same in both countries; only the time factor is different. Figure 5.8 illustrates this. As can be seen in this figure, the percentage of the population that had an iPhone in the United States of America was 15% in 2007. It is expected to grow to 95 per cent by 2015, according to the dotted line. The iPhone was introduced in the The Netherlands only in 2008. To see how the market will develop in the coming years, the pattern established by America is followed, but delayed by two years. The market potential for 2012 can be calculated from this, namely 55% of 16 million = 8.8 million.

FIGURE 5.8 Lead-lag analysis of penetration of iPhones in the USA and the Netherlands

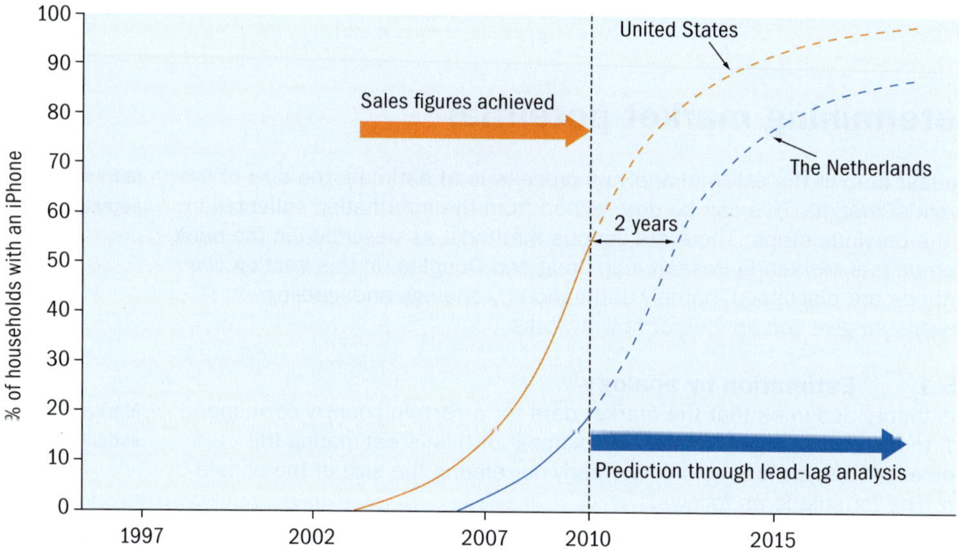

Source: Hollensen, 2007

Once this last step in the evaluation process has been taken and the market potential has been determined, it is time to take the following step, going abroad. This is discussed in chapter 6.

Summary

- After the internal analysis follows the external analysis. The external analysis consists of four steps:
  - initial analysis
  - business environmental analysis
  - market research
  - determining market potential

  After every step, it has to be seen if the outcomes provide reasons to continue the process with the following step.

- The initial analysis, researching whether there is a basic demand for the product comprises:
  - basic demand analysis
  - trade figures analysis
    - import ratio
    - export ratio
    - terms of trade
    - import cover
  - BERI index

- The environmental analysis is performed at a macro- and meso-level and comprises:
  - DEPEST analysis
    - demographic
    - economic
    - political-legal
    - ecological and ethical
    - socio-cultural
    - technological
  - competition analysis
    - number, size and financial position
    - turnover and market shares
    - marketing mix
  - supplier analysis
    - source of products
    - margin
  - distribution analysis
    - kind of products
    - way of delivery to client
    - margin
    - organisation of distribution chain

- The third step is market research. The data obtained can be divided into primary and secondary data. Significant differences in market research are:
  - availability of data
  - comparability of data
  - cultural differences

- Market potential can be determined on the basis of:
  - estimation by analogy
  - lead-lag analysis

Questions and assignments

Questions about the opening case

5.1 Make a trade figure analysis for Ikea in the Japanese furniture market.

5.2 If you look at the DEPEST analysis, in which part did Ikea make a mistake the first time they entered the Japanese market?

● www.fashionunited.nl

Turkey: from exporter to importer

Besides being a large clothing exporting country, Turkey has now also become a considerable importer. In 2009, branded clothing worth 511 million euros was exported to Turkey from the traditional EU countries. This is shown in figures from the European fashion and Textile Export Council (EFTEC).
Despite the economic crisis, which resulted in a drop in the export of fashion articles from Europe to Turkey (–7% compared to the previous year), there was still a number of countries that managed to increase exports to Turkey. Spain increased exports of fashion products by as much as 19%, achieving sales of 119 million euros in total. Spain thereby beat Italy, which saw exports decline by 19% (113 million euros in total). After Spain and Italy came Belgium (82 million euros, +2%), followed by the United Kingdom (69 million euros, –9%), Germany (+1%, 57 million euros) and France (–30%, 29 million euros).
According to EFTEC, women's clothing is the most important segment of exports from the EU to Turkey. Followed by men's clothing, swimwear and underwear.

10 May 2010

5.3 What can you say about the development of Turkey's import cover? Explain your answer.

5.4 Calculate the export ratio of clothing for Turkey if the GNP is 167 billion US dollars and the total value of exports of clothing is 11,553 billion dollars.

5.5 Do a DEPEST analysis for Turkey.

STARBUCKS
GEOGRAPHY IS A FLAVOUR.
RESPONSIBLY GROWN. ETHICALLY TRADED
Daily Offerings
100% ETHICALLY TRADED ESPRESSO.
Gold Coast

6
Market entry & international marketing

When entering an international market a company must decide whether it wishes work with a local company, take over another company, set up a joint venture with a local company or set up its own branch office abroad.
When entering a foreign market the company must decide to what extent its market strategy needs to be geared to local conditions. Should its product be geared to the local market? Can the existing advertising and promotional material be used locally? In this chapter we discuss in what ways a company can enter the international market and how its marketing strategy should be adapted.

BMW plans China production of electric Megacity car

The Chinese market will give BMW Group a big boost to implement its global strategy for new energy vehicles, Christoph Stark (from the BMW group), said in a recent interview with the Beijing News.
The German automaker even plans local production of the electric Megacity car after the start of volume production in 2013, he added.
BMW took a real road test of the Mini E in China two years ago, and has now extended the project. The Megacity will be launched in 2013, and is expected to be locally produced thereafter. The Megacity will feature a 35-kWh lithium-ion battery pack. Since an electric motor is much more compact than a gasoline engine, the car will not need a transmission, exhaust or muffler. The material used to build the car will comprise of aluminum and carbon fiber, and will match steel's strength while being half the weight of standard aluminum, according to sources.
Asked if BMW will create a new brand for its new energy vehicles in the future, Christoph Stark said it all depends on the Group's speed of development, organizational structure, production processes and whether the development cycle can meet the demand. As for the brand, he said when the timing is right, the Group will announce the news.
BMW earlier announced at the Beijing auto show that the Megacity will be sold under a sub-brand of BMW, but there was no mention of whether this is a new brand or possibly Mini.
China plays an important role in pushing forward development of new energy vehicles and electric vehicle components and parts. BMW will decide when and in what way to enter the country's electric vehicle market after having a good understanding of the local market as well as the performance of these locally manufactured auto parts and components. BMW also wants to know what kind of resources it can acquire from the industry chain here, Christoph Stark said.

Source: www.Gasgoo.com December 20, 2010

6

6.1 International cooperation

Consumers and companies now have access to the best products from many countries as a result of globalisation and shorter lines of communication. Products have become cheaper and there is great freedom of choice. Thanks to rapid technological advances, competition between countries wanting to use the latest techniques has increased considerably. The necessary investment in new technologies can be shared through the use of various types of international cooperation. Because of the ever-shorter life cycle of products, companies need help to bring new products onto the world market as quickly as possible.

Product life cycle

International market orientation involves exploring new markets and new ways of making a profit, seeking efficient production methods and obtaining a strong competitive position.

FIGURE 6.1 International market orientation: exploring new markets

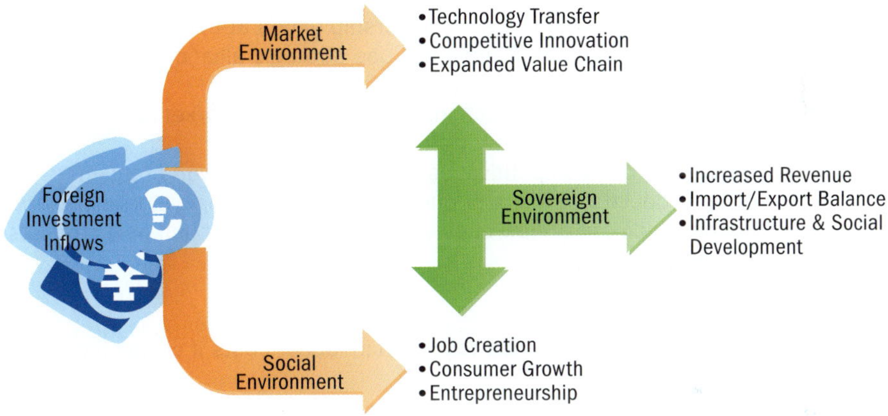

Source: www.badmannersclub.com

6.1.1 Market entry strategy

Companies enter into all types of strategic cooperation when accessing foreign markets. This is known as the market entry strategy. The goal is to defend, strengthen and expand the company's competitiveness. The market entry strategy must be in keeping with the company's international strategy and the requirements of the market in the foreign country. The strategy depends on the size and importance of the foreign market. For instance, different criteria apply to the export of heavy machinery to Eastern Europe than to the export of foodstuffs to Germany or clothing to South America. A company often enters a foreign market via:

Market entry strategy

1 import or export of the product/service
2 contractual cooperation or a strategic alliance
3 direct investment

There is a limited choice in marketing entry strategies in emerging economies. It is often difficult to understand one's contacts because of their relatively low level of education as well as cultural differences. Demand for

the product may be great but purchasing power may be small. There may be big differences in culture, climate and consumer behaviour. Currencies are sometimes weak or unusable. There is lot of competition and it requires tremendous effort to prove oneself as a new supplier.
The options also depend on the following decisions:

- Are you aiming at a small or large market share?
- Will the products be brought onto the foreign market continually or just incidentally?

Depending on the above a foreign market entry strategy must be formulated.

6.1.2 Strategic alliances

One of the fastest growing trends in the business world is the strategic alliance. A strategic alliance is an agreement between two or more companies to strengthen their market position. Knowledge and skills are exchanged and sometimes capital, technology and personnel.

Partnership

In fact, a strategic alliance is a partnership aimed at minimising risks and optimising management. Companies use strategic alliances to achieve the following:

- Benefits of scale in production, distribution, and marketing.
- An increase in market penetration.
- Improvement in competitiveness on the home and world market.
- Better product development due to shared technological developments.
- The development of new business opportunities through new products and services.
- An increase in exports.
- Product diversification.
- Reduction in costs. Direct reduction in labour costs if certain activities are moved abroad.

Defensive and offensive factors

Alliances are driven by both offensive and defensive factors. A company may want to operate worldwide in order to be able to anticipate changes in the market. This is known as an offensive alliance. The company can enter the international market by entering into a suitable alliance with an international partner.
Defensive alliances, on the other hand, are aimed at either defending or strengthening an existing position in the market by cooperating with others to combine industrial processes and production. Sometimes alliances are mistaken for mergers, acquisitions and outsourcing. Mergers and acquisitions are permanent structural changes within a company. Outsourcing is just a way for a company to purchase useful services.

Vertical chain of business
Horizontal chain of business

Alliances can also be formed within a supply chain, which can be vertical or horizontal. For instance, a vertical chain could be formed between a supplier of raw materials and the maker of the finished product. An example of a horizontal chain is an alliance between local and worldwide suppliers of raw materials.

6.2 Modes of cooperation

The literature on this subject distinguishes participating and contractual modes of cooperation. These are types of strategic alliance.
The choice depends on a company's goals and aspirations:

- In the case of participatory cooperation, the companies raise a certain amount of capital to finance the collaboration (equity joint venture).
- In the case of contractual cooperation, the companies do not raise any joint capital. The collaboration is recorded in a business collaboration agreement. This type of cooperation is cheaper and easier to terminate.

The two modes of cooperation are discussed in the following subsections.

6.2.1 Participatory cooperation

The cooperating parties will jointly invest capital to set up the partnership (figure 6.2). This includes:
1 co-makership
2 direct investment
3 joint venture
4 turnkey contract

FIGURE 6.2 Types of participatory cooperation

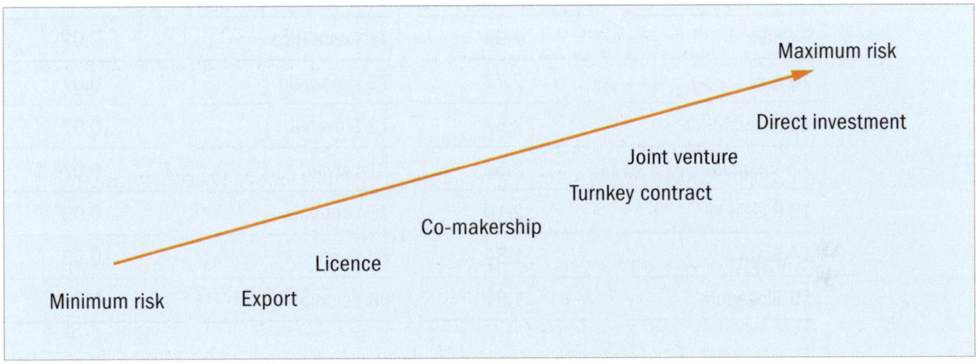

These types of cooperation are discussed one by one:

Ad 1 Co-makership
In a co-makership the supplier and customer collaborate to produce a good or service. This can be done through the exchange of personnel and knowledge or through the mutual outsourcing of production. Furthermore, the trading partners can together buy the means of production.

Ad 2 Direct investment
Direct investment (see table 6.1) means that a company buys a block of shares in another company, with the aim of obtaining knowledge of technological and market developments. The company gains a better knowledge of the situation within the local market through intensive cooperation with local suppliers and distributors. Furthermore, the investor wishes to influence company policy. Moreover, the investor controls the management

of the foreign company and can thus determine its strategy. The financial gain is: lower transport costs and savings through cheaper labour and raw materials leading to a better fiscal climate.
Research carried out by the Economist shows that in case of international cooperation, entrepreneurs choose for direct investment (and thus cooperation).

TABLE 6.1 Foreign direct investment inflows Countries, 2007–2011

Highest		**Lowest**	
Rank	*% of world total*	*Rank*	*% of world total*
1 United States	16.75	82 Kenya	0.01
2 Britain	7.54	81 Sri Lanka	0.02
3 China	5.79	80 Iran	0.02
4 France	5.22	79 Kuwait	0.03
5 Belgium	4.78	78 Cuba	0.04
6 Germany	4.41	77 El Salvador	0.04
7 Canada	4.22	76 Bangladesh	0.05
8 Hong Kong	3.20	75 Bahrain	0.06
9 Spain	2.99	74 Costa Rica	0.07
10 Italy	2.77	73 Venezuela	0.07
11 Netherlands	2.57	72 Slovenia	0.07
12 Australia	2.52	71 Latvia	0.07
13 Russia	2.10	70 Lithuania	0.08
14 Brazil	1.84	69 Cyprus	0.08
15 Singapore	1.81	68 Estonia	0.09

Ad 3 Joint venture
A joint venture is a type of collaboration with a local company in which a new company is set up. Both companies have a share in the new company. This makes it easier to approach the market. A joint venture means that the companies make use of each other's knowledge of sales and distribution systems. One of the companies contributes its technology and products while the other, for example, contributes clients. Thus this form of cooperation provides access to production technology, marketing experts, financial capital and management abilities.
Sometimes foreign governments demand the setting-up of a joint venture because they forbid direct imports or levy heavy import duties (protectionist trade policy). For instance, companies that wish to enter the Chinese market are obliged to work with local Chinese partners. The setting-up of a joint venture with a Chinese company means the company can enter the Chinese market more quickly. For instance, Nokia, the producer of mobile

phones, entered the Chinese market through a joint venture with a Chinese company.

DE TELEGRAAF, 13 APRIL 2010

PepsiCo is working on an Indian joint venture with Tata Tea

The American soft drinks and snacks company Pepsi Cola is researching with the Indian company Tata Tea the possibility of setting up a joint venture to supply the Indian market with healthy soft drinks. The shareholders of both companies must first give their consent. Furthermore the Commission on Competition must be in agreement with the venture. Tata Tea is a subsidiary of the Tata Conglomerate. The company is the second biggest supplier of tea in the world. Pepsi Cola is the market leader for soft drinks in India.

Ad 4 Turnkey contract

Design/build contract

In a turnkey contract, one company designs, constructs and tests a production facility for a client. The building is often a factory. The builder commits himself to delivering the building completely finished to the customer for a fixed amount of money. This type of contract requires a lot of preparation, because the specification of the building needs to be precise in order for a price to be established. The telecom company Ericsson signed a turnkey contract with the Turkish authorities. The Turkish government built a telecommunications facility, so that Ericsson was able to expand its telecommunications system.

TABLE 6.2 Types of cooperation – advantages and disadvantages

Types of cooperation	Advantages	Disadvantages
Co-makership	Increase of knowledge of local market; low costs and risks	Focus on product; less control and low sales pressure
Direct investment	Control of management and local market	High (preparatory) costs; big risks and difference in culture
Joint venture	Division of costs; knowledge of local market; temporary agreement	Joint control, a time-consuming process
Turnkey contract	Obtaining knowledge of local market and technology	Temporary contract and no foothold in the market

6.2.2 Contractual cooperation

The parties do not build up joint capital, but their cooperation is based on a contract. Types of contractual cooperation include:

1 agent
2 distributor
3 trading company
4 licensing
5 franchising
6 joint marketing
7 joint selling
8 piggyback-marketing
9 wholesale company

These types of cooperation will be discussed below.

Ad 1 Agent

An agent is a representative of more than one customer. Agents are self-employed independent intermediaries who act as brokers between exporters/importers (principal) and potential clients for a fixed amount of time or an indefinite period. Generally speaking, an agent does not keep any stock and is unable to guarantee fast delivery. However, in practice it is customary for the agent to keep stock on consignment. Consignment of sales is a trading arrangement in which a seller sends goods to a buyer or reseller who pays the seller only when the goods are sold. The seller remains the owner (title holder) of the goods until they are paid for in full. The unsold products can be returned to the company.

The majority of agents work on a 'no sale, no pay' basis (no payment if there has been no sale). To motivate agents, companies often pay them a monthly fixed expense allowance. Nearly 60 per cent of all export entrepreneurs use agents, initially for a year, with an option to extend the contract. The agent's legal status is fixed in the EU Directive on independent agents. EU countries keep to this Directive.

Ad 2 Distributor

A distributor is a self-employed entrepreneur who buys goods from an exporter for his own account and at his own risk, and resells these goods to his own customers. He focuses on marketing, sales and after-sales service for one or more companies. A distributor sells the imported goods after having paid any applicable import duties and taxes. As a wholesaler or retailer, it is his responsibility to comply with the regulations relating to the product and its packaging. These are discussed in detail in chapter 8.

There are three types of distributors:

1 distributors who only trade in foreign products
2 distributors who trade in local goods and foreign products
3 large distribution organisations

In table 6.3 the differences between an agent and a distributor are shown.

TABLE 6.3 Differences between agent and distributor

Agent	Distributor
Agent's fee paid by principal. Principal is responsible for fixing price and advertising	Responsible for fixing price and marketing. Possible to have the exclusive rights
Independent sales and purchase policy. No stock. Dependent on principal for service and assembly	Stock control and after-sales service
Principal influences sales and sales promotion	Is also responsible for sales and sales promotion; influences the selling price
Intensive contact with principal and customers	Hardly any contact with buyers

Ad 3 Trading company
Some companies have few resources available to commit to exporting acivities and others find exporting a daunting task because of a lack of contacts and experience. Those companies can use an export trading company. An export trading company provides services to its clients in addition to activities directly related to export activities on behalf of its clients. The bundling of these activities can prove to be cheaper because it offers the possibility of using the power of negotiations in the target market. The companies subcontract one or more activities. This company assists its clients strategically as well as operationally, including:

- providing import, export, and countertrade services
- carrying out market research of the clients' export possibilities
- contacting wholesalers, retailers or buyers. The follow-up must be done by the original company
- the developing and implementing of the market strategy

6

Ad 4 Licensing
The company (the licenser) entitles another company (the licensee) to use intellectual property such as patents, a trade or brand names, and knowledge.
A licensing agreement is an agreement whereby the licenser gives the licensee the right to exploit the license at a fee and for a certain amount of time. Such licensing contracts are also known as a "trade in knowledge" because it is not the right of ownership that is being sold but the right to use the license. The licenser retains the right of ownership, but the licensee has the right to commercially exploit the property.
The reasons for granting licenses are:
1 expansion of the market
2 exchange of knowledge between companies
3 prevention of imitation by a competitor
4 the foreign licensee can produce the product more cheaply
5 bringing the product onto the market more quickly

● www.eye-line.nl

Tommy Hilfiger licenses Safilo

The Safilo Group and the Tommy Hilfiger Group have signed a worldwide licensing agreement to work together until 2015, with an option for an additional five years. The agreement covers the design, development, production and distribution of spectacles and sunglasses.

This kind of licensing often takes place in the fashion world. Tommy Hilfiger has given Safilo a license to produce and market its sunglasses.

A fee is often paid for the privilege of obtaining such an agreement (delivery of the license). This fee is generally referred to as a 'royalty'.
In order to reach a licensing agreement, the copyright holder and the potential licensee must meet. In practice, they 'meet' by checking the copyright databanks, through a license marketplace on the internet (www 2xfr.com, www.osti.gov, www.yet2.com) or via a knowledge broker (www.ipo.org).

Ad 5 Franchising
A franchise often involves intensive cooperation between the franchiser and the franchisee. Franchising is a contractual entry mode in which one company (the franchiser) supplies another (the franchisee) with intangible property and other assistance over a period of time. The franchiser gives the franchisee the right, subject to a payment and certain clear and specific conditions, to make use of a certain sales formula. Franchise chains include McDonald's and Starbucks Coffee.

● www.thsnews.com

Starbucks new logo

World-renowned coffee franchise Starbucks' new logo is now an image-only deal, with the former "Starbucks" and "Coffee" being removed along with all other text. With more than 16,000 outlets worldwide, the kings of coffee have apparently felt that there are no words needed to announce their brand. The popularity of the coffee chain in the more than 50 countries where franchises operate will be carried solely on the shoulders of the sea-maiden who featured on the old logo. One of the main motivations behind the Starbucks new logo was eloquently put into words by the company's chairman, president and CEO, Howard Schultz, when he said: "Our new brand identity will give us the freedom and flexibility to explore innovations and new channels of distribution", which leaves listeners wondering if Starbucks has something up their sleeve that is about to be revealed.

7 January 2011

The advantages of a franchise contract are the following:
- One can enter the foreign market without having to invest too much in each outlet.
- Central buying and joint advertising can reduce costs per production unit.
- The business can be set up quickly using an existing name, with its reputation and know-how. The franchisee must pay a fee. The disadvantage is that, should the business fail, the franchiser's reputation is affected in a negative way.

Some of the big formula-exporting countries are America, Canada, Australia and several large European countries. The Chinese are highly interested in particularly successful franchisee formula. They like to import big franchise formula.

Ad 6 Joint marketing
This is a network of companies that have chosen the same marketing style in advertising or mutual service.

www.businesscourier.com

Chiquita and DANONE start joint venture marketing

Chiquita Brands International Inc. is starting joint venture marketing with the Danone Group. Internationally Chiquita Fruit will become 'just fruit In a bottle' and be marketed alongside Danone's products. Chiquita and the Danone Group have thrown their sales, marketing and supply services into a joint venture.

30 March 2010

Ad 7 Joint selling
From the perspective of an international company, a joint selling arrangement implies that the company comes to an agreement with a foreign producer of complementary goods. The producer's locally manufactured products are then added to the company's distribution channel. In return,

Distribution channel

the foreign producer adds the company's foreign-manufactured products to his local distribution channel. The advantage of such an agreement is that foreign markets can be entered without large sums of money being spent on a distribution channel. The disadvantage is that the other party's sales representatives cannot be controlled. Furthermore, an imbalance in sales can cause an unstable situation.

Ad 8 Piggyback-marketing
Piggyback-marketing means finding and using a foreign company already active in the foreign market that can add your products to its distribution channel. However, the product ranges have to be complementary and not competing.
For instance, the Dutch company Mondial wanted to sell hospital furniture in America but did not carry a range of children's furniture. The company bought children's furniture from a Danish company and could thus sell a complete range of hospital furniture in the American market.

Ad 9 Wholesale company
A wholesaler or wholesale company is a kind of intermediary that can be of interest to small and middle-sized companies: it is an easy mode of operating in the market with a relatively small outlay. A wholesale company breaks down 'bulk' into smaller packages for resale by a retailer. This may offer the manufacturer a competitive advantage, especially if he possesses limited or no knowledge of foreign markets or lacks the financial means and organisation to export. Wholesalers will often take the marketing responsibilities. Many wholesalers produce their own brochures and use their own telesales operations.
A wholesale company buys and sells large consignments of goods on the international market. The wholesaler carries a large range of products and as a result cannot pay individual attention to all of them.

The advantages and disadvantages are presented in table 6.4.

TABLE 6.4 Advantages and disadvantages of contractual cooperation

Mode of Cooperation	Advantages	Disadvantages
Agent Distributor	Knowledge of local market and low costs	Product oriented; less control and less pressure on sales
Trading company	Provides import, export and countertrade services: offers and complements each other's range of goods	Competition if other companies offer the same goods for sale
Franchise Licence	Minimal marketing efforts; expansion of brand awareness and low investment	Less control, limited protection intellectual property
Joint marketing Joint selling	Division of costs and brand awareness	Less direct individual advantage
Piggyback-marketing	Able to use the sales organisation of known exporters	Less control
Wholesale company	Specialisation and outsourcing	Product oriented; less control over sales and pressure on sales of the product

6.3 Direct mode of entry

Companies are often drawn into exporting when customers in other countries demand their goods. In this way, companies become aware of their product's international potential and get their first introduction into international business. The most obvious way to approach a market is to work with your own employees, either from your own company's home base or from a branch office in another country. The advantage is a much greater commitment from international management. However, the costs are higher. Imagine that your employee's company car costs €80,000 a year on average. With a gross margin of 10 per cent, the company must have a turnover of some €800,000 a year on average to cover this cost. There are also sales cost, office cost, administration cost, etc. At the beginning, employees often have insufficient knowledge of the market, there are few business networks and there are cultural and communication problems. It is an expensive and risky business for the company.
Other, cheaper possibilities of direct marketing are e-commerce and selling at shows, etc.
Direct types of marketing include:
a E-commerce
b trade fairs, shows, exhibitions
c sales representative or sales office

Futher details are discussed below.

E(lectronic)-commerce
E-commerce (via the internet) offers new business opportunities for small as well as large companies in both business-to-business and business-to-consumer markets worldwide. E-commerce is fast, practical and relatively cheap. For some companies, e-commerce is a distribution channel that improves or replaces traditional distribution channels. E-commerce can be defined in several ways:
- The narrow definition of e-commerce refers to doing transactions, placing orders and making payments via the internet.
- A broad definition of e-commerce includes pre-sales, sales and after-sales activities for products and services carried out by electronic means.

Prime examples of international internet sales organisations are Bol.com, Amazon and easyJet.

There are many important issues that need to be addressed when developing e-commerce. These are:
- *Visualisation*: The be-all-and-end-all of online selling is visualisation. You can keep clients if you invest in quality and user-friendliness.
- *Mutual trust*: When doing business via the internet the reliability of the other party may not be an established fact. A digital intermediary can check the identity of both parties and a safe transfer of information can take place (TTP = Trusted Third Parties).
- *Safe methods of payment:* SET (Secure Electronic Transaction) has been developed to solve the insecure payment problem. It can also be used for international transactions.
- *Language and culture:* Language and cultural barriers can be overcome

by using local offices or by employing local people. Local service providers can also be used.
- *Adapted distribution system:* This problem can be solved by linking the company's order system to that of a supplier.

Electronic buying
Via the internet and their IT systems, importers are far better able to find the right products and services worldwide with a distinct price quality ratio. The sourcing catalogue services are a well-known form of electronic buying of goods and services. These services are offered via a server through which buyers of specific types of goods can find new suppliers all over the world. Using the sourcing catalogue services, a company can find potential suppliers, products and services. Examples of sourcing catalogue services are alibaba.com, wlwonline.de, and e2open.com.

- www.haarloopbaan.nl

www.cosicarrier.com: trendy slings

While Kay Poelen was pregnant, she came into contact with the sling and saw that it had a lot of advantages. She got the idea to develop the sling further based on her own carrying experience until it was perfect, and start her own company. A year later ByKay Carriers was a highly successful international company. Since then, she has launched a website called www.cosicarrier.com. "I developed a simple website for cosicarrier, registered it with the Chamber of Commerce and started work. It was not only the sling, but also the clear and extensive instructions as well as our service to and support of clients who had questions made the company a success."

October 2009 (edited source)

Exhibition
An exhibition is a centrally located venue for large groups of suppliers and buyers. Exhibition visitors and exhibitions themselves are becoming more and more international. The goal of an exhibition is to introduce the public to a company, its products and its services. The number of international exhibitions is gigantic. There are various types of exhibitions (see table 6.5). Generally the choice is made for trade fairs, which are either horizontal or vertical exhibitions.

TABLE 6.5 Types of exhibition

Type	Characterics	Example
Trade fair	Branch information	Canton Fair, www.Cantonfair.org.cn
Horizontal trade exhibition	Specific products or techniques	Fabric Show Premiere Vision in Paris
Vertical trade exhibition	Focus on one type of product and market, concentration on the objectives for the show	AutoRai in Amsterdam
International trade exhibition	Organised around a specific international event	World Expo Shanghai 2010

Sales representative or sales office

A company can employ a person to represent the business of the employer. The representative is an extension of the foreign sales organisation, without there being any office abroad. Representation can be part of the job of an area manager, sales manager, etc. A representative is a salaried employee and is frequently in contact with the company's senior managers. Personal contacts are very important in the case of exporting. If there is no local office, the customer or potential customer is only in touch with the company's representative. That means that this person must win the customer's trust by taking into account the culture of the importing country, its traditions, the type of product, etc.

This representative keeps to the company's input, transformation and output process.

Input
Output

- Input refers to everything that has to do with the acquisition of resources, money, personnel, raw materials, and (semi-finished articles) and knowledge.
- Transformation means combining/integrating the input into a product that meets the needs of the foreign market. **Transformation**
- Output includes all the activities required to bring the product or service to the customers in the market, together with all the commercial activities.

The company and its representative can keep track of the international market when using this process.

A company can also set up its own office in a foreign country. The company then has market planning and the execution of the planning in its own hands. An agent can do a lot of the work on the advancement and support of the company abroad. An office abroad is a costly affair and the effect of cultural differences should not be underestimated. The advantage is that the company is no longer seen as a foreign.

6.4 Mergers & acquisitions

A merger can be seen as a close cooperation between two or more companies. A merger can lead to an expansion in business and distribution of the two companies, so that new opportunities are created. A merger can also lead to an improvement in the financial strength of a small company because big companies possess more capital.
There are several types of mergers which differ from a legal point of view.

- *Horizontal merger*: the joining of two companies that are direct competitors with identical product lines and markets. Through horizontal mergers, fairly large companies try to create economy of scale and an increase in that scale. The merger between Daimler Benz and Chrysler is an example of a horizontal merger.
- *Vertical merger*: the joining of a company with a client or supplier. Such a merger can give a company confidence and can increase its profitability. An example of a vertical merger is a car factory merging with a tyre company.
- *Market-extending merger*: the joining of companies that sell the same type of product in different international markets.
- *Product-extension merger*: the merger of companies with different but related products in the same market.
- *Conglomerate*: the merger of companies that cover the same business market. For example, the General Electric Company, or GE (NYSE: GE), is an American multinational conglomerate corporation, incorporated in the State of New York.

THE ECONOMIST, 11 NOVEMBER 2010

Being eaten by the dragon; what it feels like to be bought by a Chinese firm

A few years ago two executives of an international oil company were working late in its otherwise deserted office in England. A stunning young Chinese woman arrived at reception. “She was very attractive, decked out in Gucci,” one of them says. She delivered a letter from Sinopec, one of China’s giant, state-controlled energy firms, proposing a multibillion-dollar acquisition. The executive adds, a little wistfully, that she then disappeared into the night in a car with local license plates, never to be seen again. His firm was soon bought by the Chinese company. Since then Western bosses have been tapped by Chinese firms at conferences in Toronto and Cape Town and received walk-in offers in Scandinavia. Companies across Europe have solicited Chinese investment. Bankers all over the world have touted lists of Western acquisition candidates among China’s big firms. This year buyers based in China and Hong Kong have accounted for a tenth of global deals by value, including investments in oil and landmark acquisitions in industry, such as Geely’s purchase of Volvo, a Swedish carmaker. A decade ago China urged its companies to expand under the slogan “go out”. Now it is really happening.

Acquisition

Acquisitions occur between the bidding and the target company. An acquisition or takeover occurs when one company purchases another. Takeovers may either be hostile or friendly. The acquiring company usually proceeds by offering to purchase the shares from the shareholders of the target company. Often, a cash offer is made but sometimes the acquiring company may offer to trade its own shares in exchange for the target company's shares. The acquisition of a small company abroad may be a solution for companies with international ambitions, because from that position the foreign market can be explored. In some cases this acquisition augments the company's market position.
A merger or acquisition requires a heavy investment. A diagnosis of the target company must be made on the basis of the following data:

- a detailed financial analysis of its present and previous situation
- thorough research into the branch and the product
- an analysis of its success factors
- an analysis of its political and social environment

This analysis gives a good idea of the environment in which the company operates.

6.5 Outsourcing & out-tasking

Outsourcing is subcontracting. Outsourcing can be described as transferring activities to a third party that were previously carried out within the company. There are several reasons why a company decides to outsource:

- cost saving
- capacity expansion by outsourcing of products with a lower added value
- expansion of the total production capacity without major investment or high risk
- saving costs and the retention of market position through competitive pricing

However, there is a distinction between integral outsourcing ('business process outsourcing') and partial outsourcing.
Integral outsourcing means that the execution and coordination of activities is the other party's responsibility. Well-known examples are the Microsoft service desks. Microsoft signed an outsourcing pact with Indian giant Infosys to take over the responsibility for managing Microsoft's IT help desk and desk-side services operations, as well as servicing the company's applications, devices and databases in more than 100 countries.
Partial outsourcing means that certain industrial processes are moved to low-cost countries. Think of offshoring. For instance, IT companies such as Cap Gemini and ATOS Origin often move work to India or Eastern Europe. In this industry, especially in Eastern Europe and Asia, factories are often built and run by their own people. Table 6.6 gives a summary of the various forms of outsourcing together with the advantages and disadvantages. Tables 6.7 and 6.8 provide an overview of outsourcing locations.

TABLE 6.6 Types of outsourcing

Types of outsourcing	Advantages	Disadvantages
Integral outsourcing	Outsourcer: less responsibility for outsourced work	Outsourcer: less control over price and less insight into price/cost breakdown of the supplier
	Supplier: requires less knowledge about the outsourcer's project	Outsourcer: less control over the (quality of) personnel, technology and materials
	Outsourcer: project runs smoothly	Outsourcer: supplier works rather independently; commercial, technological and output risks
Partial outsourcing	Outsourcer: more control over prices, tariffs and costs	Outsourcer: needs knowledge of the companies structures in order to outsource the work
	More control over (quality of) personnel, technology and materials	Outsourcer: organizational skills in order to coordinate the outsourced work
	Coordination and control can lead to cost savings	Communication and coordination can be frustrating

TABLE 6.7 Top eight outsourcing locations worldwide

Ranking 2009	Town	Country	Region
1	Bangalore	India	Asia
2	Delhi NCR	India	Asia
3	Mumbai	India	Asia
4	Manilla NCR	Philippines	Asia
5	Dublin	Ireland	Western Europe
6	Cgebbau	India	Asia
7	Hyderabad	India	Asia
8	Pune	India	Asia

Source: Global Services and Tholons (edited)

TABLE 6.8 Top 10 candidate outsourcing cities worldwide

Ranking 2009	Town	Country	Region
1	Nizhny Novgorod	Russia	Eastern Europe
2	Bhubaneswar	India	Asia
3	Iloilo City	Philippines	Asia
4	Cork	Ireland	Western Europe
5	Thiruvananthapuram	India	Asia
6	Rucufe	Brazil	South America
7	Santa Rosa, Laguna	Philippines	Asia
8	Cordoba	Argentina	South America
9	Puerto Rico	USA	North America
10	Amman	Jordan	Middle East

Source: Global Services and Tholons

6

Out-tasking

Out-tasking means hiring external expertise to carry out certain one-off activities or jobs; as such, it could be considered the reverse of outsourcing. Out-tasking is of particular interest to small and middle-size companies for whom it is uneconomic to employ staff member with a certain type of expertise. The service provider is only the adviser, and it is the client who is ultimately responsible and who makes the final decision.

TABLE 6.9 Advantages and disadvantages of the various types of cooperation

Type of cooperation	Advantages	Disadvantages
E-commerce	Low costs	Require good distribution and after-sales service
Exhibitions	Direct contact and low costs	Marketing
Sales representative/Sales office	Direct contact with retailer and focus on market	High initial costs and differences in culture
Merger	Scale and synergy	Cultural differences, little control, time-consuming and high cost
Acquisition	Control of industrial processing and scale	Time-consuming and high cost
Outsourcing	Concentrate on own specialisation	Control of consumers and know-how is lost
Out-tasking	Employment of external expertise	Loss of know-how

6.6 International marketing strategy

In the previous sections we explained that a market entry strategy should be formulated prior to entering a foreign market. Marketing is the next step in working in a foreign market. An international marketing policy consists of international, multinational and a global marketing strategy.

International marketing

Marketing activities

International marketing means carrying out marketing activities aimed at influencing groups of people who do not form part of the national market. During the initial phase the home market is stressed. Then, focusing on its strong points, the company looks for potential markets abroad and develops a marketing strategy.

Multinational marketing

Multinational marketing is the following step in attempting to influence the foreign market. Multinational marketing means that the company adapts its policy to the culture of the country. It is typical for companies operating in various countries to act as if they are local companies. Thus no export takes place but the company works with a foreign company through a joint venture or a licensing agreement. For instance, in Muslim countries McDonald's does not serve burgers containing pork but serves only burgers made of halal meat.

Global marketing

Global marketing is also aimed at foreign markets and is sometimes called "worldwide marketing". Its aim is to achieve as much uniformity as possible. Instead of concentrating on the differences between countries and adjusting the marketing strategy accordingly, companies look at the similarities between countries. Marketing activities are standardised as far as possible. The company considers the entire world its market. Examples are Coca-Cola and Benetton.

UNITED COLORS OF BENETTON.

6.6.1 Standardise or adapt?

A company's marketing policy is not important if it only wants to dump its overproduction on the foreign market or only wishes to export goods now

and then. But if a company wants to enter the foreign market on a long-term basis, the question arises whether its marketing policy should be adapted to the foreign market or standardised. For instance, companies such as Ikea, Apple and Nike have standardised their marketing policy. What are the advantages and disadvantages of standardisation?
The advantages of standardisation are:

- Customers recognise the product when they are abroad. Furthermore, one advertising campaign appearing in all foreign markets creates an identical product **image**. Advertising costs per product unit are reduced.
- Savings in costs and increase in scale. The company profits from large-scale production. Large quantities of raw materials can be purchased; thus the costs per unit are reduced. Besides research and development costs, operational and marketing costs can be spread over a large number of products.
- No trade barriers. The product within the home market has been developed to such an extent that there are no barriers on the foreign market. The product meets all international product standards.
- Improvement in quality. The company can concentrate on its products. Personnel can be trained and investments are made in technology and machinery in order to improve the quality of the product and its production.

Disadvantages are:

- **Undifferentiated product**. Should a company bring a standardised product on the market, a competitor is bound to produce an adapted product that meets the needs of the local consumer. Furthermore, one should keep in mind that products have different uses in different countries. For instance, in some countries bicycling is a leisure activity, whilst in others it a form of transport. In the local markets consumers have their own needs and tastes.
- Trade barriers require product adjustment. This means that economy of scale is no longer possible and that costs of production rise.

A lot of international companies have developed 'world brands'. They assume that due to the internet and television the world is getting smaller and that people all over the world want the same products and the same lifestyles. An example is the MTV generation, who all want the same type of clothes and the same lifestyle.
Then there are also standardised strategies that have failed. For example Marks & Spencer, which strategy failed on the mainland of Europe. It turns out that the most effective marketing policy is the one that understands the consumer needs and wishes of the local market.

6.6.2 Think globally, act locally

Global localisation strategy

International marketing differs only slightly from marketing in the home market. Decisions must be taken on a bigger scale, and the work abroad is often risky and complex because of the many uncertainties. The best approach is to 'think globally, act locally'. This means that the global approach per country is standardized, but the product is adapted to the wishes and needs of local customers. This is also known as a global localisation strategy.
With this marketing strategy the company's policy is partly based on a global market and partly on a local market using marketing instruments.

This means that the shape, colour or taste of the product is changed or that the advertising campaign is adapted to the local consumer market. Think of the American crisp brand Pringles. The flavors are adjusted to suit local tastes: salt and vinegar for the English market and cheese for the Dutch market.

● www.grub.gunaxin.com

Top Ten Lay's Chips Flavors in China

In the western world, we all have our favorite things. Favorite beer, favorite TV shows, favorite flavor of ice cream. We get used to these things. They become the comforts of our lives. We even have our favorite flavor of potato chip, right? What happens though, when we leave the comforts of our world to go live in a completely strange and unusual land where our favorite things are thousands of miles away? It may make you happy to know that China has an abundance of Lay's Potato Chips. But before you get too excited, you need to know that the flavors in China are completely different from those of the western world. The top ten is:

10 French Chicken
9 Cucumber
8 Mexican Tomato Chicken
7 Blueberry
6 Lemon Tea
5 Hot & Sour Fish Soup
4 Little Tomato
3 Italian Red Meat
2 Numb and Spicy Hot Pot

And the number one seller in China...is... American Classic. Yep. Regular old standard issue Classic Lay's Chips.
Maybe the Chinese *are* becoming more like us!!!

6.7 International marketing mix

A marketing policy is based on the marketing mix. All elements must correspond in order to be effective. The traditional 'Four Ps' are used for market tangible products. The 'Seven Ps' model also includes Personnel, Physical evidence and Process. It is therefore better suited to industry and service companies. The international marketing instruments are:

1 Product
2 Price
3 Promotion
4 Place
5 Personnel
6 Physical evidence
7 Process

These seven marketing instruments are discussed below.

6.7.1 Product

Product policy is geared to the product that is introduced to the foreign market. The company can bring the product on the foreign market unchanged. Think of such brands as Coca-Cola and Heineken. However, the company runs the risk that the product does not appeal to the consumer. Generally speaking, the company adjusts the product to local circumstances and consumer needs. A product is a combination of tangible features such as:

- Shape, weight and dimensions: Philips, for instance, adjusted its shavers to the smaller hands of Asian people when entering this market.
- Packaging: whether a product appeals to customers' senses depends not only on the shape, but also the packaging in which the product is offered. Designers must take the cultural aspects of the foreign consumers into consideration as well as EU packaging requirements.
- Composition, taste and colour: the company must adjust its products to the cultural requirements of the foreign market. The internationally known ice cream maker Häagen Dazs adjusts its flavors' to its markets. A green-tea-flavored ice cream is on the market in Japan while Europeans enjoy strawberry-flavored ice cream.
- Range: what kind of products are to be put on the market? In India more than 75 per cent of the McDonald's' menu has been developed locally. The "Croque McDo" is the McDonald's approach to the more traditional Croque-monsieur snack found in France/Belgium or McTosti in The Netherlands.
- Instructions: in the US, a company can be held liable if the product instructions are not incomplete. Furthermore, the instructions must be written in the language of the country.
- Brand and brand image: These may not be changed too much when entering a foreign market. The chance of a brand name being associated with a rude word or taboo concept increases when it is used on the international market. The car manufacturer Fiat decided to change the name of the Ritmo to Strada when bringing it on the UK market. In the United Kingdom Ritmo is a well-known brand of condoms. That is why companies develop world brands nowadays. Under a single brand name consumers worldwide can buy more or less the same products, and the

PHILIPS

Cultural aspects

Häagen-Dazs

L'ORÉAL

advertising material is also the same. Think of the cosmetics company of L'Oréal.

www.bizz.nl

An Entrepreneur on exports: Berg Toys

Product: Outdoor toys, exported to Russia since 2004
When Henk van den Berg (CEO) built a pedal car in his parents' garage as a 16-year-old boy, he could hardly have guessed that 24 years later the top model (a Ferrari costing €1,699) would be exported to Russia by the lorry load. Berg Toys from Wekerom, The Netherlands, sells more of this top model in Russia than in his own country.

14 April 2009

6.7.2 Price

Within the marketing mix price is the only factor that can be changed in the short term without increasing the costs. In determining the price of an export product, more is required than just converting the domestic price. Transport and distribution costs and the cost of currency exchange must be taken into account. When a company imports goods, various costs are incurred that must be incorporated into the cost price.

International price strategies
There are two strategies for determining the price level of a product in a new market:
1 worldwide pricing
2 dual pricing

Ad 1 Worldwide pricing
This is a price strategy in which the sale price is the same for all countries. It is difficult to maintain this system because distribution costs and

exchange rates vary per country. For instance, should the value of the foreign currency rise against the euro, less profit is made.

Ad 2 Dual pricing
Adoption of this price strategy means that the price of the product is different in a foreign market from the price in the domestic market. Should the price be higher abroad than in the home country, it is referred to as a price escalation. Reasons may be the cost of export and the risk of fluctuations in the rate of exchange.
Sometimes the price abroad is lower than it is in the domestic country. This may be because these sales are seen as extra turnover. The company chooses to incorporate costs such as R&D and administration only in the domestic price and not include them in the price calculation for the foreign market.
In order to understand how price is determined we first need to discuss a number of basic concepts. The following concepts are discussed:
1 cost of goods
2 landed cost price
3 landed duty paid price
4 importer's price
5 wholesale price
6 retail price

6

Cost of goods
The costs of production include: cost of materials + labour costs + producer's surcharge.

Landed cost price
Landed cost is the sum of the price of goods, shipping charges and insurances. The buyer must pay certain costs depending on the INCO terms (international delivery conditions). Suppose that the buyer bought the goods Free on Board: "Free On Board" (FOB) is always used in conjunction with a port of loading. Indicating "FOB *port*" means that the seller pays for transportation of the goods to the port of shipment, plus the loading costs. The buyer pays the cost of freight transport, insurance, unloading, and transportation from the port of loading to the final destination. The passing of risks occurs when the goods pass the ship's rail at the port of shipment.

Cost price	18.45	
Transport costs	1.00	
Insurance	0.35	+
Landed cost price	19.80	

Landed duty paid price
This is the landed cost price together with the import duties and taxes levied on the goods in the exporting or importing country.

Landed cost price	19.80	
Import duty (12%)	2.38	+
Landed duty paid price	22.18	

Importer's price
If the services of an importer are made use of, his commission must be taken into account. The importer pays the landed duty paid price to the supplier and then puts a certain percentage on top (surcharge) before selling the product on to the wholesaler. This surcharge serves as a compensation for activities such as marketing and sales costs, distribution costs, general and administrative costs, and profit.

Landed duty paid price	22.18	
Surcharge (15%)	3.33	+
Importer's price	25.51	

If no importer is involved, this calculation can be ignored. The import price is the wholesaler's purchase price.

Wholesale price
This is the price the wholesaler charges his customers, the retailers. This is known as the wholesale price, shortened to WSP, which is the importer's price plus a surcharge. Here, too, the wholesaler needs a margin to cover the cost of his services. His surcharge is calculated as a particular percentage of the importer's price.

Importer's price	25.51	
Surcharge (10%)	2.55	+
Wholesale price	28.06	

In some sectors this part of the transaction is passed over, because traders do not make us of wholesalers' services. When buying – that is, importing – a trader may be big enough to bypass this step in the chain.

Retail price
The wholesale price is the retailer's purchase price. To arrive at the price the consumer has to pay, the retail price, an additional surcharge must be added. This surcharge is charged by the party that sells the product to the consumer or final buyer, viz. the retailer. This can be a chain of shops or a web shop, or even a retailer. Depending on the type of industry, this surcharge can be expressed as a percentage, or the so-called calculation number: that is the factor by which the wholesale price must be multiplied in order to obtain the consumer price.

Wholesale price	28.06	
Surcharge (40%)	11.22	+
Retail price	39.28	

or

Wholesale price	28.06	
Calculation number	1.4	×
Retail price	39.28	

Figure 6.3 shows how the price for the foreign market is determined. What is interesting is the difference in retail price between the home market and

the foreign market. This is due to factors that increase the costs of doing business (see figure 6.3).

FIGURE 6.3 Price structure, home and foreign market

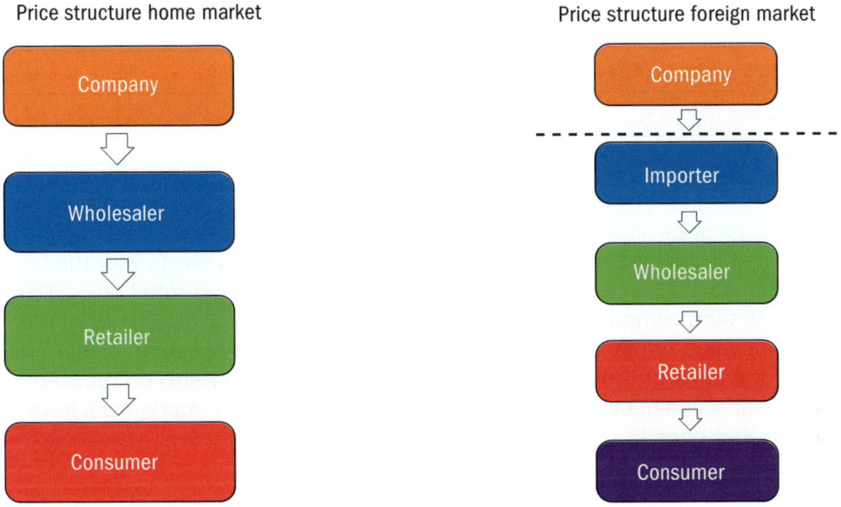

Calculating prices

Two methods are used to calculate an import or export price:

1. final price minus method
2. cost price plus method

Ad 1 Final price minus method

Price structure

The final price minus method or top-down pricing method is based on the retail price. All costs and surcharges in each link are no longer included. Calculation is done from the top to the bottom. The price that emerges, after all costs have been removed, is the calculated cost of goods. This price is then compared to the actual cost of goods. If the calculated cost price is lower, then somewhere along the supply chain cost reductions must be achieved in order to sell the product to the consumer or the cost of goods must then be reduced.

TABLE 6.10 Price calculation, home market and foreign market

Price Calculation	Home Market	Foreign Market
Cost of goods	100	100
Cost of transport		7
Insurance costs		3
Landed cost price		110
Import duty (10%)		11
Landed duty paid price		121

6

Price Calculation	Home Market	Foreign Market
Importer's surcharge (15%)		18
Importer's price		139
Wholesaler's surcharge (20%)	20	28
Wholesale price	120	167
Retailer's surcharge (40%)	48	67
Retail price	168	234

Ad 2 Cost price plus method

Mark-up factors

The cost price plus method or bottom-up pricing method starts with the cost of goods. All costs are added together to come to the retail price. This price is then compared with the predetermined consumer price and with the market value of the article. If the consumer price turns out to be higher than the price of the competitors' products, costs will have to be reduced in the supply chain, or the launch of the product on the new market will have to be abandoned.

6

Additional costs

Table 6.10 shows only the costs for transport, insurance and import duty. In fact, many other costs have to be taken into account when launching a product in a foreign country. Table 6.11 provides a few examples.

TABLE 6.11 Additional costs when launching a product

Cost of packaging, labeling, etc.	Transport costs from factory to port of departure and storage charges	Dispatch and loading costs and clearance charges	Cost of documents: Bill of Lading, Certificate of Origin, etc.
Costs clean report of findings on FOB values (see chapter 9)	Handling and settlement charges; only important when outsourcing	Bank and insurance charges	Agents' charges: shipping agent, excise and customs agent, ship broker, stevedore (see chapter 10)

6.7.3 Promotion

The company aims to inform the target group with a certain message in order to achieve specific organisational objectives. The company can reach the target group via:

- advertisements in trade magazines, flyers and general advertisements
- displays and billboards
- fairs
- personal selling
- internet

Pull or push strategy

An effective advertising policy can be developed only if the target group is known. The target group can be reached through a pull or a push strategy.

- With a pull strategy the manufacturer approaches the consumer directly. He uses advertising to stimulate demand for his products and to create a brand preference. Should this strategy succeed, the middlemen (wholesaler and retailers) are 'obliged' to carry the product in their ranges.
- In a push strategy, the 'pushing' is done by agents, importers and exporters, and representatives, who promote the products in such a manner that the distributive trade orders them. Initially, the middlemen are stimulated to order the products through price reductions and other types of support. In practice both methods are used indiscriminately.

It is important to stress the unique selling proposition (USP) and distinctive features of a product. These constitute the answer to the question why someone should buy this product, and not your competitor's product. A USP can, for instance, be a low price or advanced technology. Furthermore, the product must have added value, such as a long guarantee, good service, an online service desk or a help desk.

6.7.4 Place

In one way or another, the product must be delivered to the foreign customer. The location policy determines where the product is offered to the public and by which distribution channel. In the stage, the market entry mode is an essential factor. Additionally, the type of supplier and buyer is imperative when choosing marketing instruments. It is also wise to keep in mind that local policy for foreign retail trade is different from foreign wholesale trade. Location is the key for the retail trade; it is associated with the effort customers must make to buy the product. In order to buy foodstuffs such as milk or bread, the customer does not want to go through much effort. Customers typically make a bigger effort to buy items such as clothing, kitchens and cars. But the distribution of products is of greater importance to the wholesaler; think of transport and storage, for example.

6.7.5 Personnel

Personnel are responsible for supplying a company's products and services. The personnel represent the brand. Customers who have problems with the product contact the company's service desk. When personnel are customer-friendly and service-minded, the image of the brand improves; unfriendly personnel make the image of the company sink. Personnel who are in contact with customers must be trained to provide a high-quality service.

6.7.6 Physical evidence

Physical evidence is an essential ingredient of the service marketing mix. Consumers will form an opinion based on the customer care provided by the organisation. Services are intangible in nature. For example, a company that enters a foreign market can create a professional website and do the after-sales. Intangible aspects of service delivery–such as reputation and the opinions of other customers–are the immaterial elements of the service environment that influence customer perceptions. This creates tangible proof.

6.7.7 Process

In the marketing mix for services, a process has two components:

1 A means to obtain results; for example, to achieve a market share of 30%. A marketing strategy is subsequently built on this idea.

2 Integrating a number of processes to a general marketing process; for example, integrating telemarketing and internet marketing into a process.

Service delivery processes can improve customer satisfaction, increase customer retention, and may increase the value of a service offer.

Summary

- Market entry strategy
  Companies enter into all modes of strategic cooperation when accessing foreign markets. The goal is to defend, strengthen and expand the company's competitiveness.

- Strategic alliances
  - Agreement between two or more companies aiming to improve their market position
    - benefits of scale
    - market penetration
    - competitiveness
    - better product development
    - the development of new business opportunities
    - increase in exports
    - product diversification
    - reduction in costs
  - Defensive and offensive alliances

- Modes of cooperation
  - Participatory cooperation
    - co-makership
    - direct investment
    - joint venture
    - turnkey contract
  - Contractual cooperation
    - agent
    - distributor
    - trading companies
    - licensing
    - franchising
    - joint marketing
    - joint selling
    - piggyback-marketing
    - wholesale company

- Direct modes of entering a market
  - E-commerce
  - trade fairs, shows
  - sales representative/office

- Mergers & acquisitions
  - Merger: the combining of two or more companies, they become one
  - Acquisition: a company is bought by one or more companies that want to improve their market position

- Outsourcing & out-tasking
  - Outsourcing: passing on activities previously done by the company to a third party
  - Out-tasking: engaging external expertise to carry out regular or one-off activities

- International marketing
  - Carrying out marketing activities aimed at a particular group which is not part of the national market
  - Multinational marketing
    - Adapting marketing policy to the culture of the country
  - Global marketing
    - Worldwide marketing: attempting to achieve as much uniformity as possible
  - International marketing mix
    - Product
    - Price
    - Promotion
    - Place
    - Personnel
    - Physical evidence
    - Process

Questions and assignments

Lego is a Danish producer of toys. The Lego range is based on the age of the target group. The Lego range is known for its high quality, its modern design and the continual development of new items. In Europe Lego is directly sold to retailers by distributors. Initially, these were independent toy shops, and locations in high-class department stores. The company now also sells to the toy shop chains. Lego products have always been rather pricy, with a fairly large margin for the retailer. This high price still underpins Lego's quality image. Now that Lego it also sells to toy shop chains, the Lego distributor has noticed that he has become involved in a price war. Lego has been approached by old contacts, namely independent toy shops, with questions over the company's strategy and its consequences. A quick internet analysis showed that during the last few years the independent toy shops have achieved only 60 per cent of their Lego turnover; the department stores took 20 per cent and the toy shop chains also took 20 per cent, although they are relative new comers.

6.1 Lego has taken a decision to internationalise and is carrying out an internal analysis. Why is this necessary?

6.2 Lego's marketing activities are geared to a certain group in a large number of countries all over the world. In terms of its marketing strategy Lego is looking for as much uniformity as possible. The company would like to standardise its marketing activities. What type of international marketing should they define?

6.3 Which distribution channel does the Lego distributor make use of?

6.4 How should the Lego distributor react to the market problems described above?

6.5 Imagine that Lego would like to make direct investments. What are the advantages of such a direct investment?

7 Intercultural communication and management

In chapter 3, it was explained what was meant by culture. Because this book focuses on international business, the intercultural aspects are discussed that are important in doing international business: aspects such as communication and negotiations, as well as dealing with cultural differences. The negotiation process is discussed in the section on international negotiations, in which the negotiating strategy and the actual negotiation process is examined in depth. Three aspects of intercultural management are considered in the section on the subject. What competencies does a person need in international management, how do you manage multicultural teams and how do you manage virtual teams?

Managing across cultures

Carlos Ghosn, president and CEO of Nissan and Renault, argues that corporate culture is the key to success in the next wave of global mergers and acquisitions
Companies do not simply snap together like plastic building blocks. This is particularly true where different national cultures are involved, but even a crosstown merger can disrupt the key driver of value creation. The most important asset in any company is *esprit de corps*: the motivation of individual employees and their ability to collaborate in teams. Even in a cordial merger, it can vaporise overnight.
In 1999 Renault was a successful European carmaker, but without a market presence in Asia or North America its growth potential was constrained. Nissan had a significant presence in those two key markets, but was struggling after ten years of losses. A proud Japanese company faced the need to seek help from abroad.
The news that Renault would buy a 36.8% stake in Nissan in March 1999 met with scepticism. Observers predicted a clash between the French and Japanese cultures. And our talk of "an alliance of equals" was seen as a figleaf to cover a takeover.
In fact, aiming at alliance not absorption was the key to our chance of success. What value did Nissan offer? Given excess capacity worldwide, its plant and equipment were not the attractions. The gems were Nissan's global brand, its reservoir of skills and the loyalty of its employees. The imperative was to reinvigorate and reform Nissan's existing culture, creating a peer to Renault, not a subsidiary.

But just as we could not have merged the two cultures without destroying value, so we must ensure that both be open in response to a new global imperative: diversity. To

compete globally we must attract and motivate high-quality people close to our customers around the world. It is by no means easy for people at Renault or Nissan, but we have embraced English as a language that allows us to communicate effectively with each other and with customers around the world.
Gender is as much a challenge as geography. Especially in Japan, where the labour force and population are poised to decline in size, we can no longer afford to ignore the existence of a large population of bright, well-educated and motivated women. We need their contribution and so we are actively recruiting women at all levels. We are aware, however, that we cannot simply expect women to thrive in a culture that in large measure traces its roots to engineering fraternities. We must make space for women, and in particular we must take into account their unique needs, which will often balance childbirth with a long-term successful career.
Generational transition is in fact a further challenge. Nissan employees are learning to embrace cultural reforms such as promotion and compensation based on merit not seniority – essential features for a global company.

Source: www.economist.com, 11 January 2011

7.1 Preparing for intercultural communication

A sentence often heard is "If you are ever in the area, you must drop by." The underlying meaning can be one of the following:
- Bye /Good-bye! Don't call again!
- You are always welcome, any time.
- We'll maybe call each other in a couple of months and agree to do something.

All of these answers are correct. Whether you are really expected to be on the doorstep mainly depends on the speaker's cultural background. The language is not the problem but the expectations and assumptions implied in the words. In this section we take a closer look at cultural communication and the preparation required to work with cultural differences in an efficient way.

7.1.1 Intercultural communication

Intercultural communication

Intercultural communication means the exchange of information between people of different cultural backgrounds. It is very difficult to pass on a message 100 per cent accurately in an international environment because of cultural differences. In addition, if communication is conducted in a foreign language, 'noise' may be the result. Thus, it is very important to ask for feedback. You can then work out if the receiver has understood your message. This structure of a communication process is shown in figure 7.1.

7

FIGURE 7.1 The process of communication

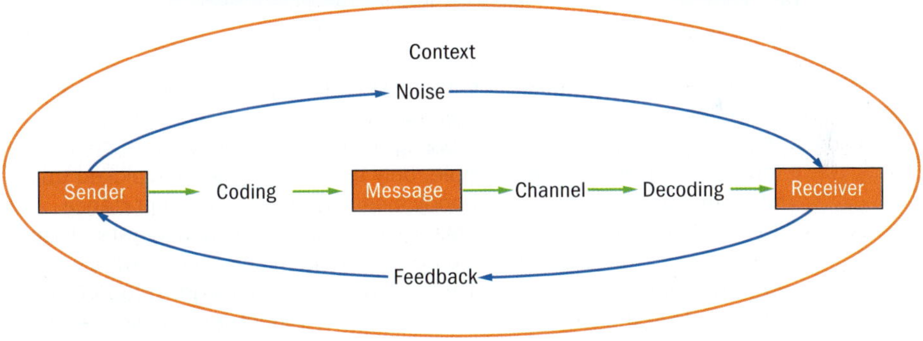

Source: Nunez, Nunez, Raya, 2007

Cultural noise

When communication with people from other cultures takes place, cultural noise is a common result. A person's culture influences the message. For example, in some cultures it is usual to talk loud during a presentation, whereas in other cultures it is important not to talk too loudly in order to avoid any inconvenience.

A number of aspects are of importance to the sender as well as the receiver for communication to take place with a minimum of noise. These aspects are:
- Awareness of thoughts or feelings. Which thoughts or feelings do you

want to express? Is it usual to express these thoughts in the culture in which one was raised?

- Translation into words or signs. Thoughts or feelings need to be translated into language or signs. To put feelings in words is often difficult, let alone in a foreign language in which you are not fluent. Sometimes it is easier to do this with signs and to ask the receiver to give feedback, to make sure that your message has been properly communicated.
- Saying or writing down words or making signs. It takes skill and courage to really do this. In some cultures, it is not easy to take the initiative if one is not the tribal chief and has hardly had any training in this skill. It is also important to look at body language, because it can support the message or it can cause noise.

Source: Nunez, Raya, 2007

The receiver will find these aspects important:

- Selecting signals. Only those signals are picked up which the receiver thinks important. The cultural background determines what is noticed. In low-context cultures, for example, only that which is said is picked up, while in high-context cultures body language is of major importance.
- Translating signals into concepts. The signals must be understood and consequently decoded. This we do by linking signals to concepts within our own frame of reference. These references differ from culture to culture. Take the OK sign. In some European countries the sign is by forming a circle with a thumb and forefinger while stretching out the other fingers. In some countries it also means OK, but in Japan the sign refers to money, in France it means zero, and in South America it is an obscene gesture.
- Interpreting information. Sounds and signs need to be stored in our brains. What do we expect? This is often prescribed by our culture. The better we know the sender's culture, the better we are able to understand him, i.e. to receive the message with as little noise as possible and subsequently the message is stored. Should the non-verbal message not correspond with the verbal information, the tendency to believe the non-verbal information is bigger. Think of a person who is crying and says that he has no pain.

In table 7.1 the advantages and disadvantages of various types of communication can be found. Study a situation and decide what type of communication suits your goal best. Remember that the 'noise risk' increase when the physical distance between the sender and receiver is bigger. In case of a foreign production sample, the written version is often better than the oral one. With the latest technology (e.g. e-mail) no time is waisted.

TABLE 7.1 Advantages and disadvantages of various types of communication

Type of Communication	Advantages	Disadvantages
Oral (direct contact between sender and receiver)	• many kinds of signals • direct feedback possible	• because of noise not all information is properly received • receiver must be able to keep up with the speaking rate of the sender
Written (no direct contact between sender and receiver)	• both sender and receiver can determine their own rate	• limitation of the signals that can be used • no direct feedback possible

Source: Schermer, 2008

7.1.2 Preparation for cultural differences

It is now clear that it is important for international business purposes that the person who is actually involved in the international business process possesses 'cultural intelligence'. This means this person must not only want to understand other cultures but should also be able to adapt to new cultures.

There are three steps in this cultural intelligence process:

1 awareness
2 knowledge
3 skills

Ad 1 Awareness

Step 1 is to become aware of the characteristics and limitations of our own culturally defined coding system and reference framework. What are the characteristics of your own style of communication and how do other cultures experience this style? The Dutch for instance have the reputation of being direct, blunt and even rude. Certain theories, such as those discussed in chapter 3, can be used to see in which area the differences lie.

Ad 2 Knowledge

Step 2 is about acquiring knowledge of the other culture. Information about other countries and their cultures can be found on www.cyborlink.com or on www.executiveplanet.com. These sites also provide information about the economies of countries, the best way of entering the market, trade figures, government regulations, literature, and useful addresses to conduct international businesses. Information on (possible) cultural differences can be found under the heading 'Culture and doing business'. Embassies can also provide a lot of information. Their information is probably more extensive and detailed. Chambers of Commerce can give you the addresses. It is also useful to acquire some knowledge of business etiquette. To do this you might consult the book *Kiss, Bow, or Shake Hands* by Wayne Conaway (2006). It is also worthwhile to write a briefing based on the data obtained and to give a copy to everyone involved in the international business deal.

● www.executiveplanet.com, edited source

Brazilian Conversation

Brazilian communication is cordial, complex, informal and highly personal.
Men usually greet each other by shaking hands and giving a gentle slap on the back. Women are usually greeted by shaking hands and a kiss near the face (air kiss).
Brazilians are known for their ability to talk naturally about intimate and personal topics. So, do not be surprised by the personal nature of questions, which is typical of Brazilians. When starting a conversation with Brazilians it is advisable to approach topics like soccer, weather, traffic (if you are in Sao Paulo), a cultural event taking place or that will take place in the city, music, and improvement of economical indicators of the country. Do not expect conversations with a high level of politicization. Topics like poverty, security, deforestation, religion, racism, corruption, social inequality, and comparisons between the Brazilian and Argentinean soccer teams should be avoided.
Brazilians are proud of being able to laugh even at themselves. Expect spontaneity. Brazilians are considered to be a bit loud because they all speak at the same time and in a tone of voice that is a bit higher than usual.
During a conversation, a Brazilian will usually interrupt to add something or make a comment before someone else has concluded his/her turn to speak. That is not perceived by Brazilians as rudeness or lack of interest in what is being said.
Brazilians touch each other a lot during a conversation. The intention is to get as close as possible. Closeness inspires trust, and trust inspires long term relationship.
Brazilians are not used to giving orders but advice, since they can get easily offended with directness as opposed to a cordial conversation.
Brazilian communication is complex, including elements of verbal and non-verbal communication and great use of body language.
Women are a recurrent subject in men's talk.

11 January 2011

Ad 3 Skills
Step 3 is implementing awareness and knowledge, from which follow the skills necessary to carry out international business. Training is possible, but if there are plans to visit the foreign country, consider the following:
- Show genuine interest in the host country and its people.
- Show understanding of the attitudes, values and way of thinking of the people in the host country .
- Be careful how you behave until you are familiar with the local ways of behaviour. Until then, it is better to listen than to talk.

- Do not be judgemental about cultural differences; do not compare their culture to your own. This may cause problems.
- Be flexible, creative and diplomatic.
- Do not expect to achieve everything at once. Be patient and persistent. To get things done some cultures require more time than others.

7.2 International negotiating

One aspect of intercultural communication is the process of conducting negotiations. As this plays an important role in international business, a whole section is dedicated to the subject. The international negotiating process is discussed in subsection 7.2.1 while negotiating strategy is discussed in subsection 7.2.2.

A negotiating process can relate to buying, sales, production, the appointment of a agent or even the setting-up of a marketing campaign. Negotiations are also necessary to obtain a patent or a licence. International negotiations are far more complicated than negotiations at a national level, because of cultural differences between the parties. In order to negotiate successfully it is necessary that you understand the culture of the other party and adapt your negotiating strategy accordingly.

7.2.1 The process of international negotiations

The international negotiating process is one in which two or more parties get together to discuss shared and/or opposing interests. The goal is to reach an agreement that is beneficial to all parties. It is not unusual for negotiations to be held in the presence of a group of staff members. This is especially the case in collectivistic cultures (see chapter 3), where it is usual to have a team of negotiators sitting at the negotiating table. Of course, it is important that the right people take part in the negotiating process. Characteristics such as stability, maturity, knowledge, optimism, empathy and a listening ear as well as flexibility are important qualities of an international negotiator.

● www.managementtoday.co.uk

Paul Beverley, PMS International Founder of the toy, novelty and homeware importer

My best....

I started sourcing goods in China over 30 years ago, back when I was operating out of one small shop on Southend seafront. Now I'd say 98% of our supplies come from China and we've got four offices there, and one in Hong Kong – as well as a 20-acre British HQ in Essex, where 300 staff work. Getting a local partner is probably the best move I ever made. He is from Taiwan and we have worked together for years now. I've learned a huge amount from him about Chinese culture, bureaucracy and the best way to do business there. When you're negotiating with a Chinese supplier, there is a way of talking that is completely different from what we are used to in the West. You might spend an hour talking about the price for one item, circling the issue rather than going straight at it – we call it dancing. Two things you must never do are to back them into a corner – if you do, they will never come out – or lose your temper. Chinese people think it's hilarious when someone starts shouting and banging the table.

My worst...
China is the only country I know where you lose money on the property market. But when we opened our first office there in Nanjing I didn't know that, so I bought the freeholds on the office, and on an apartment for the manager, too. When I sold it a few years ago, I took a bath – old buildings depreciate there just like anything else, and they were worth 60% less than what I had paid for them.
Only very recently has property started to appreciate in value, and only in Shanghai – a city that is completely different from the rest of China anyway: it's like a country within a country.
A common mistake that buyers from the West make is to underestimate the Chinese, to look down on them because so many of the people are poor. But they are incredibly hard working, and the education system there is phenomenal. A lot of the growth in our industry has been on the back of growth in China – the size and speed of the Chinese economy forces competitiveness.

4 February 2011

The negotiating process is shown in figure 7.2. The culture in which the buyer and seller have grown up and have been educated influences the process.

As you can see from Figure 7.2, the process can be divided into:
- non-task-related interaction
- task-related interaction

Non-task-related interaction

Non-task-related interaction

Non-task-related interaction has great influence in the way the relationship with the opposite party is established. It is of crucial importance preliminary to the actual negotiations. The aim of this type of interaction is to get to know each other better without talking business. Common subjects for conversation are the weather, sports, children and the family. In Western cultures, such 'small talk' does not take up much time, but in cultures with strong social structures it can take up more time than European people are accustomed to. This form of interaction can be broken down into:
1 status distinction
2 impression formation accuracy
3 interpersonal attraction

Ad 1 Status distinction

Status distinction

Someone's age, gender, education and position in the company defines the distinction in status. So, it is important that other people's positions are understood and that you know in advance how the opposite party interprets your status. There are cultures in which status plays an important role in

FIGURE 7.2 The process of international negotiating

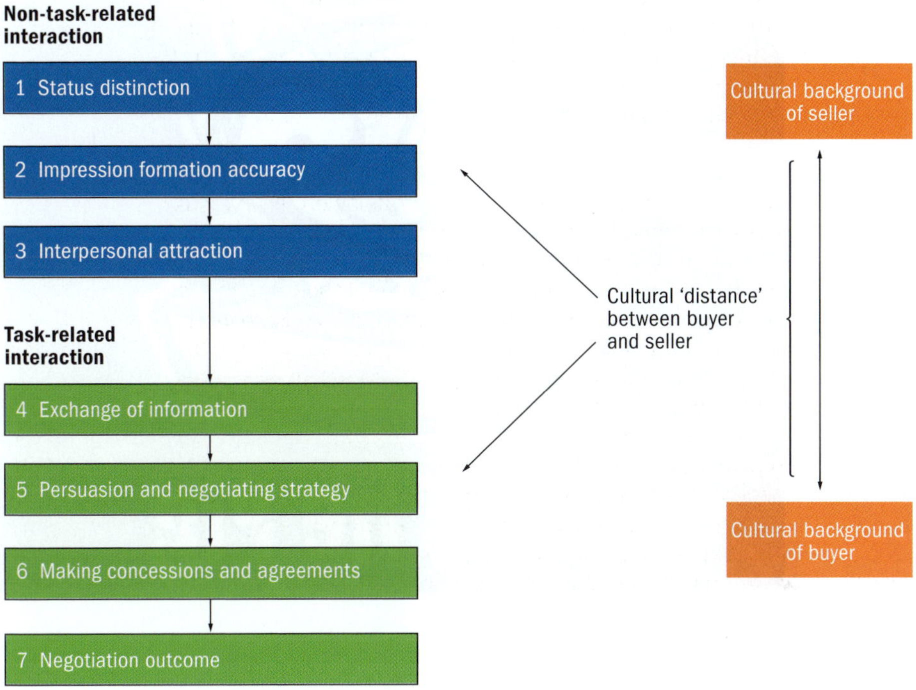

Source: Hollensen, 2007

7

negotiations. Especially in high-context cultures, (see chapter 3) a person's status is worth more than the words used by the negotiator.

Ad 2 Impression formation accuracy
Within the first minutes have made someone's acquaintance, you form an impression of the person involved. This impression will influence the negotiating process. Should a wrong impression be formed, for example because of poor non-verbal communication, this may have disastrous consequences for the negotiating process. Remember what type of the behaviour is required in another country.

Ad 3 Interpersonal attraction
On the basis of a first impression, the decision is made whether the other person is likeable or not. This has a big influence on the negotiating process. If you like someone, then you will be more inclined to compromise than if you do not. For example, in Asia people value Chinese astrology, in which the zodiac is used. Each year corresponds to a particular animal, for example a pig. It is possible that your negotiating partner asks you what sign you are. Sometimes it is better to tell a lie, because some Chinese are not attracted to particular animals, such as the pig and the snake.

Task-related interaction

7

Task-related interaction

After you have been introduced and have started to form a personal relationship, the task-related aspects of the negotiating process become more important. So then the real business begins. When operating in another culture it is sensible to let the other party decide when this phase begins. It involves the following steps:

1 exchange of information
2 persuasion and negotiating strategy
3 making concessions and agreements
4 negotiation outcome

Ad 1 Exchange of information

This is done either in writing or orally; for example, though a written offer, an interview by phone or a face to face conversation. During this stage, it is important to have a clear understanding of the negotiator's needs and expectations in order to have a good starting point. This will create an effective communication flow. Things such as packaging requirements, weights and measures, approval certification and quality standards, as well as conditions of payment and delivery are discussed. It is also important to ask the other party to provide copies of annual reports and to take into account the financial situation of the other party. The amount of information exchanged between the parties differs from culture to culture. In low-context cultures, every detail has to be discussed, while in high-context cultures not so many details need to be discussed. In some cultures, it is normal to ask lots of questions and for these to be followed by periods of silence. Be careful not to speak too much. You might reveal more information than desirable. As the exchange of information cannot often be done in either of the parties' native language, a so-called lingua franca is used. It is the language most commonly used as a means of communication between

Lingua franca

people with different mother tongues. Arabic acts as lingua franca in the Arab world. Exchanges between European people are often conducted in the 'big' languages (languages with a lot of native speakers) such as French, German or English, which are becoming increasingly known as 'international languages'. The use of a lingua franca increases the chances of noise considerably. Neither of the parties is using his mother tongue, so the possibility of misinterpretation is high. We would advise you to be well prepared.

Ad 2 Persuasion and negotiating strategy

Negotiating strategy

In this case it is a matter of persuading the other party of the logic of your position. No matter what strategy you have chosen, what matters is whether you can cash in the results. Knowledge of the market and of your own company is very important, but information about the other party can also play a role. Furthermore, it is necessary to have an understanding of the price structure (see chapter 6) so that it is clear how much room there is to negotiate in. In this stage of the negotiations price is often mentioned. Price negotiations are allowed in our Western society, though it is unusual to give more than a 25% reduction. In other cultures it is quite common to give a reduction of 50% on the first bid. Make sure you know who has to be persuaded; often it is not only the buyer. In business, very often more people are influential in the process behind the scenes; they are involved in the evaluation of a new product, and take the final decision. Do not think it is enough to persuade the person sitting opposite you. What is also important is the way you do it. In some cultures, it is normal to threaten and warn the other party until they see your point of view, while in other cultures it would absolutely be the wrong approach. Not all cultures appreciate showing emotions. A very powerful negotiating technique demands asking questions. In this case the questioner has more time to think about

his point of view. Negotiating techniques will be discussed later this chapter.

Ad 3 Making concessions and agreement
Negotiations are deemed a success if you are able to manoeuvre the negotiators from their initial point of view to an agreement in which both parties have made a compromise. This phase is also discussed later in more detail.

Ad 4 Negotiation outcome
The final goal of the negotiating process is to reach an agreement. It is usual in many Western cultures to concede quickly so that the other party can react and an agreement can be reached. This can be a simple understanding, but also a contract or a written agreement. It depends on the cultural context. Generally speaking, in a low-context culture a number of agreements must be put in formal contracts, while in a high-context culture so-called 'gentlemen's agreements' are often applied orally. Mostly these form a starting point of a long-term business relationship. In various cultures it is normal to sign a contract in the presence of all parties involved, and not, as is usual in Europe, to send the contract by mail or by e-mail.

7.2.2 Negotiating strategy

Before you start the negotiations, it is advisable to see whether you should call in the help of third parties. For example, it may be better to call in a agent who has already met the other party, and then start the negotiations. These strategies are shown in Figure 7.3.

FIGURE 7.3 Culturally responsive strategies and their feasibility

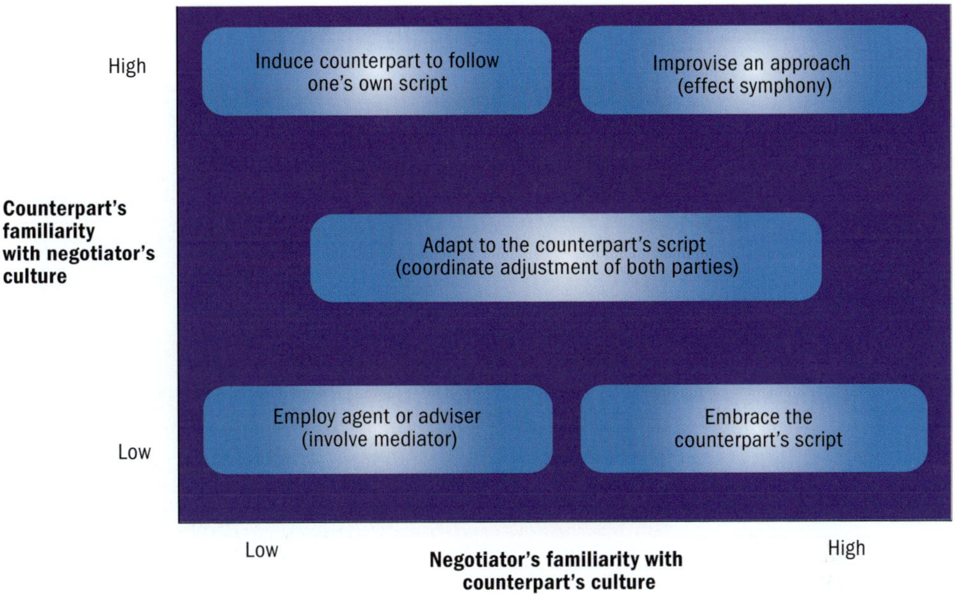

Brackets indicate a joint strategy, which requires deliberate consultation with counterpart.
At each level of familiarity, a negotiator can consider feasible the strategies desigated at that level and any lower level.

Source: http://sloanreview.mit.edu/the-magazine/files/2008/11/3524-ex2-lo.png

From this you can see that if you have no negotiating experience, it is preferable to use the services of an agent or adviser when neither party is familiar with the other party's culture. In case both parties know a lot about each other's culture it should be a combination of both cultures and an improvised approach. In the middle, when both parties know something about the other party's culture, the feasible strategies are somewhere between both cultures. The parties can decide to conduct the negotiatons alternately in each of their respective countries or establish a joint language to negotiate.

Once the decision has been taken on the type of strategy, it is important to decide on your own goal. Decide which points can be negotiated and which cannot. Provide an alternative strategy. Look for alternatives and think of these beforehand and not while sitting at the negotiating table. Figure 7.4 provides an overview of the negotiating strategies you can choose according to the position and interests.

It is important to decide your starting position. When you are just beginning you start at I, and requires quite some skills to go from I to II. You have to think how you can get from a win–lose situation to a win–win situation. It is also important to know where your counterpart can go wrong. This allows you to respond to the opposing team to your benefit. Of course, your product or service may have more to offer than that of the competition; in this case, you must make it known. Often a trial order can create an opportunity for the customer to get to know the product or service. As a

FIGURE 7.4 Different negotiating strategies

Position \ Interests	Parallelism (win-win)	Discrepancy (win-lose)
High dependability	III **Strategy** Maximum cooperation **Problem** Information exchange	IV **Strategy** 'Fight' **Problem** Achieving domination/ascendancy
Low dependability	II **Strategy** Optimal cooperation **Problem** Maintaining independence	I **Strategy** Take it or leave it **Problem** Maintaining independence

Source: Kok & Rojo, 2004

supplier, you can see how the customer reacts to the new product. At this stage of the negotiations, do not let the customer force you into exclusivity. That deprives the supplier of any chances. Once the trial order has been delivered and it meets the other party's requirements and there are follow-up orders, manoeuvre more and more to strategy II. Optimal cooperation is the final goal. You have to maintain an intensive contact with the buying party about customer wishes, specifications, quantities and designs. Price should not be the only factor; you should also compete on other factors, for example on delivery reliability.

It is, of course, the intention to manoeuvre from strategy II to strategy III. This is a rather difficult process, because in the end you may still be smaller than your competitors. The other suppliers are often business friends of the counterparty. Make sure that the counterparty invests more time in his contact with you by involving him in your story. In order to manoeuvre from strategy III to strategy IV you will have to become the best supplier, so the counterpart is strongly dependent on you. This is often associated with delivery reliability and other performing aspects. Try to find out what aspects the counterparty thinks important and make sure that you perform better than your competitors on these aspects. Then you have reached your final goal, but remember to stay on top of things if you do not wish to lose your position.

7.2.3 Negotiations and agreement

Once the negotiating strategy is known, you must look at how you are going to deal with the negotiations. At this stage, the Thomas-Kilmann model is very useful (see figure 7.5). This model shows that dealing with opposite interests always produces an area of tension between the two parties. The vertical axis represents assertiveness, the wish to force through one's own goals and realise the task. The horizontal axis stands for cooperativeness, the wish to maintain good relations in order to let the process run its course. This area of tension has been placed in an axis model in order to characterise the five ways of handling opposing interests. These are:

1 competing
2 avoiding
3 collaborating
4 accommodating
5 compromising

FIGURE 7.5 The Thomas-Kilmann Conflict Modes

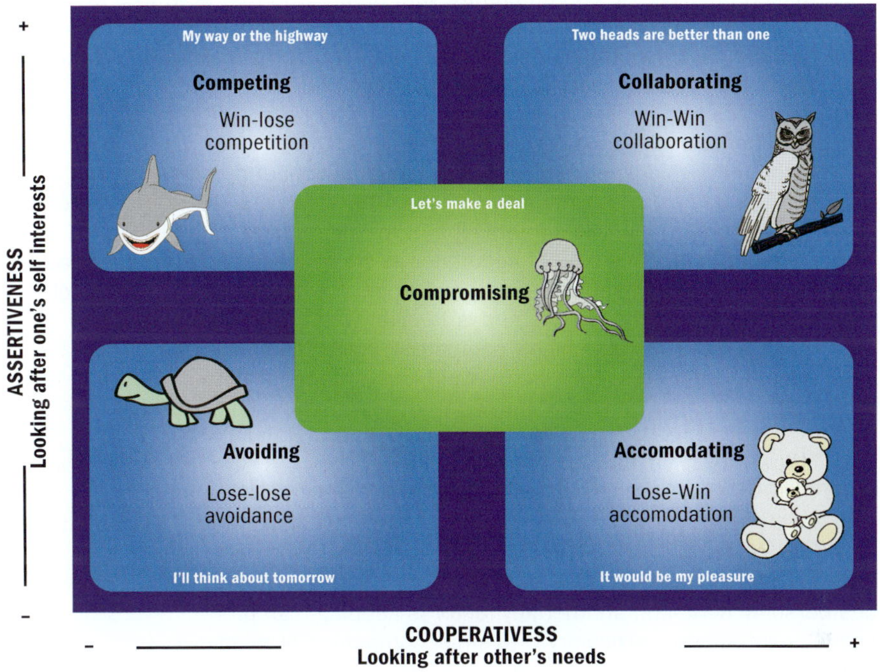

Source: Nieuwenhuis, 2009

Ad 1 Competing – 'My way or the highway'
At the top left of the figure is the 'shark': the most assertive person, who is not bothered about cooperation or the well-being of the people in his immediate surroundings, as long as he reaches his goal. You will often see this person in individually oriented societies, such as Western ones. Self-interest and status occupy a central position. All instruments of power are used to win: power to argue well, position, status and even money.

Ad 2 Avoiding – 'I'll think about it tomorrow'
Bottom left is the tortoise: the person who neither realises his goals nor shows any interest in forming relationships with other people. The turtle prefers to avoid conflicts. He also believes that he is not involved. You will often find such behaviour in collectivistic, Eastern societies. You achieve nothing in haste, but with time and patience Negotiating with this type of person can take 'forever'.

Ad 3 Collaborating – 'Two heads are better than one'
Top right is the owl: the one who tries to maintain good relations as well as realise his goals. He has found a balance between self-interest and the interest of others and continues to research all these interests, mapping them out and representing them. You often find this kind of negotiator in Asia. Long-drawn-out negotiations are no exception, but they come eventually to results.

Ad 4 Accomodating – 'It would be my pleasure'
Bottom right is the teddy bear. This type of person is always concerned about his relationship with the other and is very cooperative. Most contacts think he is nice. He can empathize with others and that is why he is a good person to talk to. However, he never realises his goals and is therefore not suitable to conduct business negotiations. You can sometimes find these types in negotiating teams in collectivistic cultures.

Ad 5 Compromising – 'Let's make a deal'
Right in the middle is the jellyfish, an animal without a backbone. The jellyfish is a calculating negotiator; the other party can achieve some of its goals provided there is something in it for him and he gets his way on several points. This type of negotiator exists in all cultures but especially in France and in central and southern Europe. He knows exactly how much room he has to manoeuvre and is familiar with the background of his opponents. He is also highly competent, clever, elegant and intent on maintaining status. He tries to avoid loss of face for both parties.

www.globalnegotiator.com/country-guides-how-to-negotiate-in-70-countries.html

How to negotiate in Arab Emirates

- Besides personal contacts, another key factor is keeping high profit margins in negotiations, particulary with small companies or middlemen who resell goods.
- As well as the price, Emirati have special interest in aspects such as education on technical rules, after-sales service, or keeping stock in the country. In this way, there are more and more foreign companies working with distributors or creating subsidiaries in the country, mainly in one of the tax-free areas.
- In the Asiatic culture, 'yes' does not have the same meaning as in the Occidental culture, since it rather means 'perhaps'. To really know what they are thinking of, it is better to ask open questions and to suggest different alternatives.
- In order to have no obligations, they use expressions like *Insh'allah* ('God willing') or *Burka Insh'allah* ('Tomorrow, God willing'). It is difficult to consider these expressions good or bad – it will depend on the conversations context.
- Negotiation process is a mix of the snail and snake strategies. Emirati take time on making a decision but once they have made up their mind, they want everything to be carried out quickly.
- It can be suprising that no more operations could be carried out even if the first one has been beneficial for the client. The reason must be

that they could have found a supplier offering better prices. To keep negotiations moving forward it will be necessary to maintain the presence in the market and to meet prices in every moment.
- To maintain commercial relations, personal contact is essential: a visit is better than a phone call. A phone call is more effective than an email.

Which approach is effective in which situation?
That depends not only on the situation but also on the culture of the other party. Each style is effective in certain situations. Good negotiators in an individualistic culture often look for a compromise but can also be very forceful. However, the seeking of a compromise or a more indulgent type of behaviour is considered better in a collectivistic culture. Figure 7.6 shows various approaches associated with certain types of behaviour. A leader must be competitive if he needs to work under time pressure, and he must be confident that he is right. It is better for him to collaborate to solve the problem if he needs the counterparty and the counterparty's interests are as important as his own. To suggest a compromise is a better temporary solution when the stakes are not too high. To accommodate is possibly an effective approach when credit needs to be built for later, and if the outcome does not matter that much. Finally, avoiding conflict can be the best scenario if the other party is more powerful and claiming to be right does not always solve anything.

7

FIGURE 7.6 Approaches used with a certain type of behaviour

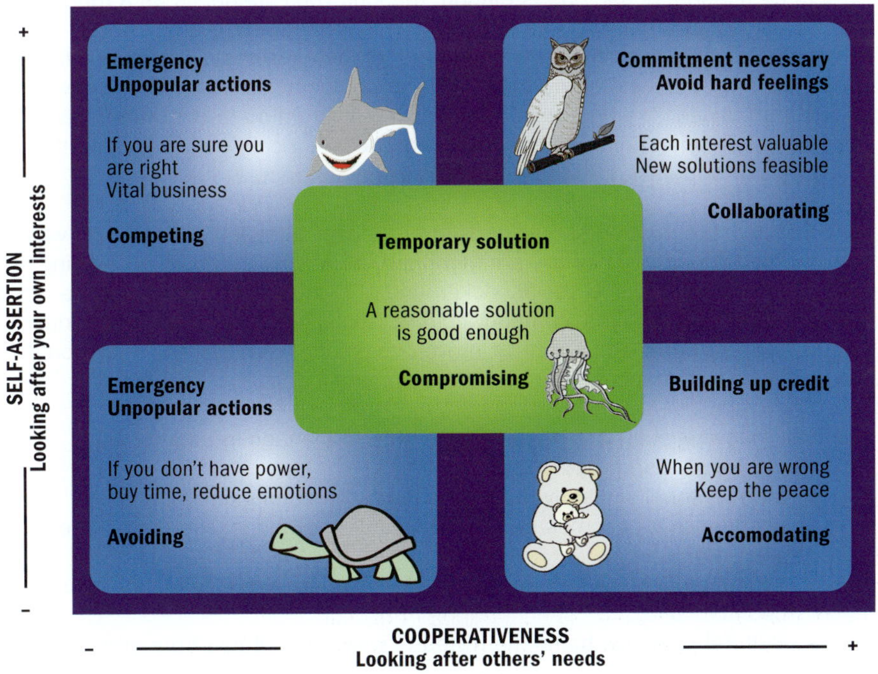

Source: Nieuwenhuis, 2009

7.3 Intercultural management

These days it has become the norm for companies to have international responsibilities as well as contacts. To establish such contacts one does not always need to travel abroad; the modern company consists of people from various cultures, who work together. More and more, people must learn to appreciate cultural differences in their working environment, not only in their own country but also abroad, and learn to cope with these differences. Managing this process is known as intercultural management. It concerns not only mutual international cultural differences, but business/ industry and corporate culture also play a role in this process (see chapter 3). The most important aspects of intercultural management are discussed in this section, in particular attention is devoted to the international manager, to multicultural teams and virtual teams.

Intercultural management

7.3.1 International manager

People often use this expression to refer to expatriates who work abroad for large multinationals. However, this type of manager plays an important role in small and medium-size companies as well as larger ones. Imagine that the company is going to expand to other countries, and to do so it needs to recruit people from other cultures. Someone has to manage this foreign office and this person must be able to manage cultural differences. However, think also about worldwide expansion through alliances and joint ventures, and through cross-border mergers and acquisitions.

Culture shock

Many international managers stationed abroad experience a culture shock. The phrase implies a sudden effect, but it is more of a latent effect. The cause is the frustration that comes to the fore as a result of encountering with a new culture and learning to cope with the differences. This effect has three phases: phase one is elation, the kind you experience as a tourist when you go aboard for the first time. This is followed by a phase of uncertainty and confusion, comparable to homesickness. This slowly fades away after a couple of months as one becomes accustomed to the new surroundings. The best thing to do is to pay attention to the matter, also when foreigners join a team. In the worst case, it can lead to an identity crisis or depression or the termination of a contract.

Effective preparation should consist of at least a 'country briefing', in which the conditions in a country are identified, as well as intercultural training, in which the history and social background of a country are discussed as well as particular customs, company culture, social behaviour, ways of conducting negotiations, etc. Should it prove necessary, individual coaching could be used to enhance personality development.

The following skills are needed to be able to manage internationally (Schneider & Barsoux, 2003):

- Interpersonal skills: by forming relationships and gaining people's confidence it becomes easier to transfer knowledge, coordinate people and control them.
- Language fluency: it is an advantage if you speak the language of the country.
- Cultural curiosity: being motivated to work with people from other cultures.

- Flexibility: being able to handle unexpected situations and uncertainty.
- Patience and respect: it takes times to get to know a different culture.
- Cultural empathy: the ability to listen to the thoughts, feelings and experiences of people from other cultures without prejudice.
- Self knowledge: the ability to interact with others without losing yourself.
- Sense of humour: this can break the ice and increase your likeability.
- Simultaneous reactivity to various cultures: being able to interact with a miscellaneous group of people.
- Being prepared to share authority: the office in the home country does not have more authority than the office abroad.
- Ability to learn fast and unlearn: to quickly absorb new points of view and try new approaches.

Global mindset

In short, a catalogue of skills is required, in which the human aspect is extremely important. People with a 'global mindset' can effectively manage beyond the boundaries of organisations, jobs and cultures. It means that the person looks for differences, learns from them and knows how to forge common interests.

● www.ft.com

Learning to cultivate a global mindset

The study of culture – once the academic purview of anthropology and sociology – is capturing a more central role at New York University Stern School of Business in a new course that aims to prepare MBA candidates for global careers. The course strives to give students an understanding of the impact that local customs and culture have on business, according to Bruce Buchanan, professor of business ethics at Stern. "We want students to appreciate that there are significant and meaningful differences between cultures and that it takes time to find out what matters to different people," he says. "With so many cultures on the planet that you're hoping to do business with, you have to do your homework. We can't give students the answers, but we hope they come away with the understanding that this is something they have to do. It doesn't just stop at the spreadsheet or the cash flow projection."

The new course follows a trend of business schools placing more emphasis on concepts such as multiculturalism and globalisation to enable MBAs to compete in an increasingly international job market. "It's a global marketplace for businesses and so it is for business

students," says John Fernandes, president of the Association to Advance Collegiate Schools of Business, the industry body.
Schools are tackling globalisation in different ways: some have introduced international exchange programmes where students spend a semester at an overseas university, others are simply giving the topic more classroom time, either in newly designed modules or incorporated into core classes on strategy and finance.

11 January 2011

7.3.2 Multicultural team

Multicultural team

A multicultural team is a team that consists of people from different cultures. Examples are the teams responsible for the development of a product (R&D departments in various countries), regional offices (office Europe) and teams that are to carry out joint ventures.

Homogeneous team

Heterogeneous team

The composition of a team largely determines its dynamism. A uniform team, of people from the same culture, generally has few disagreements and can communicate easily, is less creative, and has more standards, a higher level of coherence and an obvious informal leader. On the other hand, a heterogeneous team, of people from different cultures, has more disagreements, communicates poorly, is more creative, has fewer standards, a lower level of coherence and an dual informal leader.

Managers responsible for building teams within various cultures must first look carefully at the task the team must complete. The structure of the team must be geared to the task the team is to perform. For example, if the work is routine and clear, a uniform team is more effective. Similarities in knowledge, background, values and religion facilitate the work.
If the work is not routine, but complex and ambiguous a heterogeneous team is more effective. This is because of its diverse backgrounds, experience, knowledge and values that all contribute to a solution.

Other cultural factors play a role in group dynamics. Within an individualistic culture, it is problematic to create shared values and coherence within a team, while in a collectivistic culture this is easier to do. In cultures with wide power distances, team members should be from the same level, because those from a lower level would be intimidated or treated as inferiors. Level diversity is less of a problem in low hierarchy cultures.

Uncertainty avoidance and group dynamics can also be considered as one of the responsibilities of a team. If the task of the team is vague, ambiguous or unstructured, a team that wants to avoid uncertainty will not to be able to carry it out effectively. However, a team from a low-uncertainty-avoidance culture such as Denmark or Sweden will do the job without any problems. Finally, teams from a masculine culture work well together if financial incentives are linked to the results, while teams in a feminine culture can be motivated by goals such as improved quality of work or attitudes towards a project.

Research carried out by Brett, Behfar and Kern (2006) showed that cultural differences can cause big problems within a team. These problems often go unrecognised, until the damage caused is so serious that the team can no longer function. Points to be attended to include:

- Direct versus indirect communication: in some cultures, communication is direct and explicit but other cultures dislike this kind of communication (see table 7.2).
- Different attitudes towards hierarchy and authority: teams often have a flat organisational structure, but members from a culture with great power distances find this difficult to cope with.
- Differences in time perception between cultures (see chapter 3) and openness about the process. In Western cultures, the people are short-term oriented, and there is usually a rather short time limit.
- Trouble with accents and fluency: see the comments on the use of a lingua franca in section 7.2.

It is a skill to gear business behaviour and the cultural values of individuals towards each other. This is an essential element in the organisation's power.

TABLE 7.2 English–Dutch translations

What the English say	What the English mean	What the Dutch understand
I hear what you say	I don't agree with it and don't want to talk about it any more	He accepts my version
With the greatest respect	I think you are wrong	He is listening to me
That's not bad	It is good or very good	It is bad to middling
Very interesting	I don't agree with you I don't believe you	He is impressed
I'm sure it's my fault	It is your mistake!	It is his fault!
I almost agree	I don't agree at all	We have nearly reached an agreement

Source: http://alvinng.xanga.com/416327188/item/

7.3.3 Virtual team

A group consisting of colleagues in New York, Tokyo and the Netherlands working together on a project via internet is an example of a 'virtual team' or 'e-team'. Globalisation is creating more and more competition and forcing companies to remain on the ball. This way of working is faster, cheaper and increasingly common. One can choose the best employees even if they are located all over the world.

Virtual team

Such a team generally shares a work portal that contains a type of chatroom in which one can exchange information. Further communication takes place by telephone (if possible using a webcam or Skype) and email. A telephone- or video-conference call is used for meetings; the participants at the meeting can see each other on a screen and can talk to each other with hardly any delay.

A great advantage of working this way is 'timeshifting'. The work continues

24 hours a day. When you go home at 5 o'clock, you leave the report you are working on with your colleague in America. Because of the time difference between the countries, the colleague is only halfway though his working day and can continue working on it. When you return to work in the morning, a revised version is waiting for you.

This way of working does have a few disadvantages, especially when people from different cultures are involved. Emails, often phrased in short sentences, can cause tremendous conflicts. That is why it is important to have met colleagues face to face at least once and to have created a mutual trust. The video conference also has some disadvantages. For example, time differences: when you work with colleagues in America as well as Asia there is always one colleague who has to get up at night because of the time difference. Furthermore, a lot of technical support is required to make the conference run smoothly. There are often delays, and people can have more difficulty expressing themselves during a video conference.

Summary

- Intercultural communication is the exchange of information between two or more people from different cultures. In order to avoid 'noise' it is important for the sender:
  - to be aware of the thoughts and feelings of the other party
  - to translate to words or signs
  - to utter words or signs or write them down

  For the receiver it is important:
  - to select the signals
  - to translate the signals into concepts
  - to interpret the information

- Consider what type of communication is appropriate for what type of goal (see table 7.1).

- You need cultural intelligence in order to communicate with people from other cultures: the ability to understand other cultures and to adapt to them. The cultural intelligence process consists of:
  1 awareness
  2 knowledge
  3 skills

- Negotiating is a specific aspect of intercultural communication. The process consists of non-task-related interaction, intended to get to know each other better:
  1 status distinction
  2 impression formation accuracy
  3 interpersonal attraction

  The process also consists of task-related interaction, which includes:
  1 exchange of information
  2 persuasion and negotiation strategy
  3 making concessions and agreement
  4 negotiation outcome

- The choice of negotiating strategy depends on positions and interests (see figure 7.4).

- There are five ways of negotiating:
  1 competing
  2 avoiding
  3 collaborating
  4 accomodating
  5 compromising

- An intercultural manager must possess particular competences.

- Multicultural teams consist of people from diverse cultures. Factors that are of importance with regard to these teams are:
  - composition
  - type of task
  - group dynamics

- Virtual teams are teams of colleagues from all over the world working together on one project via a portal.

Questions and assignments

Questions about opening case

7.1 What is the lingua franca in Nissan and Renault?

7.2 What kind of negotiation strategy has Renault used for the alliance with Nissan? Motivate your answer.

7.3 State the advantages and disadvantages of virtual teams.

7.4 Research business etiquette in a country of your choice. Write a briefing on the country.

8
International commercial law

Legal considerations often play a subordinate role in international business. Profit is in trade not in legal rules. The major part of international trade does not cause any legal problems, but day- to- day reality proves differently. Business is tough and financial interests are often huge. No single, uniform international commercial law governing foreign business transactions exists. The international company must pay particular attention to the laws of each country within which it operates. Managers must be familiar with the legal systems in the countries where they do international business. They should also be aware of the nature of the legal profession, both domestic and international, and the legal relationships that exist between countries. In order to keep the risk of legal problems as small as possible when trading internationally, it is vital to dwell on a number of legal aspects which are discussed in this chapter.

Corruption: Multinationals find new ways to tackle graft

When Aldo Fumagalli decided to expand Candy, the Italian home appliances manufacturer, into Russia five years ago and open the company's first plant there, he expected the usual instances of bureaucracy and corruption. What he did not expect was that it would take weeks for the company's trucks to even make it across the border.
He recalls that the trucks spent weeks circling the country, trying to find a customs clearance point at which they could enter. Despite the fact that the customs system should operate as a federal organisation, all decisions are made on a local level, explains Mr Fumagalli.
"The local level makes its own interpretation of the law and procedures and the document that was good at one customs point was not good in another. There is no national organisation to help you".
After struggling with the problem for weeks, he decided to set up a division of the company in Moscow that would have the sole responsibility of dealing with customs clearance. The problem was solved in a matter of days.
While the customs fiasco is just one of many problems faced by Candy in Russia, the company's approach to solving it is indicative of the new approaches multinationals are employing when combating bureaucracy and corruption.
Ikea, the Swedish retailer, has repeatedly frozen new investment in the country while battling court cases and allegations of corruption, while Daimler, the carmaker, and Siemens, the industrial group, have faced allegations of bribery.
Even Mr Fumagalli's Candy has not been immune from court cases: since opening shop four years ago, it has dealt with four lawsuits over issues ranging from income tax to value added tax payments.
"The problem is that Russia is competing for investments with other Bric countries and if you have an environment that is seen as high-risk, then those investment dollars are going to go elsewhere."

Last year Transparency International, the international anti-corruption watchdog, placed Russia in 146th place beside Sierra Leone and Zimbabwe in its annual Corruption Perception Index of 180 countries.
"Russians get very upset about [the ranking] and say how unjust it is and how it doesn't reflect the improvements here.
As the Kremlin tries to improve the business environment while working on turning Moscow into a financial centre and building a technology hub, it will also have to work on improving its reputation for corruption.
"So long as this perception exists, Russia is really going to struggle."

Source: www.ft.com, 14 February 2011

8.1 The principle legal systems

Businesses live and conduct their activities within a certain framework of law based on customs and practice, on the judicial decisions of the courts and statutes enacted by governments.The legal environment is normally concerned with three aspects: home country laws, host country laws, and international laws.

1 Home country laws: important issues are conduct of the company in the domestic market and trade with third countries. Laws concerned are made to control the international activities of companies for the sake of the country. For example, many countries have established anti-corruption laws.
2 Host country laws: multinational enterprises must observe the laws of the host country. Their activities are subject to the laws and regulations of the host country, such as investment regulations, tariffs and duties, anti-dumping regulations and the protection of local industries.
3 International law: the collection of treaties, conventions and agreements between nations which have (the) force of law. International laws are particularly related to areas as patents and trademark protection, piracy laws and code of conducts for multinationals.

Legal systems

The legal systems of different countries are so disparate and complex to explore the laws of each country individually. Each country has its own legal system. When doing business internationally it is wise to have an idea of what these legal systems encompass. Four heritages form the bases for the majority of the legal systems of the world. There are two legal traditions in Europe: civil or code law and common law. Two more systems are used elsewhere in the world: socialist law and Islamic law.

8

Civil or code law

The majority of countries on the continent of Europe use this system, which is why it is often known as continental law.
Civil law is rooted in Roman law. The law in this system can be found mainly in law books and rules. That is why this is often also called professional judges' law. Agreements between business partners is based on a system of written rules of law (table 8.1).

- *Common law:* countries with a common-law tradition do not have written rules of law. In these countries, law is shaped by the decisions of judges (case law). In the common-law system there is less legislation and many things are fixed in contracts. Many common-law countries use a type of lay justice, such as trial by jury. This type of law is also called Anglo-American law.
- *Socialist law* is the official name for the legal system in a communist state. It is based on the civil-law system, with references to and additions from Marxist-Leninist ideologies. The law is based on the premise that "the government is always right" and has typically not developed a sophisticated framework of contracts (you do what the governments tell you to do) or intellectual property protection (royalties are unwarranted since the government ultimately owns everything). Former communist countries such as those of Eastern Europe and Russia are trying to advance their legal systems to accommodate issues in a free market. Furthermore, there are special courts and laws for state businesses.
- *Islamic law:* the sharia (In Arabic also shari'a) is traditional Islamic law

based on the Koran which puts forward mandates such as a prohibition of usury, or excessive interest rates. This has led some Islamic countries to ban interest entirely; in others, it may be tolerated within reason.

TABLE 8.1 The principal legal systems

	Common law	Civil law	Socialist law	Islamic law
Other names	Anglo-American, English, judge-made	Code law Continental, Romano-Germanic	Communist	Religious law
Source of law	Case law, legislation	Statutes, legislation	Statutes, legislation	Qur'an
Lawyers	Control courtroom	Judges dominate trials	Judges party members	Secondary role
Degree of judicial independence	High	High; separate from Government	Courts an extension of the state	Very limited
Policy-making role	Courts share in balancing power	Courts have equal but separate power	Courts are subordinate to the legislature	Courts and other government branches are subordinate to the Shari'a
Examples	Australia, England, Hong Kong, USA, India, Malaysia	The Netherlands, France, Spain, Germany, Japan, Mexico	China, Russia, Eastern Europe	Saudi Arabia, Turkey, the Middle East and North Africa,

Edited source: Judicial Process: Law, Courts, and Politics in the United States by David W. Neubauer, Stephen S. Meinhold/Page 24

8

● www.smh.com

Tales of Arabian nights for small businesses

A surprisingly large number of small and medium-sized businesses are exporting their products and services to the Middle East, thanks in large part to considerable support from government agencies.

But given the cultural disparities between the western and Arab worlds, the Middle East is not a market for the fainthearted, as Leigh Jasper, founder of Aconex, discovered when the business first started trading in the Middle East in 2004. Aconex develops internet-based project collaboration and document management software used in many of the large construction projects in the Middle East.
"When we started our operation there, we arrived a few weeks before Ramadan (the Muslim month of fasting), when the whole region slows down. It was tough to get meetings. At the time internet infrastructure was also primitive, although it's caught up now."
One of the greatest challenges of operating in the Middle East is getting paid on time. "We worked out it was best to negotiate partial upfront payment so we weren't out of pocket. Another hurdle was properly registering businesses in the Middle East. It took us nine months to register the Dubai business."
And, although there are specific cultural challenges around operating in Arab nations, Jasper says it's also a challenge working with genuinely multi-cultural teams. "We try to hire locally as much as possible, but many projects in the Middle East also have involvement from other nationalities. We've worked with Japanese people and Turkish contractors on some of our projects there."
Be aware of agency laws. "If you sign up a distributor in the Middle East the only way you can get out of the agreement is with the written approval of the distributor – even if they have made no sales. Some distributors will sign you up just to get a payout – it's a trap for young players."

2 December 2010

Companies often prefer to apply their own local legislation, but the foreign party can object. In order to solve the problem, international businesses often refer to international treaties or the parties can choose for the applicable law.

8.2 Pre-contract negotiations

Business contract is a legally binding agreement between two parties for an exchange of good or services that are of value. For a contract to be valid an offer must be made and accepted; this is also known as a *consensus ad idem*. In practice, this takes place when the quotation is accepted. Using a contract in business dealings helps ensure an agreement is acted on, insofar as a broken contract could result in a lawcase or out-of-court settlement and payment of damages caused by the breach. The best way to avoid a dispute or potential litigation, however, is to craft a solid agreement in which the parties are confident and have negotiated the best terms for the business.
Negotiations in international business can be protracted. In law, this is known as the pre-contract phase: the phase before the agreement has been concluded.
The negotiation process goes through several phases. They are called:

1 Initial negotiation phase
2 Consensus ad idem phase
3 Closing phase

The agreement is actually signed during the closing phase. This will not be discussed further.

8.2.1 Initial negotiation phase

The parties meet to discuss the possibility of doing business. In international business, it is very important to find out whether you are doing business with the right person.
Is the other party the director of a company or has he been granted power of attorney? Furthermore, when doing business it is important to address the following legal questions:

- Should the discussions be written down?
- Should a written contract be made?
- Does the other party representative have power of attorney?
- Is the company solvent?
- When is the agreement to be concluded and what should it contain?
- What are the payment due dates?
- Should there be an incremental payment for specific goods or services rendered once they are completed?
- How much interest on late payments?
- Is there a timeline, should the "time is of the essence" clause be used?
- What are the termination conditions?
- Should there be damages for breach of contract?
- Should there be a "liquidated damages" clause which specifies amounts to be paid if services are incomplete or deadlines are missed?
- Is the intellectual property right protected internationally?
- Who has product liability?
- Which law is applicable and how are disputes to be settled?

8.2.2 Consensus ad idem phase

Basic agreement/ pre-agreement

Until the parties reach a mutual agreement (offer and acceptance) on the essential items under discussion (product, price, product requirements, packaging, etc.), there is no agreement. Should the parties reach agreement on one or more principal points without mentioning a definite agreement, this is known as a basic agreement or pre-agreement. In principle, each of the parties can break off the negotiations.

Breaking off the negotiations

Point of departure when negotiations are broken off:

- Common law. Anglo-American law is much more reluctant to admit pre-contractual liability. The dominant perception is that in a negotiation each party has its own interests. In principle, negotiators keep full discretion including the authority to break off negotiations at any time an at will.
- Civil or code law. This Continental law assumes that relations between the parties are governed by good faith. Negotiations may have reached the stage that the parties could have expected that a contract would be signed. Yet, should the negotiations still be broken off, then according to civil law one could still act contrary to the legitimate trust of the other

party. In such a case a company can be held liable for the costs incurred and might even have to reimburse
- Islamic and socialist law. Like civil or code law, these use the good faith principle as a starting point.

Escape clause

Negotiations can unintentionally lead to an agreement. It is during this phase of the negotiations that mutual obligations come to the fore but only after both parties have signed the written contract.
The following systems are used:
- gentlemen's agreement. The terms of the agreement cannot (yet) be legally enforced.
- the clause 'subject to formal contract', 'subject to agreement'. The negotiations are being conducted free of obligation.
- the clause 'subject to board approval'. The agreement comes into force only after the Board of Directors of the company has signed the contract. Each of the parties can withdraw from the negotiations free of obligation.

Declaration of intent (Letter of intent/Memorandum of understanding)

A letter of intent, a memorandum of understanding, heads of agreement and a declaration of intent are documents used to write down the agreements made during the negotiating phase. The parties are given a sense of security before having to put more time and energy into negotiations. A letter of intent is a document which describes an intention to take some action. From the business point of view, it is defined as an agreement between two or more parties before the agreement is finalized. It is basically a compilation of key points of an agreement between two parties who intend to conduct a business transaction. While announcing a merger or a joint venture, a letter of intent is signed for the purpose of declaring that the various parties involved are negotiating a contract.

Business transaction

The key difference between a letter of intent and a Memorandum of Understanding is the nature of signatories. Memorandum of Understanding implies that all the parties involved have to be signatories, while a letter of intent only needs the party which proposes the agreement to be a signatory. Also for Memorandum of Understanding, more than two parties may be involved but for a letter of intent only two parties are involved. A letter of intent is addressed from one party to another. A party providing a business letter of intent is highly appreciated.

A letter of intent can give rise to many problems, especially if negotiations are broken off because the parties might think that it is not legally binding. But on the international scene a letter of intent is legally valid and binding on both parties.
It is possible to avoid the binding force of a letter of intent through the insertion of an escape clause: the parties declare explicitly in writing that they are not bound by the content of the letter of intent. You can download an example from the Juris International website (www.jurisint.org).

Escape clause

8.3 International contracts

A contract is an agreement between two or more people that is legally binding. It can be verbal or written. Oral contracts are ordinarily valid and therefore legally binding. However, in most jurisdictions, certain types of contracts must be reduced to writing to be enforceable. This is to prevent frauds and perjuries. For example, an unwritten contract would be unenforceable if for the sale of land.
The essential ingredients for contracts are offer and acceptance, the consideration an legal relationship:

- Offer: An offer must be made that is a proposal to enter into a contract.
- Acceptance: the offer must be accepted and must always be communicated to the person who has made the offer.
- Consideration: the consideration must have been given, for example, a price must be paid, or a promise made in return or something else that proves that both parties give some value to each other. Gifts are not legally enforceable, since the recipient of a gift gives nothing in return.
- Legal relationship: The parties must have intended to create a legal relationship.
  International agreements are based on customs other than your own and contain conditions that differ from your national law. Businessmen prefer to invoke their own national law. In order to solve this problem the International Chamber of Commerce (ICC) has drawn up a number of sample agreements. These are based as far as possible on international law. The most frequently used contracts are:
  - international sale contract
  - commercial agency contract
  - distributorship contract

You can obtain these from the ICC (http://iccwbo.org).
There are no international rules governing commercial agency or distributorship contracts. That is why the Rome 1 Decree states which law is applicable in an international conflict between parties (see below).

There are two important types of treaties governing international Sales Contracts:

Substantive law

1 The Vienna Sales Convention is a treaty offering a uniform international sales law. Its full title is the Convention on Contracts for the International Sale of Goods (CISG) (see subsection 8.3.1).

Applicable law

2 The Rome I Regulation (the law applicable to contractual obligations). The Rome I Regulation (Rome I) provides rules to determine, within the European Community (EC), which law applies to contracts that have connections with more than one country, such as cross-border business or consumer contracts. The intention is to provide clarity when the parties have not chosen the applicable law to govern the contract. This Regulation applies to contractual obligations in civil and commercial matters in situations involving a choice of the parties to a contract to choose the governing law. See section 8.4.

FOREIGN MARKETS, DECEMBER 2009/JANUARY 2010 (EDITED SOURCE)

The Netherlands music country: Big in Japan. The breakthrough of Within Temptation

The Dutch band Within Temptation monopolised the Buma Culture Export Prize from 2003 to 2006. This prize is awarded annually to the Dutch artist or band that has had the most success abroad. The band plays and sells music in 48 countries, including Russia, Germany, the UK, Japan and the US. Raymond Rijnaars, the director of AT Productions, was involved from the very beginning in the way Within Temptation conquered the world. Various things contributed to Within Temptation's international success. From 2001 the band was no longer contracted to a record company. This meant that the members of the band and the management could choose their own strategy. AT Productions concluded a partnership with a German management company.

"It takes time to build a network in a country. For an artist, the differences between Holland and Belgium are huge, let alone between Holland and Japan. A lot of thinking, creativity, blood, sweats and tears preceded the breakthrough in Germany. Thus in Portugal a number sung by Within Temptation became the title song of a kind of 'good times, bad times' saga, a Portuguese soap. In South America you always have to threaten to cancel the show a few hours before going on stage because the backstage crew do not fulfil their obligations, even though everything is specified in contracts. Only at the very last minute do they do what they are required to do. You have to arm yourself against such things. We always make sure we are on site."

8

8.3.1 The Vienna Sales Convention

The Vienna Convention on Contracts for the International Sale of Goods (CISG) came into existence in 1980 under the auspices of the United Nations. It is probably the most successful result of efforts to unify the law of international sales. The CISG has marked an important step in the development of international commercial law. The Convention has been ratified by more than 70 countries. Several European countries are not party to the Convention. These are Portugal, the United Kingdom, Ireland and Albania. Many Asian countries have also become a party to the Convention. They are China, Japan, Korea, Mongolia and Singapore.

The Vienna Sales Convention regulates when an international purchase of goods takes place, as well as the rights and duties of the parties, and the rules governing risk and delivery. It does not contain rules regarding the cost of transport, insurance, payment conditions or the transfer of ownership.

When does the Vienna Sales Convention apply?
The Vienna Sales Convention applies only in cases where the parties insert a clause into their international sales contract that the rules of the Vienna Sales Convention shall apply. If the parties do not insert such a clause then clause 1, paragraph 1 of the Vienna Sales Convention lays down whether the Convention is applicable or not. If the parties do not want to use the Vienna Sales Convention, they must state this explicitly.

When does the Vienna Sales Convention not apply?
This Convention does not apply to sales:

a of goods bought for personal, family or household use, unless the seller, at any time before or at the conclusion of the contract, neither knew nor ought to have known that the goods were bought for any such use
b by auction
c on execution or otherwise by authority of law
d of stocks, shares, investment securities, negotiable instruments or money
e of ships, vessels, hovercraft or aircraft
f of electricity.

8

What are the most important clauses of the Vienna Sales Convention?
The buyer and seller are obliged to comply with agreements made and to deliver the sales documents. Furthermore, the ownership of the goods must be transferred. Should the buyer or seller not fulfil his obligations, compliance or damages can be demanded or the agreement can be annulled.

- *Delivery and risk*. The seller has fulfilled the terms of delivery as soon as the goods sold have been given to the first carrier for dispatch to the buyer. This means that the goods should be transported by truck to a port in order to be transported further. The seller is not responsible for the loading of the goods on board the ship. This latter can be avoided by choosing INCO terms with other and conditions (see further in this chapter).
- *Ownership conditions*. The seller remains the owner of the goods sold until the goods have been paid for. Should the buyer go bankrupt or refuse to pay, the seller can reclaim his unpaid goods.

8.3.2 General conditions
Different terms are used for general conditions at international level, such as standard conditions, and buying and selling conditions. These general conditions are contractual clauses that specify the rights and obligations of both parties in the contract. It can be drawn up in various ways:

- by the company, for instance in the purchase and sales conditions

- by an independent international organisation, such as the International Chamber of Commerce (ICC)

In the General Conditions the following terms and condition are provided for:
1. terms of payment and delivery
2. complaints procedure and guarantee
3. sanctions, fines, interest and terminations conditions
4. quality description
5. allocations of tasks
6. procedures, documents required
7. permits, expertise
8. rules of arbitration
9. packaging requirements

Parties are legally bound by the terms and conditions stipulated in the general conditions:
1. Through explicit acceptance. Even though they are not mentioned in the contract, the parties still have to sign them. For instance, common law only acknowledges general conditions if they form part of the contract.
2. It is customary within the industry to which the parties belong.
3. Through tacit acceptance with reference to the general conditions. The tender, quotation and the general conditions must be written in the (usual) language of the other party.

8.3.3 International commercial terms (INCO terms 2010)

INCO terms rules are international terms of delivery rules. Governments, legal authorities and practitioners worldwide accept them for the interpretation of the most commonly used terms in international trade. They either reduce or remove altogether uncertainties arising from differing interpretations of such terms in different countries. Inco terms' rules describe mainly the tasks, costs and risks involved in the delivery of goods – excluding intangibles – from sellers to buyers.

Task allocation

Cost/risk sharing

Four groups of INCO terms

- Group E (EXW): the seller makes the goods available to the buyer at the seller's own premises. It is the only one of that category.
- Group F-terms (FCA, FAS and FOB): the seller is called upon to deliver the goods to a carrier appointed by the buyer.
- Group C-terms (CFR, CIF, CPT and CIP), the seller has to contract for carriage, but without assuming the risk of loss or damage to the goods or additional costs due to events occurring after shipment or dispatch.
- Group D-terms (DAT, DAP, and DDP), the seller has to bear all costs and risks needed to bring the goods to the place of destination.

TABLE 8.2 INCO terms 2010

	EXW	FAS	FCA	FOB	CFR	CIF	CPT	CIP	DAT	DAP	DDP
Load to truck	Buyer	Seller	Seller	Seller	Seller	Seller	Seller	Seller	Seller	Seller	Seller
Export-duty payment	Buyer	Seller	Seller	Seller	Seller	Seller	Seller	Seller	Seller	Seller	Seller
Transport to exporter's port	Buyer	Seller	Seller	Seller	Seller	Seller	Seller	Seller	Seller	Seller	Seller
Unload from truck at the origin's port	Buyer	Buyer	Seller	Seller	Seller	Seller	Seller	Seller	Seller	Seller	Seller
Landing charges at origin's port	Buyer	Buyer	Buyer	Seller	Seller	Seller	Seller	Seller	Seller	Seller	Seller
Transport to importer's port	Buyer	Buyer	Buyer	Buyer	Seller	Seller	Seller	Seller	Seller	Seller	Seller
Landing charges at importer's port	Buyer	Buyer	Buyer	Buyer	Seller	Seller	Seller	Seller	Seller	Seller	Seller
Unload onto trucks from the importer's port	Buyer	Buyer	Buyer	Buyer	Buyer	Buyer	Buyer	Buyer	Seller	Seller	Seller
Transport to destination	Buyer	Buyer	Buyer	Buyer	Buyer	Buyer	Buyer	Buyer	Buyer	Seller	Seller
Insurance	Buyer	Buyer	Buyer	Buyer	Buyer	Seller	Buyer	Seller	Buyer	Buyer	Buyer
Entry – Customs clearance, Duties and Taxes	Buyer	Buyer	Buyer	Buyer	Buyer	Buyer	Buyer	Buyer	Buyer	Buyer	Seller

Seller (green)
Buyer (blue)

Source: http://theodmgroup.com

This INCO terms table (table 8.2) reflects buyer & seller responsibility for each type of shipment under the revised 11 different INCO terms governing shipment. Green indicates the seller has the responsibility to provide the service. Blue indicates it is the buyer's responsibility.

8.4 Applicable law under Rome I

The Rome I Regulation (the law applicable to contractual obligations) applies to contractual obligations in civil and commercial matters in the event of a conflict of law. It may be applied to only a part or the whole of the contract. Provided that all the parties agree, the applicable law may be changed at any time. If the law chosen is that of a country other than that relating most closely to the contract, the provisions of the latter law need to be respected. If the contract relates to one or more member States, the applicable law chosen, other than that of a member State, must not contradict the provisions of community law. For some types of contract, the Regulation lays down options for the selection of applicable law and determines the law to be applied in the absence of choice.

Should the parties sign a contract when conducting international business and one of the parties does not meet some or all of its obligations, the injured party will take legal action. But first it must be decided what law or which rules apply to the contract. Does the local law apply or the law of the foreign country?

The Rome I regulation standardises rules that govern the law applying to cross-border contracts in the EU and defines the extent to which the parties are free to choose the applicable law. It provides rules for parties that have not specified a legal system in their contract:

1 Contracts of sales of goods: the law of the country where the seller normally resides.
2 Services contracts: the law of the country where the service provider normally resides.
3 Contracts related to immovable's: contracts "relating in immovable property or to a tenancy of immovable property" are governed by the law of the country where the immobile is located.
4 Contracts of carrier: the law of the country where the carrier normally residences.
5 Contracts on intellectual and industrial property: the law of the country where the person transferring or lending those rights normally resides.
6 Franchise contracts: the law of the country where the franchisee normally resides.
7 Distributorship contracts: the law of the country where the distributor normally resides.
8 Auction sales; the law of the place where the auction takes place governs these sales.

8.5 Product liability

Strict common safety standards applied to the products and services circulating within the internal market of the European Union. They are vital to safeguarding consumer health. The European Union has laid down general safety rules applicable to services, foodstuffs and non-food products, to be observed by producers and suppliers of these products and services. Products imported into the EU must meet these European requirements. A number of these requirements will be discussed in subsections 8.5.1 and 8.5.2.

Product liability applies to moveable industrial goods and is based on the principle of objective liability or liability without fault of the producer in cases of damage caused by a defective product. If more than one person is liable for the same damage, it is joint liability.

Producer is taken to mean:

- any participant in the production process
- the importer of the defective product
- any person putting their name, trade mark or other distinguishing feature on the product
- any person supplying a product whose producer cannot be identified.

The injured person must prove:

- the actual damage
- the defect in the product
- the causal relationship between damage and defect.

It is not necessary to prove the negligence or fault of the producer or importer.

Lack of safety, which the general public is entitled to expect, determines the defectiveness of a product. Factors to be taken into account include:

- the presentation of the product
- the use to which it could reasonably be put
- the time when the product was put into circulation.

The fact that a better product is subsequently put into circulation cannot be taken into consideration in determining the defectiveness of the product in question.

Indemnity agreement

The distributor of the product can close an indemnity agreement. An indemnity agreement is a contract where one party agrees to protect another party against certain future claims or losses; the liability is then transferred to the distributor.
The liability of the producer does not decrease even if the damage is due to a product defect or because of a fault caused by a third party. Should the blame lie with the injured party, however, the producer's liability can be reduced.

Product liability covers if the damage:

- causes death or personal injury
- damage to an item of property intended for private use or consumption other than the defective product, with a lower threshold of 500 Euros.

The producer's liability lapses after a period of 10 years, starting on the day he brings the product onto the market.

EU member states can be warned that dangerous goods have been discovered in their area through the website of the Rapid Alert System for Non-Food Products (RAPEX). Sale of the product can then be forbidden in these countries or tied to certain conditions.

● www.z24.nl

China is still the 'leading' supplier of dangerous goods. But some European goods are not always of good quality. Of the rejected consumer goods 60 per cent came from China.

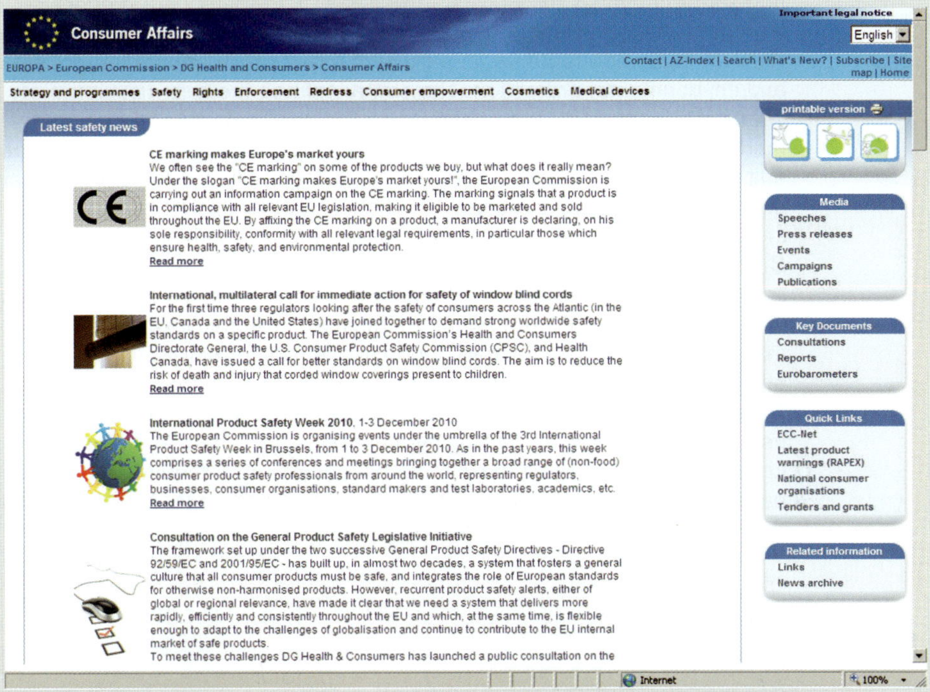

Brussels keeps a list of registered products on the RAPEX site. On the list are Chinese finger dolls, Spanish tyre-repair kits and accessories for children's car seats from the Netherlands.

16 April 2010

8.5.1 CE marking

Quality hallmark

Many technical goods must carry a CE marking (Conformité Européenne) mark. It is not a quality hallmark. The marking signals that a product is in compliance with relevant EU legislation, making it eligible to be marketed and sold throughout the EU. By affixing the CE marking on a product, a manufacturer is declaring, on his sole responsibility, conformity with all relevant legal requirements, in particular those which ensure health, safety, and environmental protection. The primary aim is the free movement of goods within the EEA. The user's manual is very important to gain a CE mark. Even if a product complies with all the CE mark requirements, it can still be considered defective when an actual claim is submitted. This mark does not cover product liability.

8.5.2 Packaging requirements

Packaging, as well as the use of paper and cardboard, is regulated by EU directive 2004/12/EG. EU countries must ensure that waste packaging material is recycled, reclaimed or burnt in an incinerator that reclaims energy.
There can be national rules on packing materials. In some countries the use of hay and straw as packaging material is forbidden. The use of some kinds of wooden packing (boxes, crates, pallets, etc.) requires a decontamination certificate. If the carrier is responsible for damage, he will demand that packaging is of good quality.

● www.zibb.nl

Product liability – 10 steps to limiting your risk

1 Have a well- staffed service counter
An exorbitant claim is often the result of frustration due to rude staff. Be pleasant even to nit-pickers.
2 Take out an appropriate insurance based on your risk profile
Do you have technically complicated products? Do you supply consumers directly or through middlemen? Do you import goods from outside the EU? Check whether your insurance policy is adequate and has not expired. Claims often loom up out of the blue years after a sale.
3 No 100 per cent!
Never guarantee 100 per cent safety in your contracts or sales brochures.
4 Meet the eventual responsibility to obtain a CE mark
The CE marking regulations comprise 23 product groups which include 'Machinery' and 'Safety of Toys'.
5 Check who should apply the CE mark
If the product consists of several semi-finished products, specify in the contracts who is responsible for which CE mark. Whoever delivers the product to the end user is liable, but based on such an agreement he can in turn make his suppliers liable.
6 Always keep a record of the technical file of the product
Then, at a later stage, you can show the state in which the product was put on the market. If it has a CE mark, it should possess a technical

file, a certificate or a declaration of conformity and a book of instructions (dated). Keep your file up to date, especially if you make changes to the product.

7 Write a good user's instruction manual
Europe demands the clear use of language (without jargon), prohibits the use of different names for the same things, and requires an explanation of abbreviations and captions under illustrations. Each product type you sell must have its own instruction manual.

8 Be honest when mentioning risks in the instruction manual
If possible, place a warning at the top of a page or a prominent place, especially if there is a danger during normal use.

9 Do not give too much information in the instruction manual
Electricians or service staff may be interested in detailed electrical diagrams, but such diagrams invite misuse when included with consumer products.

10 State clearly: you may not use the product ....
A universally known example: 'Do not use the product near a flame or red-hot object.'

8.6 Intellectual Property Rights

Intellectual property (IP) refers to creations of the mind. It includes inventions, literary and artistic works, symbols, names, images, designs used in commerce and the secret formula, such as that for making Coca-Cola. Intellectual property rights are the rights given to persons over the creations of their minds. They usually give the creator an exclusive right over the use of his/her creation for a certain period of time. Similar to another type of property, intellectual property can be traded, sold, licensed in return for fees and/or royalty payments. Intellectual property laws are designed to compensate people whose property rights have been violated. Most national legal systems protect the property rights because that is the legal rights to resources and any income the owner generate. Intellectual property laws differ greatly from nation tot nation.

Exclusive right

Despite legal protection, brands are sometimes copied exactly. This is also known as imitation, counterfeiting and piracy.

Counterfeiting

IP is divided into two categories:

1 Industrial property, which includes inventions (patents), trademarks, industrial designs, and geographic indications of source.
2 Copyright, which includes literary and artistic works such as novels, poems and plays, films, musical works, artistic works such as drawings, paintings, photographs and sculptures, and architectural designs. Rights related to copyright include those of performing artists in their performances, producers of phonograms in their recordings, and those of broadcasters in their radio and television programs.

THE GUARDIAN, 23 MARCH 2010

Google wins Louis Vuitton trademark case

European court of justice ends long-running legal battle by ruling that internet giant can use brand names in search advertising. The European court of justice ruled in favour of Google in a long-running court battle with Louis Vuitton over the use of the luxury goods company's trademarked brand names in search advertising.

However, the ECJ added the caveat that companies that use trademarked brand keywords to push sales must be more transparent about who the seller is.

Louis Vuitton, which is part of the LVMH group of brands including Moet & Chandon and Dior, had argued that Google was acting illegally by allowing other companies to bid for and use its brand names as keywords to trigger ads on its website.

Lawyers had viewed the legal battle, which has been going on for years, as potentially critical to Google as the search engine giant's business model has been built on the back of its Ad Words system.

"Google has not infringed trademark law by allowing advertisers to purchase keywords corresponding to their competitors' trademarks," said the ECJ.

Fake Louis Vuitton bags are sought-after counterfeit articles. The Brazilian designer Bea Correa made these 'real' counterfeit bags with the imprint FAKE.

8.6.1 Industrial property

Industrial property includes patents and trademarks, which are often a company's most valuable assets. Industrial property is protected internationionally under the Paris Convention for the Protection of Industrial Property (www.WIPO.int) to which nearly 184 countries are signatories.

Industrial property can be divided into the following areas:

1 Trademarks: in legal terms, trademarks are signs that serve to distinguish the goods (products) or services of one company from the goods or services of another company. The following signs are regarded as trademarks:
   - a trade names: names under which goods or services are put onto the market (e.g. Chanel, Gucci and Red Bull)
   - b picture trade mark: (Shell), labels, special types of letter or something specially laid out
   - c combinations of trade names

d shaped names: the shape of a product or of a package (perfume bottle)
e colour trade names: in unusual cases a colour or a combination of colours can be a trademark. This is the case if the public recognises a certain product or service by its colour (e.g. the Air France-KLM logo)
f sound trademarks. An advertising jingle is sometimes so well known that it can be a trademark or service mark. So musical notation may be used to graphically represent their trademark.

Trademark law is very strong. The rightful owner has an exclusive right to his trademark (monopoly). The protection of distinctive signs and geographical indication aims to stimulate and ensure fair competition and to protect consumers, by enabling them to make informed choices between various goods and services. A trademark is designated by the following symbols:
- ™ for an unregistered trade mark, that is, a mark used to promote or brand goods
- ℠ for an unregistered service mark, that is, a mark used to promote or brand services
- ® for a registered trademark

2 Innovation and the creation of technology. Inventions fall within this category (protected by patents). A patent is a right granted to the inventor of a product or process that excludes others from making, using, or selling the invention.
3 Designs: a registered design is a legal right which protects the overall visual appearance of a product in the geographical area it is registered. Drawings or designs are two types of products. We refer to drawing if the product to be protected is two-dimensional (for example the pattern or design on wallpaper, textile, tiles or crockery), and we refer to a *design* if the product is three-dimensional (for example the design of (mobile) telephones, household devices, furniture, packaging materials, building materials, sanitary fittings, toys or cutlery).

Two-dimensional design
Three-dimensional design

Import and export infringements
When importing and/or exporting goods it is important to find out whether any infringements of existing patents have taken place. Research can be done with spacenet (often written as esp@cenet, www.ep.espacenet.com). It is a free online service for searching patents and patent applications. Espacenet was developed by the European Patent Office (EPO) together with the member states of the European Patent Organisation. Every member state has an Espacenet service in its national language, and access to the EPO's worldwide database, most of which is in English. In order to find out the status of a patent the European Patent Office can be consulted (www.epo.org).

The social purpose of intellectual property right is to provide protection for the results of investment in the development of new technology, thus giving the incentive and means to finance research and development activities. A functioning intellectual property regime should also facilitate the transfer of technology in the form of foreign direct investment, joint ventures and licensing.

WALLSTREETJOURNAL, 7 JANUARY 2011

French MP blames China in Renault espionage case

RENAULT

FRANCE has ordered its intelligence services to investigate claims that Renault has fallen victim to industrial espionage on behalf of China.
The inquiry comes after the suspension without pay of three Renault executives suspected of leaking details of confidential programmes involving the development of electric vehicles. The three are alleged to have divulged programs not yet patented by Renault to intermediaries likely to have supplied the information to Chinese companies, according to a French government source. Renault fears that the technology will be copied by rivals, which will then file for a patent themselves. The French group has filed for 56 patents on electric cars and is preparing to ask for a further 149.

8.6.2 Copyright

Copyright give creators of original works the exclusive right to publish or dispose of them as they choose. Copyrights can protect:

- literary works, including novels, instruction manuals, computer programs, song lyrics, newspaper articles and some types of database
- dramatic works, including dance or mime
- musical works
- artistic works, including paintings, engravings, photographs, sculptures, collages, architecture, technical drawings, diagrams, maps and logos
- layouts or typographical arrangements used to publish a work, for a book for instance
- recordings of a work, including sound and film broadcasts of a work.

Economic rights

Economic rights give the copyright owner the opportunity to make commercial gain from the exploitation of his/her work. Copyright owners generally have the right to authorise or prohibit any of the following things in relation to their works:

- copying the work in any way. For example, photocopying, reproducing a printed page by handwriting, typing or scanning into a computer
- issuing copyrighted work to the public
- renting or lending copyrighted work to the public
- making an adaptation of the copyrighted work, such as by translating a literary or dramatic work, transcribing a musical work and converting a computer program into a different computer language or code.

Copyright is infringed when any of the above acts are done without permission of the creator, whether directly or indirectly and whether the whole or a substantial part of a work is used.

The copyright work will be protected abroad automatically in the same way that it is protected in the national law of the country. Most countries, including all western European, the USA and Russia, now belong to the Berne Convention, which is international copyright treaty. Under this agreement, the creator does not have to mark its work in any way for automatic protection to apply. However, it is sensible to mark the work with the international © symbol, followed by the name of the copyright owner and year in which the work was created.

● www.informatieprofessionals.nl

Google continues scanning French books despite a previous judgment

French publishers want to summon Google for a second time in court because of their digitalising of books for Google Books without permission of the possessor of the copyright. Four big French publishers, Gallimard, Albin Michel, Flammarion and Eyrolles, are fed up that Google, despite a court injunction, continues to scan its books and put them online. In December, a French court decided that Google had infringed the copyright of the three publishers because it digitalised books and put excerpts online without obtaining their permission. The injunction states that Google must immediately cease its digitalising of French books and pay the publishers damages of €300,000 euros. The American search engine has appealed against the injunction and, according to the publishers, it has continued scanning books.

6 April 2010

8.6.3 Company (trade) name

A company (trade) name could be a legal name used for contracts and other formal situations, such as tax related issues. Registering a company name with the Register of Companies or the Chamber of Commerce does not establish a trade name: it has to do with the use of the name for commercial purposes. There is an important distinction between the official title of the company and the name under which it may trade. It is possible for a company to be registered under the official title of the company and then start trading under a different business name. To obtain a trade name it is not necessary for a company to be established in the country or have its market in this country. This is all arranged according to the rules and regulations of the country concerned.

Often, a company name is also the name of the brand or one of the brands of the company – for example, Coca-cola and Philips. These companies carry generally a stronger position than those that only have a trade name. Even if the trade name is older than the brand name. It is important that the company name, if it is also used as a brand name, is registered worldwide (WIPO).

Assign or licence
Intellectual property rights are exclusive rights. This means that a design may not be used without the express permission of the owner of the right. Of course, the owner can allow another person to use the design (for instance, the use of a brand) for payment. This can be done by assignment or licensing of the Intellectual Property Rights (IPR). See chapter 6.
An assignment of IPR means the absolute transfer of those rights to a third party in return for payment. On the assignment of your rights to an assignee, the assignee becomes the proprietor of those rights and the ownership of the IPR would have been transferred to the assignee as the beneficial owner.
A license grants an exclusive or non-exclusive right to use the IPR in a particular territory in return for royalties. However, the owner retains all the IPR rights.

A summary of intellectual property rights is presented in table 8.3.

TABLE 8.3 Summary of intellectual property rights

	How to protect?	Protects what?	Which organisation?
Copyright		Literature, art and science (drawings, photographs, software, written texts, etc.)	Copyright comes automatically, with the © symbol
Industrial property rights	Patent	Innovative technical products or processes	• European Patent Office • World Intellectual Property Organisation (WIPO)
	Trademark	Trade/Brand names and logos	• Benelux Office for Intellectual Property (BOIP) • Office for Harmonization in the Internal Market (OHIM) • WIPO
	Designs	Drawing or design	• BOIP • OHIM • WIPO
	Company (trade) name	Name of a company	Mandatory government requirements or see 'trademark'

8

8.6.4 Maintaining intellectual property rights

Piracy

Counterfeiting and piracy have increased because of international trade – primarily in countries where copying is not against the law, because countries with emerging markets are well acquainted with this lack of legislation in this field. That is why, according to the EU-guidelines, the protection of intellectual property is necessary for the following reasons:

1 To stimulate innovation through the competitiveness of companies. If counterfeiting and piracy are not punished sufficiently, industry might lose its trust in the internal European market. Manufacturers and inventors may become discouraged and innovation and production in the EU will be slowed down.
2 To help employment in Europe.

3 to prevent financial losses and the destabilisation of markets. Financial losses from counterfeiting and piracy are considerable. They are a threat to economic stability, because they can lead to the destabilisation of the most vulnerable markets, especially the fashion and multimedia markets.
4 To protect the consumer. The consumer expects a certain quality product. Counterfeit and pirated products do not generally meet their quality standards. These products can be a danger to the health (counterfeit medication) or safety of the consumer (counterfeit toys or car- and aircraft parts).
5 Counterfeiting and piracy mean a breach of various labour laws, public health and product safety among other things.

● www.thedrum.co.uk

London branded world counterfeit capital

Research conducted by accountancy firm KPMG has identified London as one of the world's top rip off capitals. London's streets are awash with fake watches, knock-off DVDs, pirated software and counterfeit sunglasses according to the firm, with dodgy replicas retailing for around 31% of the value of their genuine equivalent.
This is a far higher ratio than in comparable cities such as New York where fakes sell for 22% of the real deals value. Indeed London is second only to Prague in the cost of fake goods, although the city ranks first when cigarettes and alcohol are excluded from the list.
Ordinarily the cost of a fake is so small that its provenance is obvious to the purchaser, in the case of London however shoppers face a sharper dilemma. David Eastwood, KPMG's head of intellectual property, said: "For products like jeans, trainers and DVDs it might not be clear to a shopper whether they are getting the real deal or a fake. Prices are usually well discounted, but not enough to make it obvious."KPMG's research also suggests that, ironically, counterfeiters are feeling the pinch from illegal downloader's just as much as legitimate record labels. Pirated music CDs have become 18% more expensive since 2007.

8.6.5 Registering the Intellectual Property right abroad?

Patents and trademarks are territorial and must be filed in each country where protection is sought. For more information on how to apply for individual patents or trademarks in a foreign country, contact the intellectual property office in that country directly. A list of contact information for most intellectual property offices worldwide can be found at www.wipo.int/news/en/links/addresses/ip/index.htm.
However, the Patent Cooperation Treaty (PCT) streamlines the process of filing patents in multiple countries. The Madrid Protocol also makes it

easier to file for trademark registration in multiple countries. By filing one patent or trademark registration application in the country, applicants can concurrently seek protection in the assigned countries. On international level *The Treaty of Paris for the Protection of Industrial Properties* 1883 (Paris Convention) allows an inventor to apply for a patent in one of the member countries using just one application. The protection is usually given for a finite term (typically 20 years in the case of patents). The World Trade Organization grants patents for a period of 20 year. This term begins when a patent application is filed with a country's patent office not when it is granted.
For copyrights, as a result of international copyright treaties and conventions, many countries do not require registration of a copyright in order to enjoy copyright protection.
Once the intellectual property rights (IPR) in a foreign country is confirmed, seek to enforce the IP rights via the civil, administrative and criminal enforcement remedies available in that country. IPR are private rights; therefore, the protection of the rights should be in accordance with the IPR laws of that country. Intellectual property laws can be complex, therefore, it is recommended that you seek local legal counsel to explore potential remedies.

● www.out-law.com

EU and US launch advice site to help small companies protect IP

8

The European Union and the US have published a web site that they hope will encourage companies to use their intellectual property rights (IPR) more fully.
The site, called the TransAtlantic IPR Portal, is also intended to help small and medium sized companies (SMEs) to protect their intellectual property assets when engaging in business abroad.
"Improved IPR protection and enforcement will result in greater employment prospects and economic growth," said the EU Commissioner for Industry and Entrepreneurship. "Counterfeiting and piracy cause great damage to businesses, not least to small and medium size enterprises. Both the EU and US are committed to helping companies compete fairly on both sides of the Atlantic." "It will enable SMEs to protect their intangible assets – brands, trademarks and patents – before entering foreign markets and to take preventive action," said a Commission statement. "It will offer advice, 'country toolkits' on IPR protection in more than 20 markets around the world and tailor-made guides for various sectors including textiles, leather, footwear, and furniture."

21 December 2010

Customs authorities

International agreements have to be made to combat the breach of intellectual property rights. These agreements also include national customs authorities to check possible breaches of intellectual property rights. Worldwide three organisations play a role:

1 World Trade Organization (WTO)
2 World Customs Organization (WCO)
3 World Intellectual Property Organization (WIPO)

The World Trade Organization (WTO) (http://www.wto.org)
The WTO aims to enable free international trade. The rules on intellectual property rights are laid down in the Agreement on Trade-Related Aspects of Intellectual Property Rights (TRIPS). All the countries affiliated to the WTO must abide by this agreement. The TRIPS aims to reduce the disruption and hindering of international trade and promotes sufficient protection of the international trade by:
- combating international trade in counterfeit goods
- creating adequate standards of protection in all member countries. Basic rules should be stipulated so that customs can confiscate the goods if they suspect they are counterfeit.

The World Customs Organization (WCO)
The WCO promotes worldwide harmonisation of (customs) procedures through the use of harmonised control systems. In the fight against counterfeiting non-EU products, the customs authorities at the outer EU frontiers can be approached to provide help. Within the EU, the owner of a Community right (brand or model) can request the customs of any EU country to act against counterfeit products found during customs checks. The Anti-Piracy Regulation states how the customs authorities should act when they discover goods that may breach intellectual property rights.

The World Intellectual Property Organization (WIPO)
The WIPO is a UN organisation. It aims to regulate and standardise intellectual property rights in line with international treaties. It is dedicated to developing a balanced and accessible international intellectual property (IP) system, which rewards creativity, stimulates innovation and contributes to economic development while safeguarding the public interest. Currently there are 184 member states.

8.6.7 Parallel importation and exhaustion

Parallel importation refers to the import of goods outside the distribution channels contractually negotiated by the manufacturer. If a manufacturer exports goods, these are often put on the market in the importing countries at a much lower price than in the manufactured country. It then becomes attractive for traders to buy the goods in the cheap countries and import them into more expensive countries, still at a lower price than must be paid for officially imported goods in the country concerned.
Legally, Intellectual property rights products may not be imported just like that into the EEA. A company should ascertain whether a formal agreement of the IP owner(s) to sell those goods abroad, that is, in another market(s) (i.e. whether the IP rights are considered to be“exhausted”) is needed. If the EEA product has been brought onto the market with the permission of the brand or design right owner, the owner cannot protect his rights. The brand or model rights are said to be ‘exhausted’. The phenomenon is therefore known as ‘exhaustion’.
Once a brand or model has been brought onto the market by the producer both within and outside the EEA, he has the right to resist the parallel import into the EEA of goods bought outside the EEA and imported into the EEA without his permission.

What type of goods can be prevented from being parallel imported?
The restriction does not apply to all goods, but only to those goods that are protected by a patent, trademark, industrial design and/or copyright.

8.7 Arbitration, settlements and jurisdiction

It is always possible for parties in international business to have conflicts with each other. Should parties not be able to solve the conflict among themselves, they can go to court or choose an alternative method of settlement. This involves employing the services of a neutral and competent third party.
The abbreviation ADR (alternative dispute resolution) is often used for a variety of methods of settling disputes.

Mediation 'Conciliation'

Mediation

The parties choose their own method of settling the conflict and play an active role in finding a solution. An independent person (the conciliator) tries to help the parties in dispute to resolve their problem. The conciliator should be impartial and should not take sides. The parties in dispute are responsible for deciding how to resolve the dispute, not the conciliator. This approach improves the chance that parties will be able to maintain the business relationship once the conflict has been settled.
It is wise that the parties make an attempt to settle the conflict among themselves, for instance through a reduction in price or the payment of compensation.

Source: www.clevelandmediator.com

Mini-trial and mediation
Mini-trial means that parties try to solve their problems with the help of an arbitrator. With this type of mediation there is neither a winner nor a loser. The parties choose their own arbitrator(s) and try to reach a compromise. The procedure is more formal and the arbitrator will always be an expert in the field and will know the case. Based on his knowledge and experience he will make a suggestion to solve the problem.
Mediation is a type of dispute solving carried out by the parties them-

selves. The parties are guided by an independent third party and trying to find a solution. Mediation does not impose a decision on the parties but allows parties themselves to come to a decision. Mediation is usually carried out when the personal relationship between parties is disrupted. The mediator is not an expert in the field but tries to restore the relationship so that parties can find a solution.

Arbitration

There are various cultures in which it is common to use arbitration to solve a dispute. The advantages of arbitration are:

- no (negative) publicity about the problem within the company
- informal, faster and cheaper than a court case
- the arbitrators are appointed on the basis of their knowledge

There are several ways of solving a conflict through arbitration. The Court of Arbitration of the International Chamber of Commerce is also an (expert) arbitrator. The International Court of Arbitration is the largest institution in the world involved in solving international commercial and business disputes. Parties often have different national, cultural and legal backgrounds and want to avoid a court case (bad publicity). ICC data show that the total number of cases the Court has heard since its inception is more than 16,000. There were 1,700 parties involved from 120 countries.

Arbitration settlement without the help of a third party: waiver or renegotiation

A waiver or renegotiation is used when delivery or payment is late. A waiver applies when one party pardons the incorrect/untimely supply or payment of the other party. Renegotiation takes place, during the term of the contract, when one of the parties does not meet its obligations.
Small and middle-size companies entering foreign markets often use waiver and renegotiation. These companies have limited capacity to meet high quality standards, produce large quantities of goods or meet strict delivery deadlines. This forces them to renegotiate the contract or ask for a waiver. Whichever method is used to resolve the dispute, the parties wish to maintain their good business relationship.

Jurisdiction

Jurisdiction is to be exercised by the EU country in which the defendant is domiciled, regardless of his/her nationality. Domicile is determined in accordance with the domestic law of the EU country where the matter is brought in court. If a party is not domiciled in the EU country of the court considering the matter, the court is to apply the law of another EU country to determine whether the party is domiciled in said state. In the case of a firm, the country where they have their statutory seat, central administration or principal place of business determines domicile. In the case of trusts, domicile is defined by the court that is considering the case by applying its own rules of private international law .The rules governing a cross-border legal dispute, in the fields of tort and contract and commercial law, international procedural law are laid down in the Lugano Convention, the convention on jurisdiction and the enforcement of judgments in civil and commercial matters.

International procedural law

Summary

- Legal aspects and international transactions
  International law:
  - civil or code law
  - common law
  - socialist law
  - Islamic law

- International negotiations
  Negotiating process:
  - initial negotiation phase
  - consensus ad idem phase
  - breaking off negotiations
  - escape clausule
  - declaration of intent
  - closing phase

- International agreements:
  - Vienna Sales Convention
  - General conditions
  - Terms of delivery: INCO terms 2010

- Product requirements and liability:
  - CE marking
  - packaging requirements

- Intellectual property rights:
  - IP is divided into two categories:
  - Industrial property: inventions (patents), trademarks, industrial designs, and geographic indications of source
  - Copyright: literary and artistic works
- Maintaining intellectual property rights
  - parallel importation and exhaustion

- Arbitration settlements
  It is always possible that parties in international business clash with each other. They can settle their disputes by:
  - mediation
  - mini-trial and mediation
  - arbitration
  - waiver or renegotiation
  - jurisdiction

Questions and assignments

● www.namaak.be

What you need to know!

When the word counterfeiting is mentioned, you may think only of glasses, bags or illegally copied CDs, DVDs and software. The reality is quite different, because no sector of the economy is spared by counterfeiters. Each year, thousands of people die as a result of counterfeiting. Antibiotics, milk powder for babies, pills, vaccines, cardiovascular medication … not one medicine escapes the counterfeiter!
Food, toys, drinks … all these product can damage your health if they are counterfeited. A counterfeit antibiotic, for instance, will not contain any active ingredient and will not cure you. A counterfeit vaccine will not render you immune. In fact even a commonplace counterfeit product like a pair of sunglasses bought from a black-market street vendor can be dangerous … Considering the price you bought them for, you can hardly expect them to protect your eyes from UV radiation! And when you wear a T-shirt that is a big-brand imitation, you had better not know with what kinds of dangerous products it was dyed. There is one thing you need to know, however: the money you spend on buying counterfeit fashion accessories will be invested by organised criminals in counterfeiting medicines, foods, drink and toys.

8.1 What can a company do to stop other companies bringing counterfeit copies of its products onto the market?

8.2 How can a company protect itself against illegal copies? Describe one method.

8.3 What are the criteria customs authorities use to ascertain how much import duty must be paid?

● www.fashionunited.nl

China rejects top brands

China has rejected clothing made by Burberry, Armani, Polo, Ralph Lauren, Max Mara and Dupont. According to Chinese officials, the garments contained chemical substances that could cause respiratory problems or eyes irritation. Of the 59 pieces tested, 25 contained too high a dose of formaldehyde, a poisonous gas, and unacceptable levels of acid. All but one of the articles had been imported. The luxury goods market in China is growing rapidly. Now it is the third largest market, after Japan and the United States. In 2010 there are 250 million Chinese who can afford luxury goods.

11 April 2010

8.4 How could the Chinese distributors reduce the quality risk of the imported branded products (Burberry, Armani, etc.)?

50
5 EURO
EYPΩ
100
500
20
200
10 EURO
EYPΩ
10

9

Risk-management, insurance and finance

The word risk means 'chance of misfortune'. Besides the 'chance' of making a profit, there is also the chance of making a loss. Business involves taking risks. Precarious conditions are on the increase and the risks attached to international business are bigger than those attached to business at home. Before taking measures that can remove or reduce the risks, it is important to research what these risks are. That is why more and more companies decide to pursue a policy known as risk management. In this chapter we discuss risk management, and subsequently the topics of insurance and finance. Insurance and finance are part of risk management.
In the last section we will discuss international financing.

Piracy is big business

Piracy still takes place all over the world. But nowhere have pirates established a more successful 'business model' than in Somalia. The chief pirate aboard a ship has the right to an expensive car, a house, a wife or a cash bonus. According to piracy expert and brokerage director Marine at Aon Risk Services, an international insurance broker, piracy takes place all over the world. "Vessels sometimes 'disappear' in the waters around China. They are then given another name or dismantled and the spare parts sold." Currently, hijackers ask for between $2.5 and $5 million per ship, but pirates adjust these amounts if they get their hands on something special.

A good example: a hijacked Ukrainian ship had among other things 33 Russian T-72 tanks, weapons and ammunition on board. At first, the pirates demanded $35 million, but they quickly lowered their demand to $3.5 million. After five months the ship's owner paid a $3.2 million ransom. A similar kind of 'auction' took place with the Saudi Arabian oil tanker MV Sirius Star, which was hijacked off Kenya. The 330-metre-long giant was carrying crude oil (valued at $100 million). It turned out that it had taken the pirates just 16 minutes to get aboard the long, slow-moving ship. The ship was finally released for also $3.2 million. "If such a ship sails at less than 10 knots, it is impossible to insure. The premium varies according to many factors: what type of ship it is, how fast it is, what the cargo is? Do you require a kidnap and ransom policy for the crew?"

The American magazine *Forbes* reported that ship owners must pay $20,000 extra insurance costs per trip. "In the case of large tankers, extra costs can reach $100,000 per trip against a 1 per cent chance that the ship will be attacked. Despite these higher costs, there is no reduction in transport along the Somali coast. Avoiding Somalia would only happen if the bulk price for crude oil was very low, because the journey would take twice as long. You have to travel past Somalia; no one is going via the Cape, right around Africa." According to the Scottish professor Peter Lehr it is a simple case of barter. "Somali pirates earn about $100 million a year in ransom money. Europeans and Asians poach fish in Somali waters to the tune of $300 million a year."

Source www.depers.nl, 9 April 2010

9

9.1 Risks

When doing international business, it is important to assess and plan for the different risks the company can face. When evaluating the risks of the potential customers, it is also important to look into risks associated with the countries in which the company is operating. Next to as physical loss or damage to goods, there should be a plan for cash flow problems to allow for the time that goods are in transit or in bonded warehouses, here or abroad and/or for heightened risk of non-payment by your customers. These risks are insurable. Other, non-insurable, risks must also be taken into account. There may be less interest in the product or service in the export or import country. National or international developments may influence prices, the interest rate or inflation rate could change. As a result, the product may be too expensive for the foreign market. This risk is also uninsurable. In international business, the risks can be divided into political risks (countries) and commercial or business risks.

9.1.1 Political risks

A political risk can simply be defined as the risk of losing money due to changes that occur in a country's government or regulatory environment. These changes can form a force majeure for parties to a contract, and removes the liability of participants to fulfill obligations due to natural and unavoidable catastrophes. This means that the agreements with the supplier or buyer cannot be carried out because of events over which they themselves have no influence.

Political risks include:

- **civil war**. This means more-or-less organised violence among inhabitants of the same state, in which a significant proportion of the inhabitants of that state are involved.

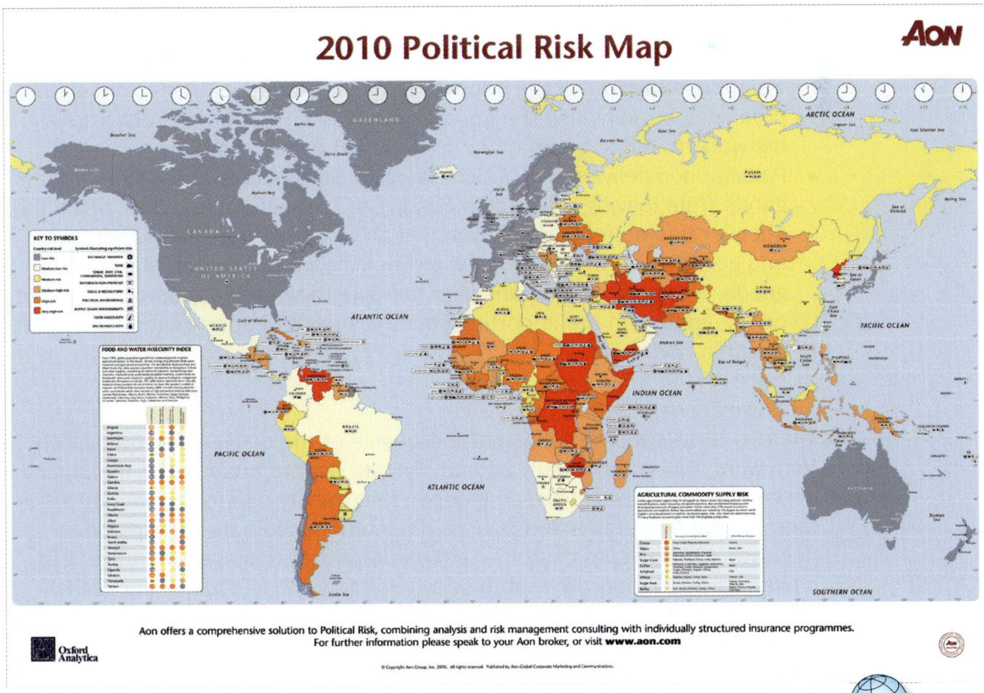

The map shown is in a larger format available on the website.

- **revolt**. A revolt means organised violent resistance against the existing authorities within a state.
- **currency shortage**. A currency shortage means a shortage of foreign currency such as dollars or euros obtained from exports. This money is needed in order to buy foreign products. The local currency is generally not accepted as means of payment.
- **moratorium**. A moratorium is a statutory injunction whereby for a certain amount of time creditors are unable to recover their money from their debtors. The authorities decide on the length of the moratorium.
- **natural disaster**. Natural disasters are caused by the forces of nature and include earthquakes, avalanches, hurricanes and floods.
- **government interference or sanction**. These are actions taken by the state.

Credit insurers, rating agencies and institutional investors are constantly occupied with mapping of political risk factors.

9.1.2 Commercial or business risks

When assessing commercial or business risks a subdivision is created according to the risks of both the buyer and the seller:
The buyer (importer) runs the following risks:
a non-delivery risk
b quality risk
c transport risk
d exchange rate risk
e risk of kidnapping, hostage-taking or extortion.

Ad a Non-delivery risk
This is the risk of circumstances arising at the suppliers' company or in his country that prohibit him from fulfilling his obligation to deliver. The non-delivery risk is subdivided into a commercial non-delivery risk and a political non-delivery risk.

- Commercial non-delivery risk. This relates to circumstances at the warehouse/factory of the supplier himself that prevent him from either producing or delivering the goods. Machinery could have broken down, his workers might be on strike or he might even have gone bankrupt.
- Political non-delivery risk. This relates to circumstances that prevent the goods from leaving the foreign country of production, and over which the supplier has no influence. Examples are natural disasters, revolt, war and government measures that prevent the production or export of goods. Besides circumstances in the exporting country there also might be regulations in the importing country, such as import restrictions, that result in non-delivery.

Ad b Quality risk
There is always a possibility that the quality of the delivered goods differs from what was contractually agreed. Should doubts arise about the quality of the purchased products, an independent quality control office can check them during production and prior to shipment. Should its findings be positive, it will give its customer a clean report of findings. The buyer can make the clean report one of the payment conditions. Quality control is important if there is a purchase agreement with a new supplier. The risk is small when doing frequently business with the same supplier.

Ad c Transport risk
International companies that buy and sell (import and export) goods become involved in transport. Goods can be damaged during transport, get stolen or lost. It depends on the agreed INCO terms whether the transport risk is to be carried by the buyer or the seller.

● www.logisticalchallenge.com

Lost at sea

As you read this, more than 50,000 Nike tennis shoes are circling the globe like a convoy of tiny striped canoes, but this flotilla of footwear is hardly alone at sea. It's been joined by thousands of Tommy Pickles cartoon heads, plastic turtles, rubber ducks, 3 million Lego pieces and, at last report, 34,000 hockey gloves. All this stuff and more is bobbing to a beach near you, said Seattle-based oceanographer Curtis Ebbesmeyer.
Each year, manufacturers around the world ship more than 100 million containers – each the size of a semi-truck – across the seven seas. Gumball dispensers, doll heads, and Beanie Babies stitched and glued in China sail across the Pacific Ocean. Made-in-Hungary frocks and Pez candies travel 10th class across the Atlantic on container ships, which carry on average 4,500 containers. But not all of them will reach port. Every year, more than 10,000 containers fall overboard and spill their cargo into the ocean. Storms are often to blame. An 8-foot by 40-foot container (2.4-meter by 12.2-meter), which can carry up to 58,000 pounds (26,000 kilograms) of cargo, might hold 10,000 shoes, 17,000 hockey gloves, or a million pieces of Lego. Far from being a curio, Ebbesmeyer's hobby gives clues to the ocean's highway of currents. Shipping companies keep meticulous records. A ship's captain is required to note where a container went overboard. If a Nike shoe washes onto a local beach, he check the serial number on the insole. It's proof that even a floating shoe leaves a footprint.
Based on his knowledge of ocean currents, Ebbesmeyer can predict when and where the goods will eventually turn up. Millions of Legos plastic pieces that spilled overboard in three containers in the Atlantic last year are expected to drift north into the Arctic Ocean and then through the Northeast Passage. In a few more years, they are expected to travel

9

south toward the 49th state, Alaska. Their expected arrival time on Alaskan beaches is 2012 and on Washington beaches in 2020, Ebbesmeyer said. In 1990, 80,000 pairs of Nikes in eight containers jumped ship during a storm in the mid-Pacific. Ten years later, some are still circumnavigating the Earth like miniature Magellans. As for the manufactured junk floating in the ocean, it's not all a waste or a wash. Those Nike shoes, for instance, they're ambassadors of goodwill, a floating thrift store. "Poor people around the world know, if you need a pair of shoes you go to the beach."

Ad d Exchange rate risk
Many companies do not realise the exchange rate risk that they run. Exhange rate risk is a potential gain or loss that occurs as a result of an exchange rate change. For instance, if a European company makes an export deal denominated in US dollars, and the euro-dollar exchange rate falls (the dollar depreciates), fewer euros will be received from the deal. Exchange rate risks can have the following consequences:

1 Economic: operating costs will rise due to changes in rates and make a product uncompetitive in the world market.
2 Turnover: the impact of currency exchange rates will reduce a company's earnings and weaken its balance sheet.
3 Transaction: if there is an unfavorable move in a specific currency between the time when a contract is agreed and the time it is completed, or between the time when a loan or borrowing is initiated and the time the funds are repaid.

To address these risks, a company can use an average exchange rate for the ongoing deals. This is all right as long as the exchange rate does not fluctuate much. If there is a long-term rise or fall in the exchange rate then this can lead to financial losses or a windfall. Another more practical option is to insist on using one's own currency for all transactions. However, asking the other party to use euros (for example) is inflexible, and forces them to take on all the risk.

Ad e Risk of kidnapping, hostage-taking or extortion
Kidnapping is knowingly restraining someone with a specific intent to do something. This may be to collect a ransom. Hostage-taking is the deprivation of a person's liberty without a ransom demand. Extortion is the threat to harm or kill a person or to damage or destroy possessions. The American insurance company AIG mentioned that about 12,500 kidnappings take place a year in more than 40 countries. During the last four years, the amount of ransom money demanded doubled, with some kidnappers demanding more than 50 million euros. For example, kidnappings take place on a daily basis in Nigeria: armed rebels and petty criminals looking for petro-dollars have set their sights on oil company employees. In Colombia, members of the rebel organisation FARC regularly kidnap foreigners, sometimes for ideological reasons, but increasingly for money.

The seller (exporter) runs the following risks:
a non-payment risk
b company risks
c risk of kidnapping, hostage-taking or extortion

Ad a Non-payment risk
The biggest risk the sellers runs is that the purchase price is not paid (continuing non-payment). Non-payment is sometimes called 'probable insolvency' and is common in southern Europe, where the customer often just 'disappears'. These are known as 'Scarper debtors'.

European Payment Index (EPI)

The debt-collection agency Intrum Justitia has been carrying out research into payment risks, payment behaviour and various credit management variables in 22 European countries. The collected data is combined with national economic data to produce the European Payment Index (EPI). This index shows payment risks by country: the lower the EPI, the better payment standards of the country. The following table shows the key indicators the EPI: the average payment period in days and the average percentage loss on accounts received payments by country.

Percentage loss on accounts received payments by country.

Country*	**European Payment Index**	**Average payment period (days)**	**Payment loss (percentage)**
Finland	125	28	1
Sweden	129	35	1.6
Norway	134	33	2
Denmark	136	37	2
Switzerland	145	42	2.3
Ireland	146	62	2
France	150	63	2.1
Estonia	152	36	2.9
Netherlands	153	42	2.5
Germany	153	49	2.1
Austria	153	35	2
UK	155	52	2.4
Belgium	156	52	2.5
Latvia	156	42	3.3
Slovakia	160	39	3
Lithuania	162	47	3.3
Italy	162	88	2.5
Poland	163	39	3
Spain	166	98	2.4

9

Country*	European Payment Index	Average payment period (days)	Payment loss (percentage)
Hungary	165	45	2.7
Czech Republic	172	49	3
Greece	180	120	3
Portugal	184	87	2.7

*Data from January, February and March 2009.

Source: Intrum Justitia, European Payment Index, 2009

Ad b Company risks
Company risks relate to:
- bankruptcy
- moratorium
- full discharge settlement
- writ of execution

Insolvency

In fact, these four company risks can lead to insolvency. Insolvency is generally defined as a financial state in which a company can no longer pay its bills and meet other obligations.

Ad c Risk of kidnapping, hostage-taking or extortion
See commercial risk.

9.2 Risk management

One of the major risks of doing business abroad is that an incorrect assessment of the risks inevitably leads to claims, disputes and court cases. Risk management can be described as the systematic and cyclic execution of risk assessment and risk control. Based on this assessment and control, precautions can be taken or adjusted. Four elements are important:
1 risk assessment
2 risk control
3 monitoring
4 continuity management

Ad 1 Risk assessment
Carrying out a risk assessment means making an inventory of the risks, analysing them and evaluating them. A total picture thus emerges of the risks the company runs.

Ad 2 Risk control
After a complete assessment of the risks has been made, precautionary measures are taken to reduce the risks. It turns out that in practice companies working internationally already have taken precautions. Think of product requirements that are in force in certain countries. Other precau-

tions are sometimes taken only after the company has been made aware of possible risks. An example is piracy along the Somali coast (see the opening case).

Precautions can be divided into two categories.

a **Preventive measures.** These are aimed at reducing the chance of something happening and/or limiting the consequences thereof. Insurance companies encourage companies to take preventive measures to keep premiums within affordable limits and to keep a grip on the risks themselves. For example seventy-five per cent of damage in companies is due to fire. Fire damage causes loss of turnover and loss of customers. The result is that about 80 per cent of the companies that suffer severe fire damage go bankrupt. Prevention can reduce this risk.

b **Financial security measures.** These are aimed at taking care of the financial consequence as soon as a risk appears. The company can keep the financial reserves on the books. A lower insurance premium does not reduce the risk. That is why the company must work out whether there are solutions with a higher yield and find out the period when the risk will come into force. An example is the importer's product liability. The importer is held liable if the product does not meet quality standards. This can make a fairly heavy demand on the finances of the importer's company or the company that hired the importer.

Ad 3 Monitoring

Monitoring means systematically and periodically collecting data on developments and trends. The company checks time and again whether the preventive measures are having the desired effect and ensures that these are updated. Monitoring keeps the company aware of changes in national and international product requirements and is useful in circumstances where the company is going to develop new products, for example. These changes may mean the insurance portfolio must be adjusted.

Ad 4 Continuity management

As far as their turnover is concerned, many companies are highly dependent on the flow of international goods. Should a link in the distribution chain fail – for example, if containers are swept overboard in a storm- the whole chain can disintegrate. The goal of continuity management is to find a way of letting the supply of goods and services (management) continue undisturbed. Then certain measures can be enforced.

Risk management can contribute to cost savings by preventing damage, reducing accidents, improving the company's risk profile and taking out the right type of insurance.

9.3 Insurance

As has been mentioned before, taking out insurance can cover risks in international business. Insurance can be sub-divided into indemnity insurance and insurance of fixed sums.

Indemnity insurance
Sum insurance

The goal of indemnity insurance is to minimize the financial risk of the policyholder. An insurance of fixed sums means insurance under which the insurer is obliged to pay a fixed sum of money on the occurrence of an

insured event. The cover is limited to the life or health of a person, and pays out a predetermined amount should a claim arise based on the occurrence of the insured event. Thus, should the insured person die or have an accident, a fixed amount is paid out.
In international business indemnity insurance is important.

Parties
An insurance contract is a contract under which one party, the insurer promises the other party, the policyholder, coverage against a risk specified in the insurance contract. The insurance policy is an agreement between the insurer and the policyholder. The policyholder is not only the person or entity whose risk is being insured but also the person or entity who concludes the agreement with the insurer. You can take out insurance directly with an insurer or through an insurance broker.

Broker

The broker stands between the insurer and the policyholder. Other names for a broker include insurance representative, insurance agent and insurance adviser. The broker gives advice and mediates when a policy is being negotiated and settled.

Policy
The insurance risk surveyors advise the insurance companies about risk, based on technical knowledge and good practice. Once the risk assessment has taken place and the candidate accepted, then the insurance contract can be made. The contract is laid down in a formal document known as an insurance policy. It includes all clauses, terms, exceptions and conditions of the insurance contract.

Coinsurance
Coinsurance is generally widely used in the European insurance market. Coinsurance is a method by which insurance companies control the risk of insuring against catastrophic events or extending insurance to individuals or businesses likely to create sizable claims. The risk is shared based on percentages between the insurance companies. Often, one insurance company will lead. The leading insurance company is responsible for administering various aspects of the insurance policy, such as premium, claims and the insurance documents. Coinsurance is used when it is impossible to place the entire risk with one insurer.

An example:
A trading vessel is valued at 10 million Euros. No single insurer is prepared to accept 100 per cent of the risk. With coinsurance the risk can be spread among a number of insurers.

9.4 Types of insurance

When choosing a type of insurance one has to consider the needs of the company, the risks it runs, and how they can be covered. The financial potential of the company should also be taken into account.

Table 9.1 shows the types of insurance taken out by international companies.

TABLE 9.1 Types of insurance

Risk category	Insurance
Quality	• Product liability insurance • Product recall insurance • Product extortion insurance
Transport	• Transport insurance • Average Grosse • Carrier liability insurance • Seller's interest insurance
Exchange rates	• Currency (term) contract • Currency option contract • Exchange rate clause • Exchange rate risk insurance
Kidnapping, hostage-taking or extortion	• Kidnap and ransom insurance
Non-payment	• Credit insurance • Export credit insurance

We will discuss these types of insurance below.

9.4.1 Quality risk

To cover a quality risk a number of types of insurance have been developed:
a Product liability insurance
b Product recall insurance
c Product extortion insurance

These are discussed below.

Ad a Product liability insurance
The company can be held liable for defects, faults and flaws in services provided and products. To protect itself against product liability claims by third parties, the company can take out a product liability insurance. This insurance is also important for importers of goods from outside the EU because from a legal standpoint they are regarded as the producer.

There are two types of coverage: occurrence and claims made.
- **Occurrence coverage**. With occurrence coverage, the damage for any incident that occurred while the policy was in force is covered, even if the claim is not made until some years after the policy has expired.
- **Claims made coverage**. This means that only the claims actually made during the duration of the policy are covered.

Ad b Product recall insurance
Product recall is the recall of products that have been damaged to such an extent that they are dangerous if used. Damage is often the result of an accident or inattention at the production or distribution stage. But damage can also be intentional (sabotage, for example, by a dissatisfied worker). A recall is generally made by the manufacturer of the damaged product, sometimes by the wholesaler or by a retailer (shop). The company's reputation can be jeopardized if a product has to be recalled, for example by negative publicity in the media.

Contaminated products insurance

There are various type of product recall insurances, such as contaminated products insurance (CPI). This provides coverage for:

- an accidental (unintended) production fault, as a result of which products endanger the public health or damage other products (accidental product contamination)
- an attempt to (criminal) tamper with products so that they are unfit for use or damaged (malicious product tampering).

● www.northumberlandview.ca

Recall Children's Sleepwear

Fact Sheet

Brand	**Description**	**Sears Item Number**	**Sizes**
Sesame Street	Cookie Monster on a blue hooded velour sleeper	36849	12M/20lbs 18M/26lbs
Sesame Street	Elmo on a red hooded velour sleeper	36850	12M/20lbs 18M/26lbs
Small Paul	Blue hooded sleeper	39259	9M
Small Paul	Pink hooded sleeper	39496	9M

Hazard Identified

The recalled sleepwear does not meet the design and flammability requirements for children's sleepwear under Canadian law. Children's sleepwear that is loose fitting or that has loose edges can contact ignition sources such as stove elements, candles, and matches more easily than tight-fitting sleepwear. Once ignited the sleepwear can burn rapidly and cause severe burns to large areas of the child's body resulting in shock and sometimes death.
Consumers are advised not to let their children wear the recalled sleepwear and should immediately take the product away from children. The recalled sleepwear can be returned to the nearest Sears Department store for a full refund if accompanied by a sales receipt or Sears Card statement, or for the lowest selling price without a receipt.

January 2011

Ad c Product extortion insurance
Product extortion means that companies become victims of extortion: a threat to damage, destroy or to contaminate its products to induce the company to pay a ransom to the blackmailers. Under these circumstances, a company cannot operate normally. This is the kind of risk product extortion insurance deals with. Product extortion insurance covers the payment of a ransom should a company be threatened. Worldwide various multinationals

such as Heineken and Coca-Cola have been confronted with this type of extortion.

9.4.2 Transport risk

The decision whether or not to take out transport insurance depends on the following:

- the agreed conditions of delivery (INCO term)
- the value of the articles
- the continuity of the flow of goods (can the goods quickly be replaced?)
- the mode of transport

There are several types of coverage. The best coverage depends on the type of goods, type and means of transport, packaging and destination:

a Transport insurance
b General Average insurance
c Carrier's liability insurance
d Sellers' interest insurance

Ad a Transport insurance
Insurance covering the transportation of goods is simply known as transport insurance. There are several coverage options. Standard transport insurance covers nearly all possible risks (except those related to a good's own defect) that can arise during transport, including the periods of loading and discharge of cargo.

All-risk cover

The most commonly used transport insurance is all-risks (the most comprehensive coverage) for:

- a one-off transport insurance (policy)
- a single shipment (loose item)
- continuous transport insurance policy (turnover policy) for road transport
- transport insurance of transport of cargo by sea when each shipment must be declared (customs declaration policy).

The storage of goods carries its own risks. This can also be insured.

Ad b General Average insurance
A General Average covers on a container vessel, owners vessel, charterers and cargo the interests that will be exposed to extensive delays. Coverage is designed specifically to reduce delay and administrative burdens on owners and other interests in connection with a General Average. Even if the goods of one of the parties are undamaged all the parties may be required to pay for the damage. This is the case if damage to cargo has been caused deliberately and sacrifices have been made to retain the ship and its remaining cargo.

Ad c Carrier's liability insurance
According to the terms of a transport contract a carrier has a duty to deliver goods to the destination in the condition in which he received them. Should the carrier neglect his duty to care for the goods, the claimant or the transport insurer can hold him liable. The carrier pays damages in accordance with the following terms:

- *AVC (General Transport Terms – National Road Transport)*. The AVC state that the carrier's liability is up to an amount of 3.40 euros per kilogram of damaged or lost goods. Under certain conditions the carrier cannot be held liable.

- *CMR* stands for "Convention relative au contrat de transport international de marchandises par route" which translates as "Convention on the Contract for the International Carriage of Goods by Road. Under CMR the liability for loss or damage to a load is strictly limited to 11,80 Euros per kilo of damaged, lost or stolen goods, or the actual value – whichever is lower.

There is also the possibility that carrier arranges for transport without the AVC or CMR conditions. Liability is no longer limited to the above-mentioned amount and the carrier could face considerable claims if the goods do not arrive at their destination or arrive damaged. He can take out carrier liability insurance to guard against such an eventuality.

Ad d Sellers' interest insurance
When the buyer is responsible for the transport insurance (as in the case of a FOB purchase) but the seller cannot rely on him doing this properly, it is wise for the seller to take out extra insurance: sellers' interest insurance. This is an additional transport insurance bought by the seller and provides cover if the CFR, FOB or FAS buyer has not purchased (adequate) transport insurance.

9.4.3 Exchange rate risk

There are various methods of limiting exchange rate risk:
a currency (term) contract
b currency option contract
c exchange rate clause
d exchange rate risk insurance

These methods will be discussed below.

Ad a Currency (term) contract
A contract is signed with a bank that on a certain date a currency exchange transaction will take place at a predetermined price, sometimes known as a forward contract. This clearly shows what the foreign currency transaction will cost. The time at which the currency term contact is signed is very important. A lot of companies wait to cover exchange risk until the currency market starts to move, but they often find that they have already suffered a loss because of currency fluctuations.

Ad b Currency option contract
A currency option is the right to buy or sell a certain amount of foreign currency for an agreed exchange rate during or after a predetermined period. A premium must be paid for this right. This type of contract is not used for the purchase or sale of foreign currency but for the right to do so. A currency option covers a limited number of foreign currencies. The costs are higher than for a currency term contract, but there is also more flexibility.

Ad c Exchange rate clause
With an exchange rate clause, the seller fixes the value of the goods in its currency. If the rate of the invoicing currency in the contract increases, the price of the export is increased for the purchaser on the basis of the new exchange rate. The buyer and the seller agree that both parties shall bear

the loss or take the profit should there be changes in the exchange rate. Thus the negative exchange rate development is compensated for the new purchaser price.

Ad d Exchange rate risk insurance
This insurance covers the risk that foreign currency loans yield less because of a fall in value of the currency against the euro.
Insurers often offer two possibilities:
1 An exchange rate risk insurance that takes account of certain currency ranges. As soon as the exchange rate rises above the upper limit, creating a profit, the surplus must be paid to the insurer. Should the rate fall beneath the lower limit, the insurer must reimburse the exchange loss.
2 An exchange rate risk insurance where an average rate is agreed.

The premium is calculated according to the total amount outstanding (principal and interest) starting from the date the contract comes into force.

EXAMPLE

In this currency risk example, we imagine that there has been a drop of 10 per cent in the value of a foreign currency against the euro.
Should a company have reached 10 per cent of its turnover in dollars, and the dollar falls by 10 per cent against the euro, then the company's turnover will be 1 per cent lower than expected.
Suppose that the company previously had a 2 per cent profit margin; in that case, this 1 per cent reduction in turnover means a halving of its profits (to 1 per cent). If the company had a profit margin of 20 per cent, then this reduction in turnover of 1 per cent would mean a reduction in profit of 5 per cent.

Source: internationaalondernemen.nl

9

9.4.4 Risk of kidnapping, hostage-taking or extortion

The consequences of kidnapping, taking hostage and extortion are covered by the kidnap and ransom insurance. Ships and goods have a monetary value, but the price of human life cannot be measured. This is the reason why the kidnap risk for human beings is limited: to, say, 10 million euros per insured incident. Should a kidnapping take place, the ransom will be paid up to the maximum available insurance amount. This insurance is meant particularly for international businesses active in Latin America and Africa.

9.4.5 Non-payment risk

The seller runs the risk that the purchase price will not be paid. The risk can be covered through credit insurance.
It covers the risk of financial loss that can occur when trade credit is offered by a company to its corporate customers – thus providing a set period of credit after the provision of products or services before payment is due.This provides coverage for:

- commercial risks, for instance the customer may be unable or unwilling to pay
- political risks, for instance a shortage of the contract currency in the customer's country, or government intervention, or a natural disaster.

Contract risk

Credit insurance can take effect on the moment of delivery or on the moment the sales contract is concluded. In the first case it covers the non-payment risk, in the second case it provides co-insurance of the contract risk. This form of insurance can be very useful to companies that sell customer-specific products.
The seller concludes a sales contract with a customer for the delivery of specially designed products, e.g. with a customer-specific logo. These are delivered six months later. If in the meantime the customer has gone bankrupt, specially designed products cannot be sold to another company. These costs can be covered by credit insurance.

Alternatives to credit insurance

There are various alternatives to credit insurance, such as letters of credit (L/C) and cash against documents (CAD). We will discuss these later in this chapter. An L/C also carries a non-payment risk. If an L/C is opened by a foreign bank according to the buyer's instruction, but it is not confirmed by bank of the seller, the seller still runs the risk that the bank that opened the L/C does not meet its obligations. This is seen as a political risk.
CAD also carries risks. What happens if the buyer does not collect the documents and leaves the goods at the airport or in the port? They must be stored, and eventually returned. This is a financial risk. This can also happen with documents against acceptance and documents against payment.
The best possible security is pre-payment, but customers rarely agree to this. The customer must wait and see whether, after payment, he will have his goods delivered. On the other hand, with open credit the supplier must wait to get paid.

- http://global.atradius.com

Atradius, Structured Insurance Facility (SIF)

The Structured Insurance Facility (SIF) provide coverage for transactions with countries which are "off cover", or in which the requirement of an unconditional payment guarantee from the central government is waived.
This facility is only available for transactions with private sector buyers or banks. When analysing applications for cover, Atradius will pay close attention to risk-mitigating factors, which may differ per transaction and country.
There are three country categories:
1 "off-cover" countries, whereby exceptions can be made on a case-by-case basis for private sector buyers or banks
2 "off-cover" countries, whereby exceptions can be made on a case-by-case basis for private sector buyers or banks if they generate foreign currency income or have access to foreign currency
3 "off-cover" countries, whereby no exceptions can be made, given political and/or economic conditions.

Countries with high transfer risks are normally classified as 2. For transactions with these countries it is therefore important that buyers/ borrowers independently generate foreign currency income or have access to foreign currency.
Transactions with private sector buyers/borrowers must be structured such that they are not affected by the risks that led to the off cover status for the country concerned. Risk-mitigating factors could include a higher down payment, an escrow account structure, mortgages on real estate or ships, or pledged accounts receivable.
Given that this facility is for transactions carrying higher risks than those covered under our regular country policy, the total facility is limited to €200 mln. The limit per country is €30 mln (maximum obligo) and per transaction €15 mln (loan amount). The maximum repayment period is 7 years.

9

9.5 Finance

International payments are a necessary part of international business. A bank often acts as a go-between in financial transactions, depending on the method of payment the buyer and seller have agreed to. Entrepreneurs starting out in international business often make the mistake of going to the bank at a very late stage in business negotiations. It is of prime importance to settle all financial matters before making any agreements. The choice of payment terms forms an important part of the negotiations with the foreign party in order to cover the debtor and/or country risks.
The choice of payment terms is dependent on the following:
- The relationship. The buyer must be creditworthy and payments must be

on time and without problems. Only then can the exact payment condition be chosen.

- The complexity of the method of payment. It is easy to arrange that the customer will pay 30 days after receipt of invoice. In the case of documentary credit, agreements must be made with the opposite party and the bank. These must be in writing and then the agreements have to be carried out.
- Distance. If the other company is round the corner, it is easy go there yourself or employ a debt collector. But it becomes a more difficult if the other party lives in Rome or Singapore. That is why payment terms will depend on the partner country.
- Culture. Culture also determines payment behaviour. Paying as late as possible is considered a scandal in some countries; in others it is normal practice.
- Market. A salesman knows that in every country he must take account of his competitors. If his competitors give 60 days' credit, he will not be quick to ask for cash on delivery.
- The political situation. Doing business in country suffering from continual political upheaval requires cast-iron payment terms.
- The economic situation. A country with a weak economy could become a threat. A company may require hard currency to pay for goods supplied. Think of some countries in Africa.
- The demands made by banks and insurance companies. To finance or pay a company, a bank can demand that the company use documentary credit or take out insurance. When insuring a non-payment risk the insurance company will generally demand that the system of payment that has the least risk is chosen (see figure 9.1).

FIGURE 9.1 Various forms of payment

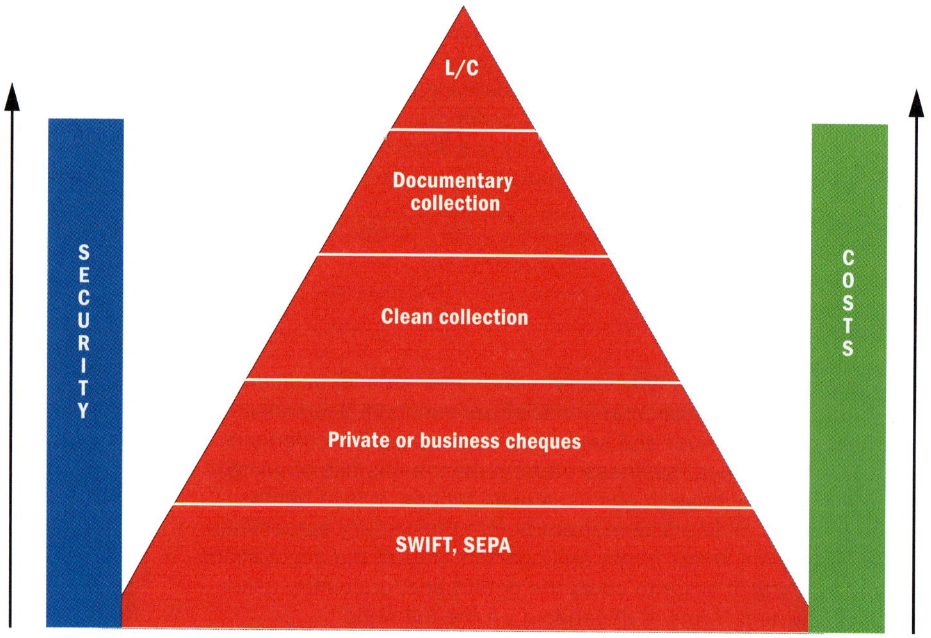

The most common forms of payment are:
- clean payment
- clean collection
- documentary collection
- documentary credit (letter of credit)
- international bank guarantee.

9.5.1 Clean payment

Clean payments are transfers to or from a foreign country for which the bank does not require any (commercial) documents. In the clean payment method, all shipping documents are handled directly between the parties. The role of banks is limited to clearing amounts as required. The clean payment method offers a relatively cheap and uncomplicated method of payment for both importers and exporters. There are basically two types of clean payments:

Shipping documents

1 Advance Payment: in the advance payment method the exporter is trusted to ship the goods after receiving payment from the importer.
2 Open Account: in the open account method the importer is trusted to pay the exporter after receipt of goods.

The main drawback of open account method is that the exporter (seller) runs a risk if payment is to be made after the goods have been inspected. If payment has to be made prior to inspection, then the risk for the importer (buyer) is whether the goods will be delivered on time.
Payment in foreign currency is one of the disadvantages of clean payment. There is always an exchange rate risk.
The advantages of clean payment are:
- simple procedure
- quick settlement
- low costs

Clean payments can be made in the following ways:
a via the SWIFT network
b Single Euro Payment Area (in Europe with SEPA countries)
c by cheque or bill of exchange

Ad a SWIFT
Through SWIFT, transfer of funds to various countries can be completely automated; SWIFT is a worldwide computer network used by banks to keep in direct contact with each other. This makes the process of money transfer more efficient, secure and with lower cost. Thus, SWIFT makes the process of transferring funds worldwide easier.

Ad b SEPA
The Single Euro Payments Area (SEPA) (see table 9.2) is the area where companies and other economic players will be able to make and receive payments in euros (whether between or within national boundaries) under the same basic conditions, rights and obligations, regardless of their location with one account.

TABLE 9.2 SEPA countries

Belgium	Iceland	Poland
Bulgaria	Italy	Portugal
Cyprus	Latvia	Romania
Denmark	Liechtenstein	Slovenia
Germany	Lithuania	Slovakia
Estonia	Luxemburg	Spain
Finland	Malta	Czech Republic
France	Monaco	United Kingdom
Greece	The Netherlands	Sweden
Hungary	Norway	Switzerland
Ireland	Austria	

Source: AbnAmro

SEPA offers benefits for companies. Companies can do business in the SEPA countries and save bank costs because the SEPA payment service is based on global ISO (International Organisation for Standardisation) standards. This means for businesses: common standards, faster settlement and simplified processing will improve cash flow, reduce costs and facilitate the access to new markets. Companies can rely on a single set of euro payment instruments covering the SEPA- countries.

Ad c Cheque and bill of exchange
Bank cheques can be used to make payments: the drawer writes the details including the money amount, date, and a payee on the cheque, and signs it, ordering their bank, known as the drawee, to pay the company the amount of money stated. The advantage of a bank cheque is that it gives a company the possibility to put pressure (regress) on the buyer's bank because he has signed the cheque.

9.5.2 Clean collection

When clean collection has been agreed to within the terms of payment, the seller must give his bank authorisation to collect money from the buyer. The clean collection document can state that the collection rules of the International Chamber of Commerce, the ICC Uniform Rules for Collection 1995 (URC 1995), apply.
Essentially the same rules apply as for clean payment, but the seller's bank has a more active role to play with this type of payment. The bank is ordered to collect payment without having to deal with the business documents.

EXAMPLE

American businesses use a variety of payment systems, such as cheques, electronic payments and credit cards. The payment conditions in the US are nearly the same with respect to risks and collateral as elsewhere in the world. The choice of payment method depends on the credit-worthiness and reliability of the person with whom one does business. Payments between the Netherlands and the US are generally done via bank transfer. Otherwise, the US is the country of the cheque. Payments made by cheque are called open account payments. Bills of exchange and documentary collection are used less often. Documentary credits are only used with very large amounts.

9.5.3 Documentary collection

A number of documents are attached to each international contract. These include shipping documents and certificates of origin. A buyer (importer) needs these documents – especially the bill of lading – in order to gain possession of the imported goods. The buyer pays for goods at delivery. In case of a documentary collection banks, therefore, act as intermediaries to collect payment from the buyer in exchange for the transfer of documents that enable the holder to take possession of the goods. The procedure is easier than a documentary credit, and the bank charges are lower. The bank, however, does not act as surety of payment but rather only as collector of funds for documents.
This system is known as documentary collection and all banks handle documentary collections according to international rules of the ICC. The documentary collection procedure is shown in figure 9.2.

9

FIGURE 9.2 Steps in the settling of a documentary collection

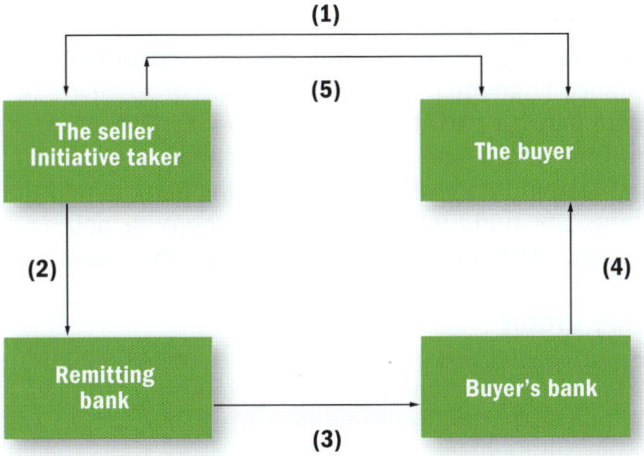

The documents required under a documentary collection are fundamentally the same as those in a documentary letter of credit transaction:
- commercial invoice
- insurance papers
- shipping documents such as bill of lading, airway bill and forwarding agent's certificate
- certificate of origin.

There is a choice of three types of documentary collection:
1. cash against documents (CAD)
2. documents against acceptance of a long-term bill of exchange, known as documents against acceptance (D/A)
3. documents against payment (D/P).

For this type of payment method a relationship based on trust between parties is very important. The banks involved in a documentary collection do not guarantee payment or assume any credit risk, as they do in documentary credit transactions. The banks act merely as intermediaries to facilitate payment for a shipment. Since the banks are under no obligation to authenticate documents, it is possible that the seller will send a short shipment, the incorrect goods, or inferior goods. The only recourse available to the buyer is through direct contact with the seller or legal action.

Ad 1 CAD (cash against documents)
One of the clauses in the sales agreement states that the buyer must pay in cash and that at the same time he hands over the cash he receives the documents. A third party is involved (generally the bank), which retains the documents until the buyer's payment has been received. This means that the buyer cannot take possession of the goods without paying.

Ad 2 D/A (documents against acceptance)
The buyer is given the documents after accepting a (long-term) bill of exchange. The bill of exchange is presented to the importer at maturity, when it has to be paid. D/A is a less secure method of payment for the seller than CAD, because the acceptance of a bill of exchange does not provide a watertight guarantee that the bill will be paid.

Ad 3 D/P (documents against payment)
In D/A terms the collecting bank is permitted to release the documents to the buyer against acceptance (signing) of a bill of exchange or signing of a time draft at the bank promising to pay at a later date (usually 30, 60 or 90 days). The completed draft is held by the collecting bank and presented to the buyer for payment at maturity, after which the collecting bank sends the funds to the remitting bank, which in turn sends them to the principal/seller. In fact, this type of payment is impractical and is not often used.

9.5.4 Documentary credit

Negotiations

The confidence of the exporter increases considerably if during business negotiations parties decide to use documentary credit (letter of credit) as a payment method. This is known as a letter of credit (L/C).
L/C is a contractual agreement between the (issuing) bank, on behalf of one of its customers, authorizing the advising or conforming bank to make payment to the beneficiary. Note, however, that banks only check docu-

ments; they do not trade in goods. The issuing bank, on the request of its customer, opens the letter of credit. The issuing bank makes a commitment to honor drawings made under the credit. The beneficiary is normally the provider of goods and/or services. Essentially, the issuing bank replaces the bank's customer as the payee.
Only after the supplier has complied with the documents and duties mentioned in the L/C will the bank pay the amount mentioned.

BUITENLANDSE MARKTEN, OCTOBER 2009

The challenge: He who wants to conquer a foreign market must take risks: first pay, then deliver. Or is it the other way round?

GOS International sells printing machines for plastic items such a yoghurt pots and butter tubs to 60 counties worldwide. The country that is burnt into director Vincent Tukkers' memory is Russia.
"The Russian government has very strict import requirements and government rules lean towards protectionism: 'us first'. The Russians casually put our sales contracts to one side and substituted a bulky version written in Russian and English. Russian law applied. Because the Russians didn't want to sign a contract according to Dutch law, it finally became a contract according to Swiss law. A nice neutral solution.
I would like to give other small and medium-size companies some advice. Make sure that you have a good Russian agent on the spot. And also make sure that you have a watertight contract and have agreed the payment terms. You must have all the payments written into the letter of credit, payment and all, before you ship your goods. In Russia, business does not always run smoothly."

9

FIGURE 9.3 Opening a documentary credit

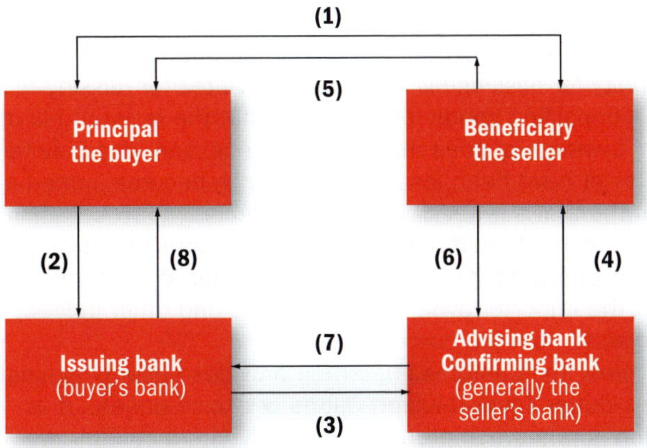

Generally, the quicker the payment, the better the price you can negotiate (payment reduction). This can result in a lower sales price (more profit).

9.5.5 International bank guarantees

Legally speaking, a bank guarantee is a conditionally accepted liability to pay, also known as a security guarantee. At the request of the principal, the bank (guarantor) guarantees money in favour of the beneficiary. The bank guarantee is used to exact observance of one's obligations.
Bank guarantees are used a lot in European countries because they are cheaper than credit. The US and many Asian countries prefer the stand-by letters of credit. In principle, they have the same function as bank guarantees: they provide assurance of the completion of the business transaction, because should the buyer not pay then they are activated. The difference is that with documentary credit the documents must be presented before a certain date.

Bank guarantees are divided into:

1. Guarantees that provide the assurance of compliance with financial obligations. These are:
   - *Payment bond.* This gives the supplier/accepter (beneficiary of the guarantee) a guarantee that payment will take place after completion of the duties mentioned in the contract within a predetermined time and for the invoiced amount. Internationally, this is referred to as a garantie de paiement or Zahlungsgarantie.
   - *Advance payment guarantee.* In this case the customer is guaranteed that the paid advance will be paid back if the goods are not delivered or the service is not carried out.
   - *Bond guarantee (bid bond).* A bid bond provides the assurance that the commitments in the offer will actually be met.
2. Guarantees that provide the assurance of compliance with non-financial obligations. These are:
   - *Performance bond.* The customer guarantees to perform the contract in accordance with its terms and conditions, at the agreed upon price, and within the time allowed.The meaning of fulfilment depends on the type of contract and the agreements made.
   - *Maintenance guarantee.* This provides the certitude that the maintenance and warranty undertakings of the supplier or builder regarding goods delivered or work completed will be carried out.
   - *Letter of indemnity for missing bill of lading (guarantee for missing bills of lading)* When importing goods it is possible that the relevant bill of lading (proof of ownership) goes missing. The necessary documents could arrive later or have been lost. The goods can become immediately available if there is a letter of indemnity for missing bill of lading. This protects the shipper/captain/carrier from the possible negative consequences of delivering goods with a missing bill of lading. With this guarantee, the importer avoids storage costs and other indirect costs and/or claims from the customer.
   - *Customs guarantee.* The customs guarantee provides security against unpaid customs duties (import-export duties or excise duties). It is often used when goods are imported temporarily into a country. A claim can be made if there is no evidence that the goods have been re-exported within the specified period and the resultant customs duties have not been paid.

9.6 International financing

During the start-up of an international business, various financial sources can be tapped. Government subsidies may be available, and commercial banks and development banks may be able to provide credit. Development banks belong to the World Bank Group or local banks without a profit motive. They stimulate the economy of emerging markets. We will now discuss the various sources of finance.

F-capital and Business Angels

This means "Family and Friends": they provide the F-capital. They are also known as business angels. This informal risk capital community co-finances the majority of new businesses.

Financing of venture capital/risk capital

Companies that carry on international business and undertake foreign investment can make use of venture capital or risk capital. This capital is supplied by third-party investors (investors outside the company). Because of the risk, the investor demands a rate of interest on their investment. The risk of failure is high. Profit expectations and sound operational management are very important. In some cases, the investor or venture capitalist becomes the owner of the company.

Multilateral banks

There are multilateral banks worldwide (see table 9.3), each one active in a specific geographical area. These banks provide credit and offer other services, such as investment funds, payment guarantees and lease facilities to small and medium-size companies. They stimulate entrepreneurship and promote an open democratic market economy. These banks include:

1. European Bank for Reconstruction and Development (EBRD). This bank finances projects undertaken by banks, industries and companies in countries from Central Europe to Central Asia (www.ebrd.org).
2. European Investment Bank (EIB). The EIB is a non-profit, policy driven bank. The EIB facilitates the aims of the European Union by providing long-term guarantees and capital services to companies. Companies must first contact a local intermediary bank (www.eib.org).
3. International Finance Corporation (IFC). This organisation fosters sustainable economic growth in developing countries by providing finance to private investors and by giving advice to companies and governments in emerging markets in Sub-Saharan Africa, Europe, Central Asia, Latin America and the Caribbean, the Middle East and North Africa (www.ifc.org).
4. Asian Development Bank (ASDB). This bank offers help to Asian countries to reduce poverty and improve the quality of life of the population. The ASDB also gives direct support to private businesses in developing countries by equity investments, guarantees and loans (www.asdb.org).
5. African Development Bank (AFDB). Its goal is to reduce poverty and improve the living conditions of Africans. It aims to develop sustainable economies (www.afdb.org).
6. Inter American Development Bank (IADB). The IADB was set up to support the process of economic and social development in Latin America and the Caribbean. The bank is the most important source of multi-lateral financing in the region (www.iadb.org).

TABLE 9.3 Financial possibilities of multilateral banks

	EBRD	EIB	IFC	ASDB	AFDB	IADB
Region of activities	Eastern Europe and the East	EU and a number of developing countries	World wide	Asia	Africa	Latin America
1 Large credits* (direct)	5.25 million euros	25 million euros	$40 million	X	$9 million	X
2 Smaller credits (via intermediaries)	X	X	X			
3 Investment equity, venture-capital funds	X					
4 Payment guarantees: trade facilitation programmes	X		X	X		
5 Leasing	X		X			
6 Investments			X			

*The sums mentioned concern the minimum project size.

Source: www.internationaalondenemen.nl

9

Factoring

Factoring means financing based on the debt portfolio of a company. The company passes the administration of its debt portfolio to a factoring company. This company in turn provides the company with advances.
The advantages of factoring are:

- Flexible financing to cash flow (max. 90 per cent of a debt portfolio).
- Better financial ratios: to improve the solvency and liquidity of the company.
- Expertise of factoring company on the area of foreign markets (payment terms, delivery and payment conditions, etc).

The disadvantages of factoring are:

- The financial position of the company is an open book, because the whole of the customer portfolio has to be passed on.
- It forms an extra link in the contact between the company and its customers. The commercial relationship between the company and its customers can be disrupted.
- The factoring company decides which companies will be supplied and the maximum amount of credit they will be allowed.
- It can create a negative picture. The company's customers can see factoring as a sign that the company's financial position is unstable.

The costs of factoring consist of a commission for the factoring company and payment of interest. Factoring can be expanded with risk coverage, which in practice means credit insurance.

International leasing

Another form of financing for companies which want to go international is leasing. The meaning of the term leasing differs from country to country. Generally speaking, a lease agreement denote an agreement in which one party (the lessee) makes use of the right to use a leased object for an agreed period and against a certain amount of compensation payable to the other party (the lessor). From an international point of view, a company, which uses the lease construction, can work the market from two sides:

Compensation

1 *Leasing as a financial resource*. A lease is an agreement between (the lessee) and the finance company (the lessor). The lessee has to pay a periodic fee, usually monthly, for the use and possibly ownership of equipment. The lease object could be office computers, company cars or more specialised equipment, such as a forklift truck. Furthermore, it leaves the company free to build cash reserves to finance/expand their business. There are several forms of leasing. We will not discuss these in detail.

2 *Vendor leasing (sale of capital goods)*. Is also known as lease asset servicing or vendor programs in which the vendor offers leases. Leasing is used as a sales instrument to improve vendor sales volume. Customers can view the vendor as a one-stop shop where they can fulfill their orders and get financing, rather than having to seek financing beforehand from a bank or other lending institution. Thus a new (international) market option is opened.
For example, a producer of forklifts concludes a direct leasing agreement with his customer in Vietnam, or he sells his products to a local leasing company, which in turn leases them to the customer in Vietnam.

9

Summary

- Because of variables such as transaction complexity and foreign business partners, there are increased risks attached to international business.

- Risks
  - Political risks
  - Commercial or business risks
  - Non-delivery risk
  - Quality risks
  - Transport risks
  - Exchange rate risk
  - Risk of kidnapping, hostage-taking or extortion
  - Non-payment risk
  - Company risks

- Risk management
  - Risk assessment: total picture of all risks
  - Risk control:
    - preventive measures
    - financial security measures
  - Monitoring: collecting data systematically and periodically
  - Continuity management: the delivery of products and services despite a catastrophe or other major disruptions

- Insurance
  - Can be divided into indemnity insurance and sum insurance
  - Parties: policyholder and insurer
  - Policy: an insurance agreement set out in a contract
  - Coinsurance: insurers and brokers come together to conclude insurance policies with high risk or with a large insured amount

- Types of insurance
  - Quality risk:
    - product liability insurance
    - product recall insurance
    - product extortion insurance
  - Transport:
    - transport insurance
    - general average insurance
    - carrier liability insurance
    - seller's interest insurance
  - Exchange rate risk:
    - currency (term) contract
    - currency option contract
    - exchange rate clause
    - exchange rate risk insurance
  - Risk of kidnapping, hostage-taking or extortion
    - Kidnap and ransom insurance
  - Non-payment risk
    - credit insurance
    - export credit insurance

- Finance
  - International payments: payment methods include:
    - clean payment
    - clean collection
    - documentary collection
    - documentary credit
    - international bank guarantees
  - International financing: there are various sources of finance for international businessmen:
    - F-capital and Business Angels
    - venture capital/risk capital
    - multilateral banks
    - factoring
    - international leasing

9

Questions and assignments

● www.vmt.nl

Unilever recalls sausages

A small amount of cheese was found in Unox Party sausages because of a production fault, wrote Unilever on Saturday in an advertorial in national and regional newspapers.
The cheese contains milk protein, which can cause a reaction in people who are allergic to it. People who are not allergic can safely eat the sausages.
According to Unilever the fault affected a maximum of 2,100 Party sausages in small tins with a use-by date of 02-2013. The company is asking consumers to cut out the label and send it to Unilever so they get a refund.

9.1 Imagine Unilever exports its products to America. How could the American importers limit the quality risk of the imported meat product?

9.2 Why is it so important during negotiations with an exporter to discuss INCO terms?

Imagine that Unilever has the sausages produced in Poland and asks the ABN Amro bank to draw up a documentary credit in favour of the Polish company. The Bank of Poland in Warsaw, where it is made available for payment, confirms this.
The Polish company sends the goods, completes the required documents and sends them to the Bank of Poland with a documentary letter of credit. The Bank of Poland checks the documents, finds them in order, but refuses to pay because:

a they first want to check the documents with ABN Amro bank in Amsterdam
b Unilever must first request payment of the ABM Amro bank

9.3 How do you judge these two pleas?

● www.forbes.com

Doing Business In Egypt: Protecting Your Assets

Current political unrest in Egypt is a reminder of how quickly some nations can spinout of control. Entering into joint ventures with local/ foreign partners is a way to reduce exposure to confiscation risk since the presence of nationals can take a company under the radar, although it is not a guarantee that the risk is eliminated. If cost-effective, political risk insurance is another option covering the risks of confiscation, political violence, insurrection, civil unrest and discrimination, among other things.

February 2011

9.4 Based on the political risk what kind of insurance would you advice companies?

9.5 Explain why it is important for a company to reduce this risk?

Ferrymasters

10 Logistics and customs

The final step in the process of doing international business is discussed in this chapter: the logistics of supplying and receiving goods and services. In order to understand what logistics are we first look at the bigger picture, viz supply chain management. The various modes of transport are discussed together with the advantages and disadvantages involved. We will then look at the legal aspects of a transport contract. And finally, a brief explanation follows on how customs authorities operate, and the usual document flow in international trade.

Warm glow of the chill factor

Source http://www.ft.com

Snow, ice and sub-zero temperatures all over the northern hemisphere – it is a great winter for Kilfrost. One-third of the de-icing and anti-icing fluids that aircraft worldwide must use to fly safely in cold weather are made by this small, privately owned family business. The trade-secret ingredients that have made Kilfrost a renowned brand with sales to more than 50 countries in five continents – "the magic pixie dust" as Gary Lydiate, chief executive, describes this crucial intellectual property – are made solely in a riverside factory at the end of a country lane in the peaceful Northumberland town of Haltwhistle.

The recent heavy snow and very low temperatures, from the US to the UK and Russia among others, have underlined the importance of de-icer, which is carefully coated on aircraft wings and tails in cold weather before they can take off safely. Recent difficulties at Heathrow and elsewhere were caused not by de-icing issues, Mr Lydiate stresses, but by the volume of snow on runways.

Since taking over as chief executive in 2006, Mr Lydiate has overseen changes in the pattern of buying raw materials. He set up large storage facilities near the mouth of the River Tyne for monopropylene glycol (MPG), a vital constituent not made in the UK that must be imported from Rotterdam in 2,000-tonne shipments.

The MPG storage facility enables the Haltwhistle factory to increase output very quickly when needed; the call for de-icer at big airports such as Frankfurt, Heathrow and Schiphol, all of which Kilfrost supplies, can go from nothing to 500 tonnes a day. In the three months leading up to mid-December, Kilfrost's European customers, including airports, airlines and air services companies, have already used 20,000 tonnes of de-icer, far more than usual.

Because severe weather makes transport difficult, Mr Lydiate has boosted Kilfrost's blending and storage capacity in mainland Europe, and it has manufacturing plants in continental Europe, the US and Japan. However, R&D and "pixie dust" production happen only at Haltwhistle. "I've recruited people from Australia and Canada to make sure we get the right people in," he says. Since Mr Lydiate arrived, the workforce has tripled to 74, including 12 in the US and four in the new Beijing office.

Source: www.ft.com, 13 January 2011

10

10.1 Logistics for international business

Logistics is an important element in international business. The products or services that are sold or bought must be transported from the production location to the buyer's. Logistics involves everything to move the goods from the factory to the buyer: not only the transport itself but also arranging and managing the transport. Logistics is part of supply chain management (SCM) that plans implements, and controls the efficient, effective forward and reverse flow and storage of goods, service and information between the point of origin and the point of origin of consumption in order to meet customers requirements. Figure 10.1 shows an overview of a supply chain.

Logistics

Supply chain management

FIGURE 10.1 Supply chain

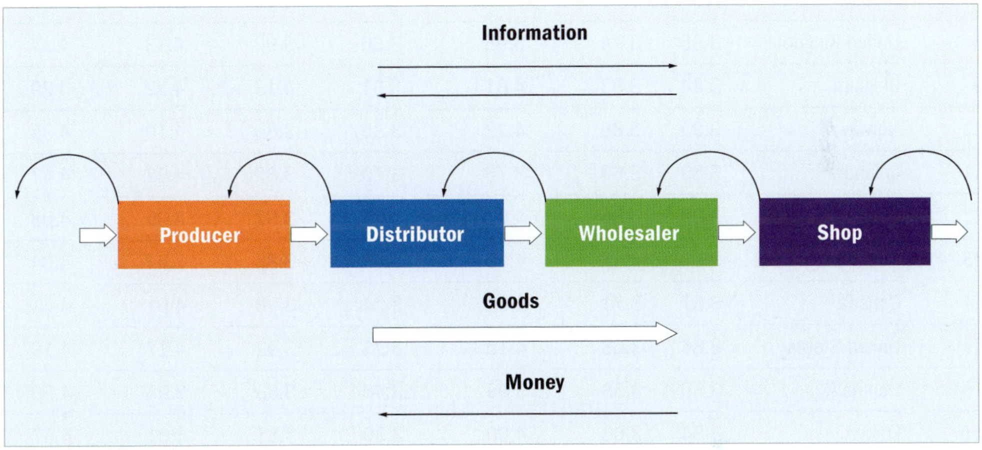

Source: Grit & De Geus, 2006

In this chapter we primarily focus on logistics, because it is out of the scope of this book to discuss the supply chain in depth. Of course it is important to keep the supply chain in mind, since it can lead to changes in the logistical choices of a company.

10.1.1 The position of Europa in logistics

Europe plays an important role in logistics. European countries are heavy traders with high import and export levels. Research by the World Bank in 2010 shows that 13 of the 20 best logistical countries in the world are European countries. Germany takes first place, Sweden, the Netherlands and Luxembourg take third, fourth and fifth place.
As shown in table 10.1, European countries score well in the areas of customs, infrastructure, international forwarding, competence and timeliness.

10

TABLE 10.1 Logistics Performance Index 2010

Int. LPI Rank	Country	LPI	Customs	Infra-structure	Interna-tional ship-ments	Logis-tics compe-tence	Tracking & tracing	Time-liness
1	Germany	4.11	4.00	4.34	3.66	4.14	4.18	4.48
2	Singapore	4.09	4.02	4.22	3.86	4.12	4.15	4.23
3	Sweden	4.08	3.88	4.03	3.83	4.22	4.22	4.32
4	Netherlands	4.07	3.98	4.25	3.61	4.15	4.12	4.41
5	Luxembourg	3.98	4.04	4.06	3.67	3.67	3.92	4.58
6	Switzerland	3.97	3.73	4.17	3.32	4.32	4.27	4.20
7	Japan	3.97	3.79	4.19	3.55	4.00	4.13	4.26
8	United Kingdom	3.95	3.74	3.95	3.66	3.92	4.13	4.37
9	Belgium	3.94	3.83	4.01	3.31	4.13	4.22	4.29
10	Norway	3.93	3.86	4.22	3.35	3.85	4.10	4.35
11	Ireland	3.89	3.60	3.76	3.70	3.82	4.02	4.47
12	Finland	3.89	3.86	4.08	3.41	3.92	4.09	4.08
13	Hong Kong, China	3.88	3.83	4.00	3.67	3.83	3.94	4.04
14	Canada	3.87	3.71	4.03	3.24	3.99	4.01	4.41
15	United States	3.86	3.68	4.15	3.21	3.92	4.17	4.19
16	Denmark	3.85	3.58	3.99	3.46	3.83	3.94	4.38
17	France	3.84	3.63	4.00	3.30	3.87	4.01	4.37
18	Australia	3.84	3.68	3.78	3.78	3.77	3.87	4.16
19	Austria	3.76	3.49	3.68	3.78	3.70	3.83	4.08
20	Taiwan	3.71	3.35	3.62	3.64	3.65	4.04	3.95

Source: World Bank, 2010

10

If you look at volumes in Europe, Rotterdam jumps out immediately. Antwerp, Hamburg, Marseilles and Amsterdam also handle large volumes, but follow Rotterdam at a great distance. The Netherlands is one of the main gateways to Europe: Rotterdam is the largest European port and Schiphol is the third largest air cargo port in Europe (figure 10.2).

FIGURE 10.2 Main European cargo ports

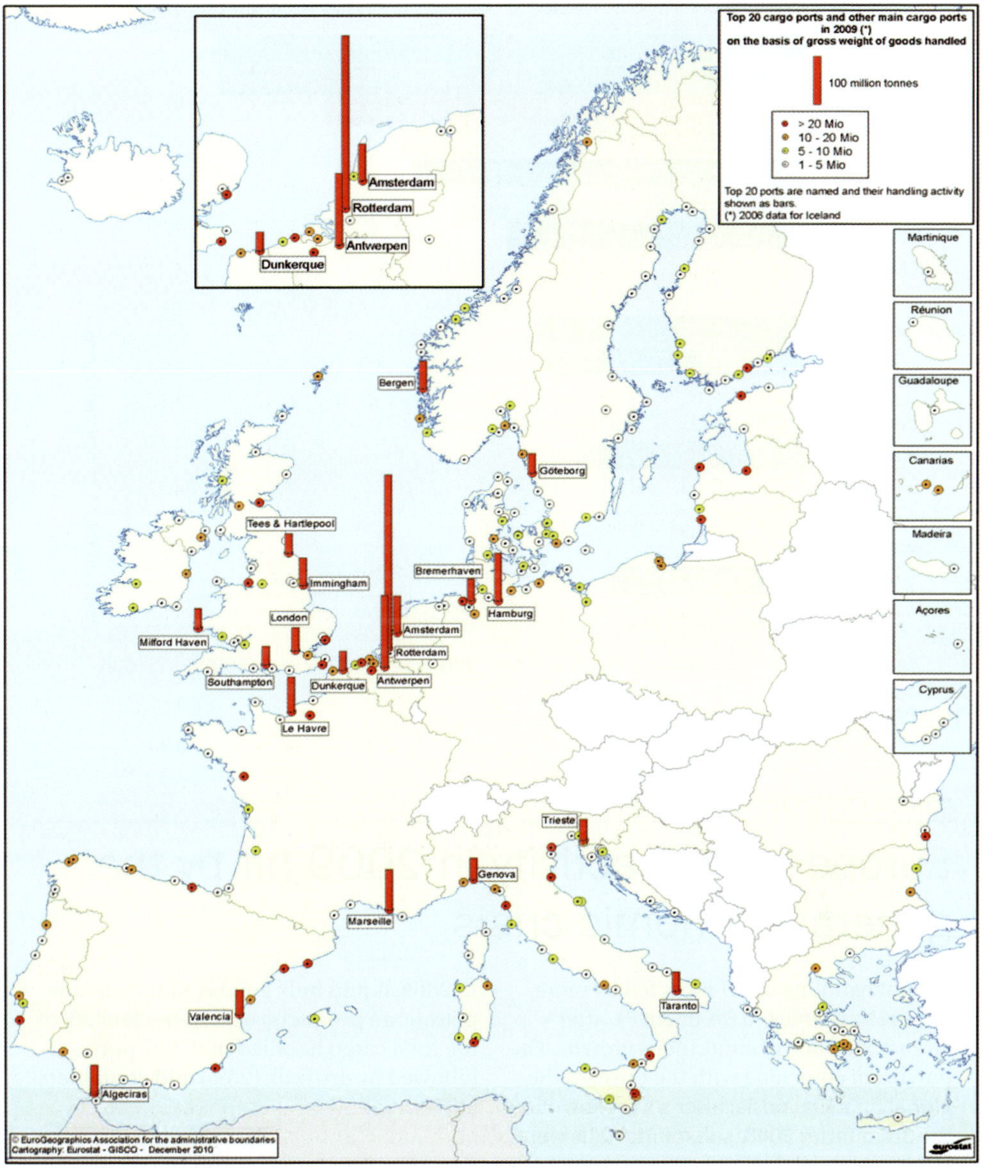

Source: Eurostat 2010

After Shanghai and Singapore, Rotterdam is the biggest harbour in the world, as can be seen in figure 10.3. In 2008, 421.1 million metric tonnes (1,000 kg) of goods and more than 10 million containers were processed. Most of the goods were destined for Europe (more than 51 per cent) (figure 10.3).

FIGURE 10.3 Top 20 ports in the world

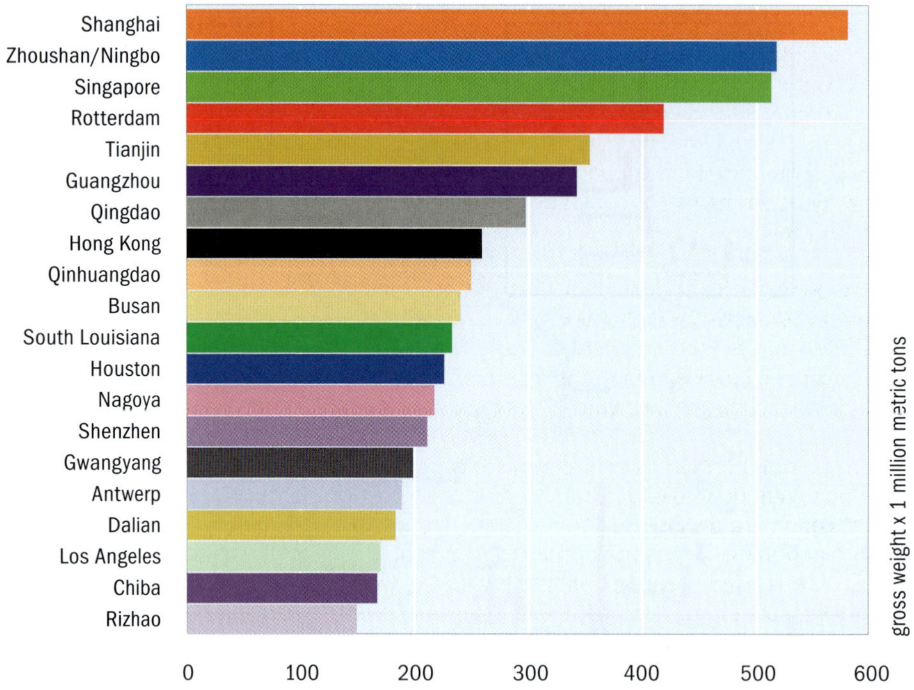

Source: Haven in cijfers, 2008

EUROSTAT STATISTICS IN FOCUS 65/2010

European port activity in 2009 hit by the general economic crisis

Freight handling in EU ports fell by more than 12% in 2009 (-0.5% in 2008), after almost a decade of continuous growth. The downturn coincided with the onset of the global financial crisis: after a slowdown in the 3rd quarter 2008, substantial falls were registered in all the following quarters (notably -16% in the 2nd quarter 2009).

In 2009, the total weight of goods handled in EU-27 maritime ports is estimated at 3.4 billion tonnes, the same level as in 2003. Of these, 62% were goods unloaded (64% in 2008).
At 501 million tonnes, the United Kingdom had the highest share (15%) of goods handled in EU-27 ports, followed by Italy and the Netherlands.

In 2009, liquid bulk goods (which include petroleum products) accounted for 42% of the total cargo handled in EU-27 ports, followed by dry bulk (23%) and containers (18%).

Rotterdam, Antwerpen and Hamburg - all located on the North Sea coast - maintained their positions as the three largest EU ports in terms of both gross weight of goods and volume of containers handled.

In 2009, more than 60% of EU-27 seaborne goods transport concerned an extra-EU-27 partner port. International intra-EU-27 transport represented 25% and national transport 11%.

10.2 Transport strategy

Goods bought or sold abroad must be shipped to/from the home country. Generally the supplier mentions in his offer whether the shipment will take place by road, water/sea or air. The problems of transport, and all that goes with it, are underestimated by many companies. Furthermore, costs fluctuate widely depending on the mode of transport. A company may request an adjustment in the transport mode that is more price-appropriate. It goes without saying that a company in international business must have a transport policy.

Transportation choice

Whoever is responsible for organising the transport depends on the delivery terms, i.e. the INCO terms (see chapter 8). The mode of transportation depends on a number of factors, such as costs, type of goods, the speed required and accessibility. Per kilometre/mile air transport is most expensive, but the fastest. Transport by ship is the cheapest, but it takes a lot of time.
Sometimes road transport costs five times as much as rail transport. However, a truck goes door-to-door from the producer to the importer's warehouse. If goods are transported by rail, the question is always how the goods are to reach the railway station in the first place. The lower the value and the bigger the volume of the goods, the higher the proportion of cost dedicated to transport them. It is worth calculating whether importing goods from a foreign country is worthwhile. Air transport is economic only in the case of high-value, low-volume goods. A pipeline is used to transport oil products and chemicals. A pipeline has the advantage of continuous supply; the disadvantage is that pipelines cannot be built everywhere. An overview of all these aspects is found in figure 10.4.

The mode of transport means should primarily be customer-oriented. This is particularly important for exporters. In the country of destination itself, road transport will largely be used to deliver the products to the customer's doorstep.

10.2.1 Parties involved in transport

Once the mode of transport has been made, the date of delivery has to be agreed upon. In international trade, the term ETA is often used. This means 'estimated time of arrival', that is the time when the ship, truck, train or aircraft arrives at its destination port, terminal or country. This is determined by the INCO terms. Because the day or hour of arrival cannot always be predicted, the 'estimated time of departure' (ETD) is often used to describe the day the goods are to leave the supplier's warehouse.

Contract of carriage

Once the delivery date has been agreed, the goods are transported to meet the agreed time and date. A contract of carriage is drawn up by the three parties involved:
1 carrier of the goods
2 consignor
3 consignee

FIGURE 10.4 Factors affecting mode of transport

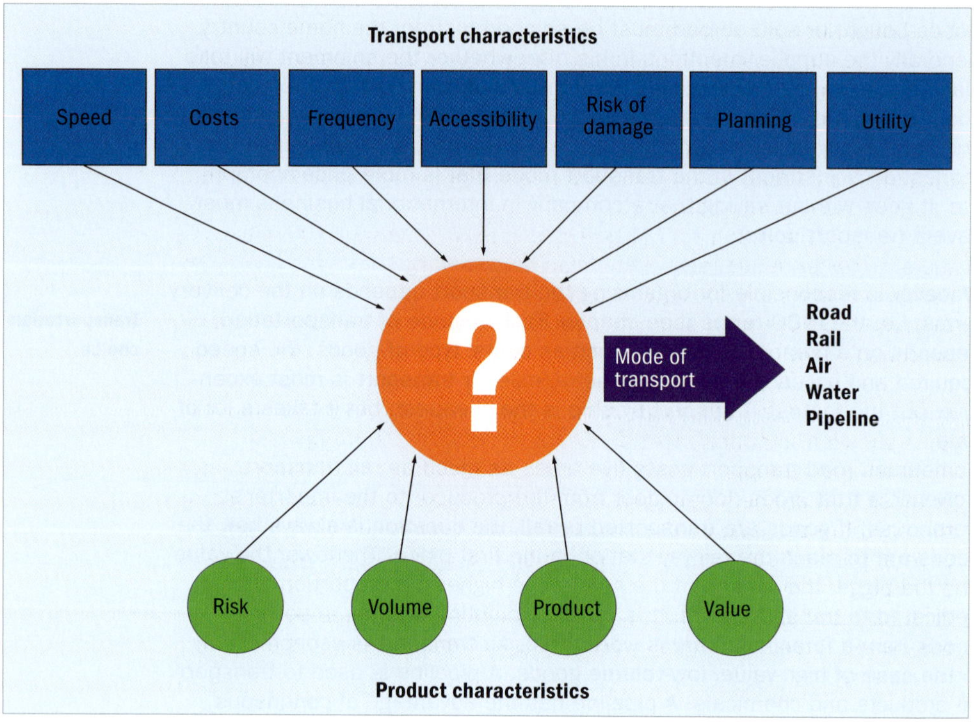

Source: Grit & De Geus, 2006

Ad 1 Carrier of the goods
The carrier is required to deliver the goods at the agreed destination in the same condition in which he received the goods.

Ad 2 Consignor
The consignor is the person who actually delivers the goods to the carrier. Some carriers use the term 'sender' or 'shipper'. Often, the consignor is the seller.

Ad 3 Consignee
The consignee is the person to whom the carrier must deliver the goods and who is entitled to accept the goods.

A contract of carriage must mention the following details:
- place and date the document was drawn up;
- names and addresses of the consignor, carrier and consignee;
- description of the goods, if possible according to the Combined Nomenclature (chapter 2);
- place and date where the goods have to be unloaded
- brands, gross weight and, if possible, net weight
- type of packaging
- measurements
- quantity
- INCO terms
- product requirements

Assistance
Other companies are involved in the transport process in addition to the three parties already mentioned:
- **Shipper**: one that makes the contract of carriage with the carrier. Usually the sender of the goods.
- **Shipping agent**: deals with the road, water or air transport of goods. In addition, the shipping agent takes care of permit applications, quotations, insurance and booking charges in shipping, and collects shipments from various clients (groupage).
- **Ship owner**: is the owner of a seagoing vessel. The captain is employed by the ship owner. A seagoing vessel can be owned by two or more people: this is known as a shipping company.
- **Shipbroker**: represents a shipping company and is responsible for loading on behalf of the ship of the owner. The shipbroker is the one who makes agreements with shippers.
- **Stevedore**: is the one who loads and unloads the ship. He is the shipbroker's subcontractor and must ensure that the goods are properly handled. For example, he should see to products that need ventilation, or those that are heat sensitive. He is responsible for the distribution of the weight of the load on the vessel, and cargo to be released when several ports of call are visited. In aviation, this function is performed by an airport handling agency.
- **Cargo interested party**: anyone who has an interest in the load. That may be the owner of the bill of lading, the consignee, the owner and the insurers of the cargo.

10.2.2 Transport activities
Transport involves not only the actual transportation of goods, but also other activities such as packaging, transhipment, storage, reconditioning and information processing.

Packaging

Packaging

One aspect of transport is packaging. Packaging means one or more receptacles to preform their containment and other safety functions. On the packaging often instructions are to be found on how to handle the cargo. In the case of fragile or breakable goods the packaging often notifies which way up they should be loaded. It is logical that when transporting goods the volume and weight of the shipment should be kept to a minimum. However, the packaging must be strong enough to prevent the goods being damaged. It is also wise to look at the type of packaging, and whether it will remain in a good condition in its country of destination. For example, in a humid climate the stackable properties and strength of the cardboard are reduced. When importing products into Europe you must bear in mind that in some countries a packaging tax is levied. Importers must also pay tax on the packaging of imported goods if they remove the packaging. Packed goods being exported are free of packaging tax. In case of private label goods the producer of the goods has to pay the packaging tax. Germany requires recyclable packaging and in some countries the use of straw and hay as a filling is forbidden. More and more countries require decontamination certificates for wooden crates.

There are two types of packaging that require further explanation:

1 container
2 pallet

Ad 1 Container

These are mainly used for transport by water. A container is a metal box for the transport of goods, as shown in the photograph.

Containers have various standard measurements, the most common types being:

- 40 ft container (about 12 × 2.4 × 2.6 metres)
- 20 ft container (about 6 × 2.4 × 2.6 metres)

The 20 ft container is used frequently. The great advantage of containers is that they make small consignments quite cheap to transport . Recently, however, there has been a lot of publicity about gasses and vapours found in containers. Sea containers are often treated with pesticides in their country of origin in order to kill harmful insects and larvae. Cargoes from Asia and Africa that are carried by ship are often fumigated. This applies to containers carrying food, clothing, shoes, toys and furniture, as well as goods packed in wooden crates.

Ad 2 Pallet
A pallet is a platform that can be moved by a conveyance such as a truck, fork-lift or crane.
There are several sizes of pallet, but frequently the following are used:

- euro pallet (80 × 120 cm) (in united kingdom is 100 x 120cm common)
- wholesaler pallet (80 × 100 cm)

A euro pallet is shown in the picture below.

Transhipment and storage
During the transport process, goods may be stored several times as they wait to be transferred from one type of transport to another, from lorry to train or from boat to train. This is called transhipment. It is possible, for example, that goods cannot be transported onwards immediately when a ship enters into the port, so they must be temporarily stored in a storehouse.

Reconditioning of goods
Reconditioning literally means 'to restore to good condition'. Goods can be damaged during transport. A good example is textiles becoming crinked in transit. This means that it might be necessary to make the goods shop ready again.

Information processing
Information processing is the handling of the documentation required to organise transport. International transport without transport documents is impossible. Every mode of transport requires a different type of document. Each type of transport document has to conform to certain requirements. We shall go into this in more detail in section 10.3.

10.3 Modes of transport

The mode of transport chosen depends on a number of aspects that have been discussed in section 10.2. In this section we discuss the differences between the various modes of transport and look at the various transport documents required.

Before we discuss the various modes of transport we will first look again at the basis for calculating freight rates (table 10.2). Have done so could be made already a first choice.

TABLE 10.2 Calculation of a freight rate based on various modes of transport

	Weight	**Volume**	**Transport**	**Kilometre**	**Package**
Mode of Transport	Road, rail, water and air	Road, rail, water and air	Water	Road	Road
Details	per kilogram, per 10 kilogram to 100 kilogram in a scale: per 100 - 1000 kg For instance groupage and big shipments	per occupied room aboard a ship or aircraft: per m3 or per 40 cubic feet (1 foot = 30,48 cm)	per container for instance does one talk of a 'lump sum' or a fixed sum per full 20 ft or 40 ft container	the distance determines for instance of a rush delivery via courier service	per package if more than one destination is to be called at

Road transport

Heavy or large-volume goods are generally transported by ship. Light or compact goods are generally transported via rail or road. In the majority of countries road transport is cheaper than rail transport. This depends on the price of fuel and, for instance, the tolls levied on motorways. It should be mentioned that rail transport is much more environmentally friendly because of the lower CO_2 emissions.

Table 10.3 gives an overview of the advantages and disadvantages of each mode of transport

TABLE 10.3 Advantages and disadvantages per mode of transport

Transport/ Quality	**Road**	**Rail**	**Air**	**Water**	**Pipeline**
Speed	+	-	++	-	--
Cost	0	+	--	++	+
Frequency	+	-	0	-	++
Accessibility	++	+	-	-	-
Risk of damage	0	-	0	0	++
Planning	0	0	0	0	++
Utility	+	+	0	++	--

Source: Grit & De Geus, 2006

The various modes of transport are discussed more in detail in the following subsection.

10.3.1 Road transport

Road transport is used to transport goods if the distance is not too large: for example, products made in Europe. When using road transport, the customer can have his goods brought right to his doorstep.
Two concepts are used in road transport:

- **FTL (full truck load)**. This abbreviation stands for a complete truck load,

often called a complete load. The consignor of a complete load sends one complete truck to one consignee.
- **LTL (less than full truck load)**. These letters indicate an incomplete truck load. The truck contains goods for various consignees. Transport usually takes longer.

Documents required for road transport

CMR

During commercial domestic road transport the carrier must use an authorised bill of lading. The document required for international road transport is the international bill of lading, known as the CMR (Convention Relative au Contrat de Transport International de Marchandises par Route) document. The CMR document is also valid for domestic transport if this is part of the international transport. When the carrier signs a CMR document it takes on temporary responsibility for the goods and can be held liable in the event of damage. When accepting the goods the consignee must sign the carrier's copy.
The CMR document is non-negotiable, that is to say that the transfer of the goods takes place by actual delivery of the goods and not via the transfer of the bill of lading. A example of the document can be found on the website.

- www.economist.com

Logistics in Africa

Aside from a few niche industries such as cut flowers, which are air-freighted from Kenya and Ethiopia to auctions in the Netherlands, African trade has not changed much since the end of the colonial era. Unprocessed raw materials go out; finished goods come in. The trade imbalance is vividly illustrated by the ships sent from Asia to pick up empty containers left at African ports. Within Africa, moreover, it is difficult and costly to move goods. The continent has only a few broken-down railways. It has nothing resembling a transcontinental motorway. Even the British colonial dream of a road connecting Cape Town with Cairo failed.
Today, getting a container to the heart of Africa – from Douala in Cameroon to Bangassou in the Central African Republic, say – still means a wait of up to three weeks at the port on arrival; roadblocks, bribes, pot-holes and mud-drifts on the road along the way; malarial fevers, prostitutes and monkey-meat stews in the lorry cabin; hyenas and soldiers on the road at night. The costs of fuel and repairs make even the few arterial routes (beyond southern Africa) uneconomic. A study by America's trade department found that it cost more to ship a ton of wheat from Mombasa in Kenya to Kampala in Uganda than it did to ship it from Chicago to Mombasa.

But several companies are trying to make the best of Africa's creaking infrastructure to construct transcontinental logistics networks. Among them are DHL, Maersk, Dubai World and Chinese companies supplying oil and mining projects in Angola and the Democratic Republic of Congo (DRC). The clear leader so far is Bolloré Africa Logistics, a division of Bolloré, a French industrial conglomerate.

13 January 2011

10.3.2 Rail transport

Rail transport is less flexible than road transport. Door-to-door service can be provided only if a combination of modes of transport (multimodal transport, see 10.3.6) is on offer. Rail transport is used mainly for bulk freight, goods not packed individually, and containers. Rail transport is economic only if the distances covered are large. An example of a big project in this field is the Channel Tunnel that connects mainland Europe with Britain.

Multimodal transport

Documents required for rail transport

The transport document required for international rail transport is the international rail bill of lading, known as the CIM (Convention Internationale concernant le Transport des Marchandises par Chemin de Fer) document. A CIM document is associated with an international treaty, called COTIF, and applies to all railways that have become a party to the treaty. In principle they are bound to transport all types of goods unless the goods have extreme measurements, are very heavy or are dangerous goods not packed according to the regulations. An example of this document can be found on the website.

CIM

10.3.3 Air transport

Air transport has a lot of advantages and the volume is rising. The most important advantage is speed. The cost of this type of transport is often the biggest impediment to its use. High-quality goods and perishable or seasonal goods are mostly transported by air. Air transport is also used if products are not ready in time for water transport.

Documents required for air transport

Airway bill

The transport document required for air transport is the airway bill (AWB) or air freight bill of lading. This is non-negotiable. The carrier and the consignee must both sign the AWB. The AWB is to accompany the goods and is also the receipt and insurance receipt as well as the proof of the transport agreement. A copy of the document can be found on the website.

10.3.4 Water transport

Water transport

Water transport can be divided into inland navigation and maritime transport. Inland navigation means that goods are transported via rivers, canals and lakes, while in maritime transport goods are transported via oceans and seas.
Both can transport bulk goods and mixed cargo, but the quantities differ. Ships used for maritime transport are often bigger, and can ship bigger quantities at the same time. In terms of volume, water transport is the biggest shipper of goods.

Two terms are used in this mode of transport:

- FCL (full container load). This means that the whole container is meant for one consignee. Because some companies have made agreements with customs (see subparagraph 10.6.3) these containers can be shipped to the customer with seals intact and customs will carry out clearance later on. It saves time.
- LCL (less than full container load). This means that the container contains shipments for various consignees. Generally customs clearance takes quite a long time because the container must first be unloaded and only then can the goods be sent to the consignees.

Documents required for water transport

Bill of lading

The transport document required for transport by water is the bill of lading (B/L) or seawaybill. The bill of lading:

1 Is the shipping company's proof that the goods have been received for transport to their destination.
2 It represents the goods. It is transferable: transferring the B/L to another person means making this person the owner of the goods. So like a cheque it may be endorsed affected ownership of the goods actually being carried.
3 It is receipt signed by the carrier confirming whether goods matching the contract description have been received in good condition.

Reference is sometimes made to a 'dirty/foul bill of lading'. This means that upon delivery of the goods it turns out that the goods do not correspond with what has been agreed to in the B/L. The carrier must record this on the B/L. Prior to shipment, any such defects must be put right. The B/L will be described as 'clean' if the goods have been received on board in apparent good condition. A sample B/L can be found on the website.

SCHOENVISIE, FEBRUARY 2009 (EDITED)

Original

Last summer, one of our customers had two orders for Chinese products. The first order was shipped in June, but for some unaccountable reason it left without a B/L. At the request of the customer the second order was shipped with another of his orders made in another factory with which we do not do business. For this order a B/L was written, but unfortunately with the wrong data, which our manufacturer had erroneously passed on to the carrier: the name of the ship relating to Order 2 was written on the B/L but the quantity related to Order 1. B/L can only be written out once so a revised version is impossible. The goods were shipped but with the wrong document.

After many negotiations, the goods were finally released by customs, and we were able to deliver them to the customer. Unfortunately, the customer refused to pay without the original B/L. We are still running round in circles trying to find a solution to this dilemma, so that the customer will pay his bill, but this 'original' story does not yet have a happy ending.

10.3.5 Pipeline transport

Pipeline transport

Pipeline transport is transport via pipes that are above, on or under the ground or on the seabed. Liquids, gasses and solids can be transported by pipeline. Pipelines are used all over the world to transport crude oil and liquid gas.

Documents required for pipeline transport

No specific document is needed for this mode of transport. Customs do require special permission to deliver these products.

10.3.6 Multimodal transport

Thinking in terms of separate modes of transport is gradually becoming a thing of the past. These days, goods must be brought from A to B quickly, safely and as cheaply as possible. Multimodal transport combines and integrates various modes of transport in order to offer the customer a user-friendly, door-to-door service. Containers are often used, but also roll-on and roll-off systems. The Channel Tunnel is a good example, where lorries drive onto and off the train.

Documents required for multimodal transport

Combined bill of lading

The transport document used for multimodal transport is a combined bill of lading. This document covers the cargo before, during and after transport. An example of the document can be found on the website.

10.4 International transport law

Which law applies if, for instance, a consignment of goods is sold by a Brazilian company to a German buyer and, on arrival, it turns out that they cannot be sold because of water damage. If the Brazilian company has

taken out solid transport insurance, it can try to recover damages from the shipping company.
A number of international treaties with uniform rules cover the liability of the carrier. Each treaty covers one specific mode of transport:

- Ship (B/L transport): The Hague Visby Rules (Rotterdam Rules from 2011)
- Airplane: Warsaw Convention
- Truck: CMR (Convention on the Contract for the International Carriage of Goods by Road)
- Train: CIM (Convention Internationale concernant le Transport de Marchandises par Chemin de Fer).

The Rotterdam Rules and the CMR differ from the other treaties mentioned. No complaint can be lodged or an appeal made against these treaties. In the rules on the liability of the carrier the basic assumption is made that the carrier is responsible for the damage to the goods before and/or during transport, independent of the question whether the carrier can be blamed for the said damage. No matter the circumstances, the carrier must guarantee that the goods reach their destination undamaged (results obligation). The carrier's results obligation means that he is liable prior to and during the transfer of the goods: including the transport vehicle he uses during the transportation and for the people who assist him.

Rotterdam Rules
In 2011, a new UN treaty came into force on sea transport: the Rotterdam Rules. The treaty contains modern, clear rules on the transport of goods by water, making world trade more efficient.

The Rotterdam Rules give international transport law a certain amount of security. They apply to door-to-door transport. The same law applies to road transport, rail transport and transport by water. This system has advantages for container transport. The existing treaties on sea transport do not take account of this modern mode of transport. The Hamburg Rules (1978) only apply to port-to-port transport. The Hague Visby Rules (1968) apply

only from the moment the hoist is attached to the cargo during loading to the moment the hoist is removed when the goods are unloaded.
The Rotterdam Rules increase the carrier's liability. The duty of the carrier to provide a seaworthy ship will now apply to the complete trip instead of only at the beginning of the voyage. The amount of money to which the carrier can restrict his liability has been increased. The Rotterdam Rules have two other important advantages:

- Electronic transport documents are now allowed. This will make the transfer of the transported goods much quicker and the transaction costs will decrease.
- There are fewer possibilities for defence, so the number of court cases will no doubt fall. Under the Rotterdam Rules, the carrier is also held liable for damage resulting from a navigation error.

10.5 IT and logistics

Like every department of a company, the logistics department uses IT. IT is used to help trace goods (tracing) and to recall them if something goes wrong (tracking). Another important reason for IT is time; in logistics, as in other areas, time is money. Various new IT systems are being developed, including supermarket-style barcoding. These new IT systems are discussed in the following subsections.

Tracing
Tracking

10.5.1 ERP

ERP stands for Enterprise Resource Planning. ERP is software that integrates information from several departments, such as finance, sales, purchasing and distribution, into an ERP system forming one single database. The advantage is that all corporate processes are connected and the information is available to all users. Changes need only be entered into the ERP system and they can be seen in all departments (where previously customer data needed to be changed in both sales and finance departments, for example). The introduction of ERP is very expensive. The software often has to be custom made. Examples for ERP systems for Small and Medium-Size Enterprises (SMEs) include Syntri, Exact and SAP with Business One.

10.5.2 RFID

RFID is the abbreviation of radio frequency identification – identification using radio waves. RFID uses radio signals to locate and identify merchandise, batched products or transportation assets fitted with special electronic tags. This is due to the RFID 'tags', also known as the smartlabel or intelligent tags.

The tags enable the automatic track-and-trace of merchandise/assets through out the supply chain.

www.ft.com

Does IT work? Leaner use of logistics keeps supplies moving

The past few years have brought strong increases in revenue for the transport and logistics sector; it has enjoyed double-digit growth for most of this decade, according to PwC, the professional services firm. The current break in growth, as the economic downturn hits, may well prove temporary, but in the meantime, logistics and distribution managers – and the third-party logistics companies that carry an increasing percentage of the world's goods – face pressures to contain costs and drive efficiencies throughout the supply chain. At the same time, companies, especially those in retail, want to reduce their stock holdings. But they also want to avoid shortages and disappointed customers.

Now, though, supply chain risk is a foremost concern among logistics managers. Companies are increasingly worried that their suppliers might fail, or even if they do not, that they will be unable to ship their products. Non-economic factors, from piracy to the threat of swine flu, are also forcing companies to look again at their logistics planning.

Other, longer-term investments in logistics technologies are being put on hold, however. Spending on tools such as radio frequency identification (RFID), or for larger items, GPS-based tagging, has dropped back.

It is not just the economy that has affected spending on such systems. RFID, in particular, attracted a lot of attention at the beginning of the decade, with large retail groups such as Marks and Spencer and Wal-Mart using the technology to track goods in their warehouses and stores.

However, the cost of the chips, their reliability and the difficulties companies faced dealing with the vast amounts of data created by RFID have forced them to review their plans.

13 January 2011

One of the best-known RFID applications is the new passport. All European passports and identity papers issued since 26 August 2006 have an RFID tag containing all personal data shown on the passport. The invisible RFID tag even contains the passport photo.

10.5.3 EDI

EDI is the abbreviation for Electronic Data Interchange: the electronic exchange of messages. This technique enables streams of information to be sent between computer systems of various parties involved in a business transaction, such as the supplier, the buyer and even the bank, the customs authorities and the insurance company (see figure 10.5). The advantages are speed and accuracy. Companies can respond to fickle consumer behaviour, for example, in the supermarket sector. Repeat orders can easily be placed because suppliers also receive the sales figures. However, in the field of international business the integration of EDI is slow, mainly because legal aspects pertaining evidence and fraud need to be solved. Furthermore, suppliers and buyers are apprehensive as to what the receiving party of the data may do with them.

FIGURE 10.5 Exchange of data between companies

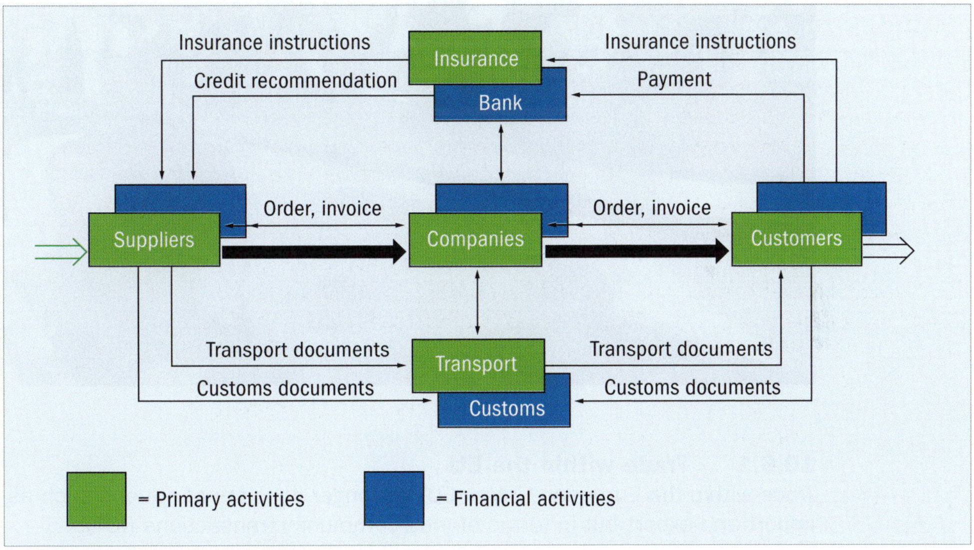

Source: Visser & Van Goor, 2009

10.6 Customs

As mentioned in section 10.1, Europe is famous for distribution and transport. Every day, millions of tons of goods enter and leave the region: by road, sea and air. It is obvious that these movements of goods must be checked. This is the customs authority's field of activity. Customs are part of the tax authorities. Customs have three tasks:

1 To stop certain types of goods at the frontier, such as weapons and counterfeit goods, and goods being exported into countries where international sanctions apply.

10

2 To enforce legal and general rules and regulations; goods cannot enter and remain in the European Union without import duties being paid. Yet such goods can be transported within the European Union and also processed and stored (to be exported again at a later stage). The rules that apply state that Customs must ensure that duties are paid. Sometimes when goods are exported, customs duties are refunded. Customs check whether the goods really have been exported to prevent a tax refund when not applicable.
3 To impose and collect taxes: include import duties, excise tax, value added tax, and the tax on cars and motorcycles. Customs calculate how much tax is to be paid (levied) and make sure that this tax is actually paid (collection).

Customs must apply political, administrative and legal rules. Some are decided on a European level and partly on a national level. In the following sections the practical aspects of dealing with customs is discussed. In particular, the flow of documents is very important.

10.6.1 Trade within the EU

Trade within the European Union (EU) no longer consists of notions such as import and export but in terms of intra-community transactions (ICT):
- Imports from another EU country are intra-community acquisitions (ICA).
- Exports to another EU country are intra-community deliveries (ICD).

Intra-community transaction

Intra-community transactions do not require customs documents; after all, there is free movement of goods and services within the EU.
The disadvantage of ICT is that companies must comply with all sorts of administrative obligations. The principal rule of the VAT system is that deliveries from one business to another are taxed in the country where the transport of the goods ends, or in the country where the buyer lives. It is known as the destination principle. This means that goods are to be delivered at a 0% rate while the buyer in the destination country must declare VAT according to the rates and rules that apply in the country concerned. In accordance with the new VAT system, the following administrative obligations apply:

Destination principle

- Invoice requirement. The invoice must state the VAT identification number of the company and the VAT number of the supplier(s). Should the goods be supplied within the EU, the supplier must check whether the VAT number of the foreign buyer is correct. This can be done via the website : http://ec.europa.eu/taxation_customs/vies/
- VAT declaration. The VAT declaration must be made in the country in which the buyer lives depending on the volume you bought. If you have sold goods, no VAT has to be paid.
- Intra community registration. The owner of a company is required to keep a record of all temporary transfers (such as the transfer of goods to another EU country).
- Registration for Intrastat statistics. Companies must periodically format and submit Intrastat declarations. The Intrastat system is a system that is used to record Eurostat statistical information concerning the trading of goods between the Member States of the European Union.

The tax office requires proof of a delivery within the EU. This can be:
- purchase order
- order confirmation
- delivery order contract
- invoice
- transport document
- freight bill (of the carrier)
- receipt

Origin principle

If a business delivers goods to consumers who do not have VAT identification numbers, the EU origin principle applies; the delivery is subject to tax in the country where the purchase takes place. VAT is to be calculated when the goods are sold. It makes no difference whether the goods are sold to a private individual within a country or abroad. In both cases VAT has to be levied based on the country of production origin.

10.6.2 Trade outside the EU

Trade outside the EU does involve export and import. Certain rules and regulations also apply to this type of trade.

Export

When you export goods to countries outside the EU, you have to deal with both tax authorities and customs authorities. In many cases you can invoice the export goods to businesses at 0% VAT. As an exporter, you are expected to provide proof to the tax authorities on request. These documents to proof export outside the EU can be:
- copies of an invoice made out to the foreign customer
- evidence of payment made from abroad
- copies of transport documents
- a signed waybill
- invoices from carriers
- an EU export document
- an import declaration made abroad
- correspondence with foreign customers
- internal freight documents (logbook)

Depending on the INCO terms, the duty (for export), levies and taxes are for

the account of the exporting company. The amount of import duty payable in countries outside the EU can be found on the website
http://mkaccdb.eu.int
based on the Combined Nomenclature (see chapter 2). An example can be seen in the following figure.

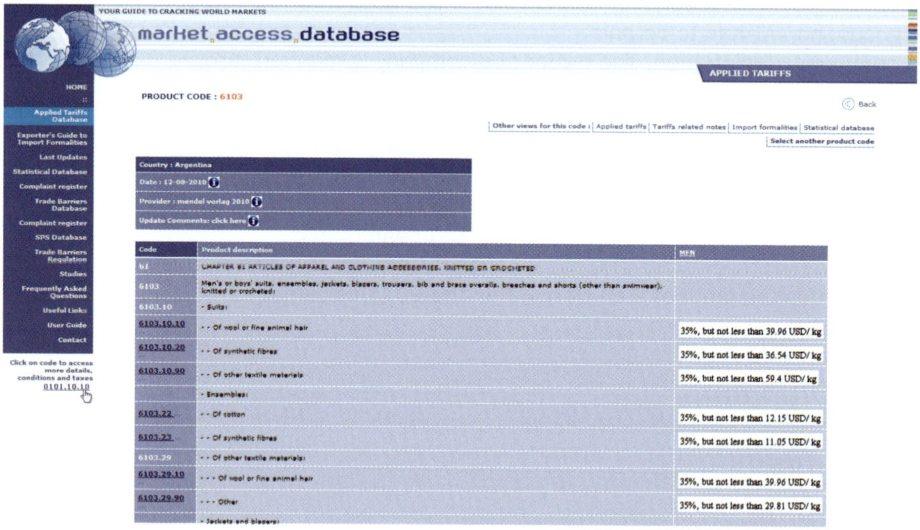

Code	Product description	MFN
61	CHAPTER 61 ARTICLES OF APPAREL AND CLOTHING ACCESSORIES, KNITTED OR CROCHETED	
6103	Men's or boys' suits, ensembles, jackets, blazers, trousers, bib and brace overalls, breeches and shorts (other than swimwear), knitted or crocheted:	
6103.10	- Suits:	
6103.10.10	- - Of wool or fine animal hair	35%, but not less than 39.96 USD/ kg
6103.10.20	- - Of synthetic fibres	35%, but not less than 36.54 USD/ kg
6103.10.90	- - Of other textile materials	35%, but not less than 59.4 USD/ kg
	- Ensembles:	
6103.22	- - Of cotton	35%, but not less than 12.15 USD/ kg
6103.23	- - Of synthetic fibres	35%, but not less than 11.05 USD/ kg
6103.29	- - Of other textile materials:	
6103.29.10	- - - Of wool or fine animal hair	35%, but not less than 39.96 USD/ kg
6103.29.90	- - - Other	35%, but not less than 29.81 USD/ kg
	- Jackets and blazers:	

Source : http://mkaccdb.eu.int/

Import
If goods are imported from outside the EU to an EU member state, the customs authorities must approve them before they can be put into circulation. This means that:

- Import declaration must be submitted to Customs.
- Import duty or other taxes must be paid.

10

● www.telegraaf.nl

iPad target for customs at Schiphol

AMSTERDAM – For some time to come customs officials at Schiphol airport are going to be keeping an especially close eye on passengers flying in from the United States. People who have bought one or more iPads there may have to pay VAT on the gadgets.

Purchases to a value of $567 may be imported tax fee, so a 16GB iPad can cross the border without problems. The 32GB and 64GB versions of the iPad, however, cost $599 and $699 respectively, so 19% VAT is applicable. Customs do not want to talk about a hunt on the iPad; "We work risk based. Now that the iPad has been put on the market in America, we are keeping an even closer eye on things. But we also do that when the dollar is very low. We also look at flights from Asia to check for counterfeit goods," says a spokesperson.

15 April 2010

An import declaration can be made with the "Single Administrative Document" (an example can be found on the website) or via an electronic declaration. Customs use the data to calculate taxes and duty, and also to decide whether other laws or regulations apply. The amount of import dues depends on the Combined Nomenclature and the country of origin of the goods. Import duties are the same throughout the EU.

Furthermore, VAT must be declared and paid to the tax office of the EU country into which the goods were imported. Customs first calculate the import duties on the basis of the customs value (purchase price + freight costs + insurance premium up to the place where the goods entered the EU), known as the CIF price. After that, they calculate the VAT. Thus VAT is always the last levy, raised on the total value of the shipment. The tariffs on imports from countries outside the EU can be found on http://ec.europa.eu/taxation_customs/dds2/taric/taric_consultation.jsp?Lang=en&Taric=&QuotaAuthorities=false&EndPub=&MeasText=&Area=&Regulation=&LangDescr=&MeasType=&SimDate=20110419&StartPub=&OrderNum=&GoodsText=&ContextPath=&redirectionDate=20110419&Level=&Expand=false.

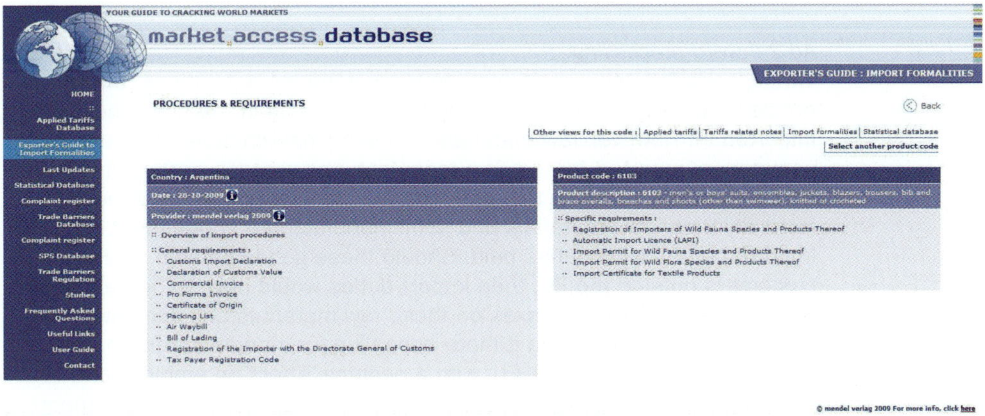

10

European Binding Tariff Information

It is possible to ask for European Binding Tariff Information (EBTI) before goods are brought into free circulation. Using this information you can work out in advance how much duty needs to be paid. To obtain this information, one must send a sample and description of the goods, or a photograph, to customs and ask them to determine the CN code. The customs authorities of the other member states are bound to observe this division.

10.6.3 Customs regulations

Bonded goods

Free circulation goods

When goods are brought into the EU, they are called bonded goods. In order to bring the goods into free circulation and change their status from bonded goods to free circulation goods, the applicable duties must be paid and the commercial policy measures will have to be applied.

Besides import, export and re-export other things are of importance in international trade in goods. When goods enter the EU, it is not always known what the final destination of the goods will be. There are regulations under customs that goods can be stored. There are also rules that make it possible to treat or process bonded goods in and outside the EU. The customs rules preclude the payment of import duties or provide for a reduction on import duties.

Various customs regulations exist. Those to be discussed in this section are:
1 customs warehousing
2 inward processing
3 outward processing
4 temporary importation

Ad 1 Customs warehousing
Customs warehousing allows the owner to hold imported non-EU goods in the EU and choose when he pays the duties or re-export the goods. This is to avoid double taxation.

The owner of the custom warehouse is responsible for any irregularities of the goods held under a bonded warehouse ruling. A good example of the use of customs bonded warehousing is foreign companies like Nike and Harley-Davidson, which have their distribution centres in the Netherlands. From here they can send goods to customers all over the world.

Ad 2 Inward processing
When goods fall under customs bonded warehouse regulations, they may not be processed normally. The goods must remain in the state they were imported in. However, raw materials and semi-manufactured items are sometimes imported for use in a manufacturing process or they undergo a certain treatment (finish) that changes the composition of the goods. Normally these raw materials and semi-manufactured goods must be imported and import duties paid. Should these goods be sold again to customers outside the EU, then import duties would have to be paid again. However, if the EU levied taxes on these raw materials and semi-manufactured goods, it would make it more appealing for manufacturers to finish these goods outside of the EU, with a negative effect on employment. Therefore products imported and then processed are exempt from import duties and anti-dumping levies. The proviso is that the final product is exported again. This is known as inward processing. Figure 10.6 is a schematic diagram mapping out what it involves.

FIGURE 10.6 Schematic diagram of inward processing

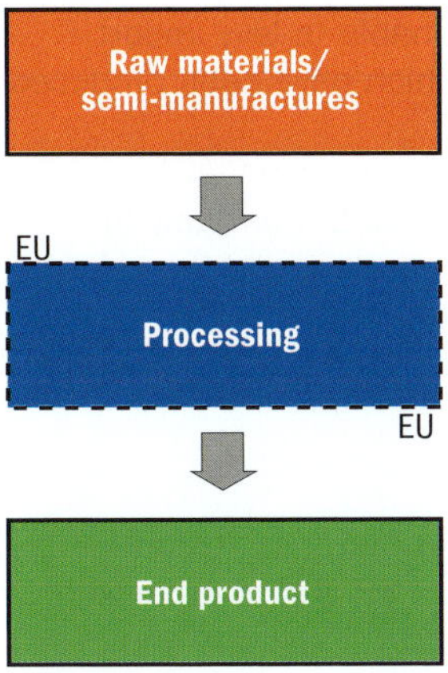

An example of inward processing is the manufacture of shoes in Europe containing imported leather from China, which are subsequently exported for sale in America. Should the export conditions attached to the final product not be met – that is they are not exported from the EU, but instead are distributed inside the EU – then import duties must be paid for the imported raw materials or semi-manufactured goods. For inward processing relief you need a customs permit. Such a permit is issued only if the raw materials or semi-manufactured goods concerned cannot be acquired in the EU, or cannot be acquired of the same quality or at the same price. The petitioner must prove this when applying for a permit (tender, trade statistics).

Ad 3 Outward processing
Outward processing (figure 10.7) is the mirror image of inward processing. Outward processing relief makes it possible to export goods temporarily for them to be processed, adapted or repaired outside the EU. The products

FIGURE 10.7 Schematic description of outward processing

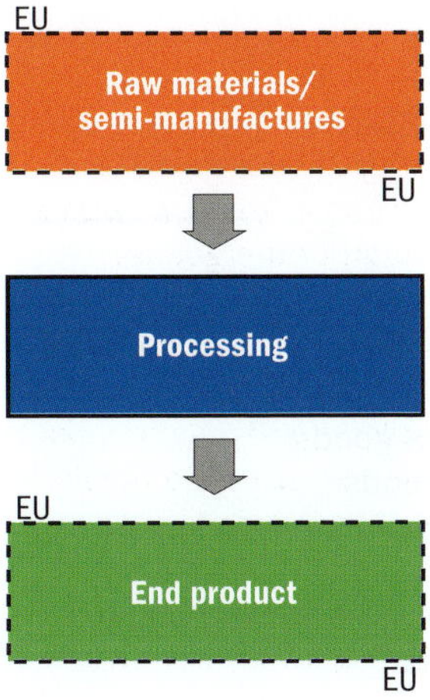

made of these EU raw materials or semi-manufactured goods can then be re-imported into the EU with partial or total exemption of import duties. The idea behind the exemption is that it would unreasonable to levy import duties on goods imported from non-EU countries which have been produced from previously exported EU goods.

An example of passive improvement is the export of cloth from Italy to Pakistan to make blouses. The blouses are then imported, and the value of part of the goods that has temporarily been exported from the EU, i.e. the cloth, is exempted from import taxes. Import duties must be paid on the remaining value of the blouses.

Ad 4 Temporary importation
Temporary importation means that goods may be used in the EU-community without payment of duty or VAT under certain conditions and re-exported afterwards in the same state as they were in at import. The condition of the temporarily imported goods should stay and remain in the condition in which they were imported. Goods that come under these regulations include those shown at exhibitions, and the containers in which the goods are transported.

10.6.4 Customs documents

Every transaction to do with international trade involves customs and their rules and regulations apply. Despite the absence of frontiers within the EU, a number of documents are always required for import as well as export. The following screenprint gives an example of the documents needed for export to other countries.

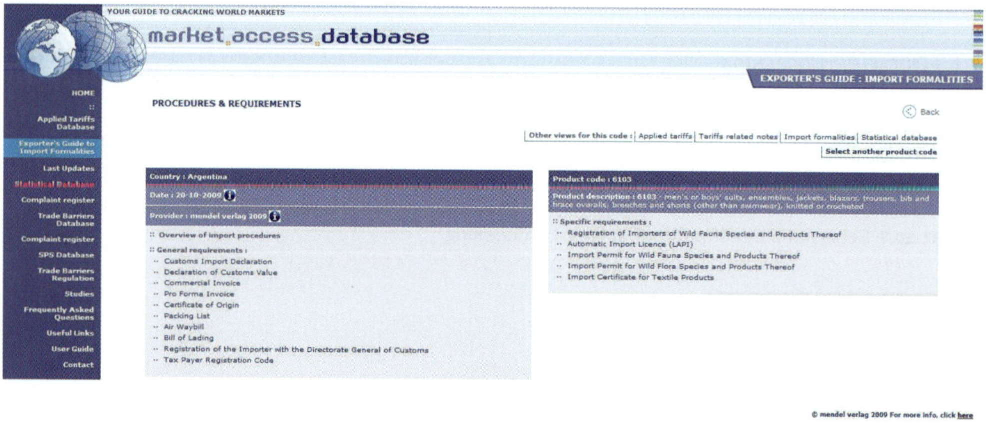

These documents can be divided into various categories, all with their own identification mark:

1 transport documents: relating to the transport of goods
2 documents of origin: showing the origin of the goods
3 permits: granting official permission from the government to import or export
4 administrative documents: required by administrative bodies for the recording of such things as prices and quantities
5 other documents: for various purposes

Transport documents

The first four of these have already been discussed in section 10.3. They are:

- CMR
- CIM
- bill of lading
- airway bill
- TIR carnet

The final document, the TIR carnet, is discussed below.

TIR carnet

Sometimes an extra document is needed for transport outside the EU. This is the TIR (Transports Internationaux Routiers) carnet. This document is needed to transport goods through various countries or when goods transported to the EU pass through the territory of non-EU countries. Having a TIR carnet, trucks need not be cleared through customs at each frontier. Transit is much faster. The TIR system not only covers customs transit by road, but can be combined with other modes of transport (for example, rail, inland waterway and even maritime transport), as long as at least one part of the total transport distance is covered by road.
TIR carnets are issued by a transport organisation. An example can be found on the website.

Documents of origin

A document of origin is written proof of the origin of goods and is required for goods originating from certain countries. The documents are mandatory for importers from certain countries and sometimes for exporters to the countries. The following documents are now discussed.

- certificate of origin
- EUR-1
- EUR-MED
- form A certificate of origin

An example of these documents can be found on the website.

Certificate of origin

This document states from what country the shipped goods originate, but "originate" in a certificate of origin does not refer to the country the goods are shipped from, but to the country where the goods are actually made. This document is needed to export to certain countries when, because of reason of trade policy, it has been decided to protect their own industry or agriculture. It is also required for countries that are being boycotted. This document is not needed within the EU.

EUR-1

An EUR-1 certificate is a type of certificate of origin used to obtain a reduction of or an exemption from import duties. The certificate is meant to show the origin of goods when importing from certain countries. The European Union has drawn up the list of countries for which this hold good. Companies importing low-value shipments are allowed to present a so-called declaration of origin provided on the invoice by the manufacturer of the goods.

EUR-MED
The EUR-MED is a variant of EUR-1 valid for the countries that signed the Pan-Euro-Mediterranean agreement. The agreement makes it possible to include raw materials from all partner countries in the regulation of origin (accumulation). The list of countries include the EU countries, Norway, Iceland, Faroe Islands, Liechtenstein, Switzerland, Morocco, Tunisia, Algeria, Egypt, Jordan, Lebanon, Syria, Israel, the West Bank and Gaza strip and Turkey.

Form A
This certificate is used to apply for lower import tariffs in accordance with to the preferential tariff measures (see chapter 2). A lower tariff is applied if the products originate from countries with which the EU has signed trade agreements. All certificates of origin are issued in the country of origin by an authority such as the chamber of commerce, consulate or notary.

Permits
In certain cases, an export or import license must be obtained from customs. Some goods may not be exported or imported at all or may be exported or imported only in small quantities. Other goods are permitted only if certain (strict) conditions are met. The relevant permits must often accompany the shipment.

Import license
This permit is required for the import of certain products. An import license can be obtained from your local customs organisation. An import permit is issued only if an export permit has been issued by a qualified body in the exporting country. Should a company import the same category of goods several times a year, it can obtain an import permit valid for one year. The imported amounts are deducted each time from the total amount authorised.

Export license
When goods are exported, an export license is sometimes required from customs. This applies to goods of which only a small amount may be exported, such as weapons.

Commercial documents
Apart from documents checked by customs, trade documents are needed, same as for domestic shipments, such as:
- invoice
- packing list
- pro-forma invoice
- order confirmation
- quotation
- clean report of findings (see chapter 9)
- insurance certificate

Example of an invoice

LEEFLANG & ZN. BV milling cutters

Westzijde 318 *tel.: +31-75-6814818*
1506 GJ ZAANDAM, the Netherlands *fax: +31-75-6162882*

Chamber of Commerce Amsterdam registration no: 123457
VAT--number: NL003567823B01

INVOICE FOR : Khatiam ltd.
FAKTUUR VOOR : mr. Samak Na Ayutthaya M.R.
106 Wireless Rd.
Bangkok 10330
Thailand

Documentary credit nr. ABC01234

Goods description:

Marks and no's Merken en nrs.	Description Omschrijving	Number Aantal	Unit price Stuksprijs	Total amount Totaalbedrag
Leeflang de Luxe 1-200	Milling cutters	2,000	USD 95.00	USD 190,000
Leeflang Standard 201-400	Milling cutters	2,000	USD 75.00	USD 150,000
Grand total:		4,000		USD 340,000

(In writing: Fourthousand milling cutters, total invoice amount Threehundredandfortythousand US Dollars only).

All as per order no. 567 dated 12.01.2004

Each milling cutter packed in a box and per 10 pieces packed in strong seaworthy (desinfected) wooden cases with waterproof linings as marked above. The total number of 400 wooden cases have been loaded in two 40 ft. sea containers.

Total gross volume of the cases: 120 m³, total gross weight: 12,000 kgs.

Further details as per attached packing list.

Country of origin: The Netherlands
Shipped per container vessel Whale II on 4th February 2004 all as per attached Bill of Lading.
Port of shipment: Rotterdam
Terms of delivery: FOB Rotterdam Incoterms 2000

Conditions of payment: As per above mentioned irrevocable Documentary Credit nr. ABC 01234.

Source: http://www.kvk.nl/Images/factuur_tcm16-125719.pdf

10

Other documents

A few other customs documents are needed or useful in certain circumstances, namely:

- *Single Administrative Document (SAD).* The SAD is a customs declaration in the EU and in Switzerland, Norway and Iceland. The document covers the placement of goods under any customs procedure:
  - import
  - warehouses
  - transit in the EU
  - export
  - inward and outward processing

An example of this document can be found on the website.

- *ATA carnets*. An ATA carnet (Admission Temporaire/Temporary Admission) is an international customs document with which it is easier to temporarily import and export to a number of countries outside the European Union (EU): the United States, Canada, New Zealand, and a number of African and Asian countries. It is used for goods such as exhibition materials, product samples and machinery for one-off jobs. These goods are returned to the EU after a certain amount of time. If you have an ATA carnet you have fewer costs, and procedures are simpler. With an ATA carnet you are entitled to import and export certain goods an unrestricted number of times in one year. It can be used in several countries. An example of this carnet can be found on the website.
- *ATR certificate.* An ATR certificate is a customs document used for trade between EU countries and Turkey. The EU concluded a customs agreement with Turkey so that most goods can be imported in either direction without the payment of import duties. The goods need to originate from the EU or Turkey. The ATR certificate cannot be used for certain types of goods, including most agricultural products and some products made of steel. The point is that in case of these products the origin is important and is required on the EUR-1 certificate. An example of an ATR certificate can be found on the website.

Summary

► Logistics is the term that refers to everything that must take place to bring goods from the factory to the customer. Logistics is part of supply chain management.

► Europe is an important international player in the field of logistics.

► The choice of the transport mode depends on the transport and product characteristics (see figure 10.4), such as speed, cost, volume and value.

► Activities that are part of the transport chain are:
- packaging
- transhipment and storage
- reconditioning
- information processing

► The six different forms of transport are:
- road
- rail
- air
- water
- pipeline
- combination

Each mode of transport has advantages and disadvantages (see table 10.3) and requires specific transport documents.

► Information technology (IT) can facilitate logistics:
- ERP
- RFID
- EDI

► International business within the EU does not require customs documents. Doing business with countries outside the EU does.

► Customs regulations are:
- customs warehousing regulations
- inward processing
- outward processing
- temporary importation

► There are various categories of document:
- transport documents
- documents of origin
- permits
- commercial documents
- other documents

► Transport documents are:
- CMR (road)
- CIM (rail)
- Airway bill (air)
- Bill of lading (water)
- TIR carnet

► Documents of origin are written proof that goods come from certain countries. There are four of them:
- certificate of origin
- EUR-1
- EUR-MED
- form A certificate of origin

► Certain goods require permits:
- import license
- export license

► Administrative documents, also known as trading documents:
- invoice
- packing list
- pro-forma invoice
- order confirmation
- offer
- clean report of findings
- insurance certificate

► Other documents are:
- SAD document
- ATA carnet
- ATR certificate

Questions and Assignments

Questions on the opening case

10.1 What mode of transport will Kilfrost choose for the de-icing liquid? Motivate your answer.

10.2 What kind of transport documents are needed to transport the liquid?

BUITENLANDSE MARKTEN, JULY 2010

'One customs office? Not in Moldavia'

Mike van Kampen, owner of Fresco Meubel, had never heard of the country. For the last three years his company has not only been settled there, but he has also lived there: Moldavia.

"In Holland my biggest problem was finding young skilled cabinet makers," says the 36-year-old businessman. "My employees were all about 55 years old and many of them were going to retire pretty soon. It was time for Fresco Meubel to move. I soon started to think about Eastern Europe, because there, good cabinet makers were still in good supply. That is how, three years ago, I came to Chisinau, the capital of Moldavia, the poorest country in Europe. The average monthly wage is about 100 Euros."

"Here the biggest obstacle is the bureaucracy"

"It took a lot of perseverance to get all the necessary permits. Permission has to be obtained to import each piece of furniture. And for each small change you had to get a separate contract. Thankfully, we were able to recruit local people to sort out these matters for us. Via a friend of mine, I came into contact with a consultancy whose owner was going to move to Moscow. After a little persistence and by offering them good prospects and a good salary, I was able to employ the accounts manager and the manageress of the consultancy. I noticed the big differences in company culture between Holland and this former Soviet republic."

"The final letdown was that we were unable to use materials from Moldavia such as leather, polyether and wood. The quality of these Moldavian materials is unsatisfactory for use in our high-grade furniture. Our wood comes from Russia. It is transported to our factory in Venlo, where they make furniture kits, which are then put together in Moldavia. They are then transported back to Holland, to the customer. These days, as a Dutch furniture maker, you have to either import foreigners to work for you, or move your factory abroad."

10.3 Describe what the situation would be if Fresco made use of outward processing relief. Motivate your answer.

10.4 Find out how much import duty has to be paid for furniture from Moldavia. CN code is 9403 6010.

10.5 Find out which documents are needed to export furniture to Canada. Use the CN code from question 10.4.

Bibliography

Books

(2005) *Starten met internationaal ondernemen, Transport en douane*. Den Haag: Ministerie van Economische Zaken.
(2009) *Haven in cijfers*, Havenbedrijf Rotterdam NV.
(2010) *World Economic Outlook*. Washington, DC: IMF Multimedia Service.
Albaum, G. & Strandskov, J. & Duerr, E. (2002). *International Marketing and Export Management* (4de editie). Essex: Pearson Education Limited.
Bakker, A.C. (2006). *Juridische aspecten van internationale koop* (5de druk). Groningen: Noordhoff Uitgevers.
Ball, D.A., McCulloch, W.H., Frantz, P.L., Geringer, M.J. & Minor, M. (2004). *International Business, the Challenge of Global Competition* (9de editie). New York: Mc Graw Hill.
Cateora, P.R. & Graham, J.L. (2008). *International Marketing* (13de internationale editie). New York: McGraw-Hill Companies.
Caterora, P. & Graham, J. (2008). *International Marketing* (13de druk). New York: McGraw-Hill.
Connerley, M.L. & Pedersen, P.B. (2005). *Leadership in a diverse and multicultural environment: developing awareness, knowledge, and skills*, California: Sage Publications.
Crane, A. & Matten, D. (2007). *Business Ethics* (2de editie). Oxford: Oxford University Press.
Daniels, J.D. & Radebaugh, L.H. (2001). *International Business, Environments and Operations* (9de internationale editie). Upper Saddle River: New Jersey: Prentice Hall.
De Weerd-Nederhof, P., Van Looy, B. & Visscher, K. (2004). *Innovatie(f) organiseren* (1ste druk). Deventer: Kluwer.
Dekker, H.C. & Groot, T (2002). *Management van strategische samenwerking* (1ste druk). Deventer: Kluwer.
Despota, K., Dobson, R. & Zinnbauer, D. (red) (2009) *Global Corruption Report 2009, corruption and the private sector*. Cambridge: Cambridge University Press.
Emden, E.L.A. van (2005). *Bankgarantie* (5de druk). Deventer: Kluwer.
Gonealves, E. & Karkkainen, A. (2010). *Eurostat statistics in focus*. European Union.
Griffin, R.W. & Pustay, M.W. (2002). *International Business, A managerial perspective* (3de internationale editie). Upper Sadlle River: Prentice Hall.
Grit, R. & de Geus, J. (2006). *Management en logistiek*. Groningen/Houten: Wolters-Noordhoff.
Groeneveld, R. (red) (2009). *EVO Logistics Yearbook, 2009 edition*. Utrecht: EVO.
Groot, H.J. de & Stein, P.A. (2002). *Grondtrekken van het Handelsrecht* (9de druk). Deventer: Kluwer.
Hall, S. van (2008). *Contracten in de internationale handel*. Groningen: Noordhoff Uitgevers.
Hill, C.W.L. (2006). *Global Business Today* (4de editie). New York: McGraw-Hill/Irwin.
Hofstede, G. & Hofstede G.J. (2005) *Allemaal andersdenkenden: omgaan met cultuurverschillen* (18de druk). Amsterdam/Antwerpen: Contact.
Hollensen, S. (2007), *Global Marketing* (4de druk). Essex: Pearson Education.
Hollensen, S. (2008). *Essentials of Global Marketing* (1ste druk). Upper Saddle River, NJ Pearson Education Inc./Prentice Hall.

Hollensen, S. (2010). *Internationale marketing*. Essex: Pearson Education.

Hoogenraad, P. & Scholten, H.J. (2004). *Juridische aspecten van de export*. (5de druk). Groningen: Noordhoff Uitgevers.

Jagersma, P.K. & Ebbers, H. (2004). *Internationale Bedrijfskunde, van exporteren naar globaliseren*. Amsterdam: Pearson Education Benelux.

Kauri & Vokakenniscentrum (red.) (2005). *Kompas voor duurzaam internationaal ondernemen*.

Kelly, Ph. (2009). *International Business and Management*. Hampshire: Cengage Learning EMEA.

Keuning, D. & Lange, R. de (2007). *Grondslagen van het management* (4de druk). Deventer: Kluwer.

Kok, A. & Rojo, M.J.B. (2004). *Succesvol internationaal onderhandelen*. Utrecht/Zutphen: Thieme Meulenhoff.

Kok, A. & Rojo, M.J.B. (2005). *Een goed exportplan, Essentials*. Utrecht: Thieme Meulenhoff.

Kotler, P., Keller, K.L., Robben, H. & Guens, M. (2007). *Marketing Management, de essentie (*3de druk), Breukelen: Pearson Education Benelux.

Kotler, P. & Armstrong, G. (2009). *Principes van Marketing* (5de druk). Pearson Education Benelux BV.

Moratis, L. & Veen, M. van der (2006). *Basisboek MVO*. Assen: van Gorcum.

Mulders, M. (2007). *75 Managementmodellen*. Groningen: Wolters-Noordhoff.

Nibe-SVV, (2007). *Verzekeringsleer*. Amsterdam: NIBE SVV.

Nieuwenhuis, M. (2009). *The art of management, deel 2 cultuur en mensen* (7de druk).

Nunez, Ir. C. & Nunez Mahdi, Drs. R. & Popma, Drs. L. (2007) *Interculturele communicatie, Van ontkenning tot wederzijdse integratie*. Assen: Koninklijke Van Gorcum BV.

Palacios, F.M. & Steeman, H. (2001). *Internationale Handel*, EduActief.

Peng, M.W. (2009). *Global Business*. Canada: South-Western Cengage Learning.

Plemp, S.J. (2005). *Verzekeringsrecht naar titel 7.17 BW*, (1ste druk). Groningen: Noordhoff Uitgevers.

Rustenburg, G., Hoften, R. van & Steenbeek, A. (2008). *SalesManagement* (3de druk) Groningen: Noordhoff Uitgevers.

Rustenburg, Gb. (red), (2007). *Strategische en operationele marketingplanning, Kernstof-B (*4de druk). Groningen: Wolters-Noordhoff.

Schermer, K. (2008). *Interculturele samenwerking en communicatie* (1ste druk), Groningen/ Houten: Wolters-Noordhoff.

Schneider, S. C. & Barsoux J.- L. (2003). *Intercultureel Management* (2de editie). Pearson Education Benelux.

Smal, J.C.A. & Tak, A.A.M.M. (2008). *Marketing Kernstof-A (*6de druk). Groningen: Wolters-Noordhoff.

Stokes, D. & Wilson, N. (2010). *Small Business Management and Interpreneurship* (6de druk). Hampshire, Cengage Learning EMEA.

Trompenaars, F. & Hampden-Turner, C. (1998), *Over de grenzen van cultuur en Management* (3de druk). Amsterdam/Antwerpen: Contact.

Trompenaars, Fons & Woolliams, Peter (2005). *Business en cultuur, samenwerken in het tijdperk van globalisering*. Amsterdam/Antwerpen: Business Contact.

Veldman, J. (1998). *Internationale Handel*. Groningen: Noordhoff Uitgevers, Fenedex.

Veldman, J. (2009). *Export Management*. Groningen: Noordhoff Uitgevers.

Visser H.M. & Goor, A.R. van (2009). *Werken met logistiek, op weg naar Supply Chain Management*. Groningen/Houten: Noordhoff Uitgevers.

Vos, B., Dijkstra, G. & Van den Berg, K. (2008). *De meerwaarde van Maatschappelijk Verantwoord Ketenmanagement, van moeten naar willen*. Assen: van Gorcum.

Wall, S. & Rees, B. (2010). *Introduction to International Business* (3de druk). Upper Saddle River, NJ Pearson Education Inc./Prentice Hall.

Zunta (Ed.), *Discover BRIC* (2010). TNS.

Wall, S., Minocha, S. & Rees, Bronwen (2010). International Business (3de editie). Essex: Pearson Education Limited.
Weele, A.J. van (2008). *Inkoop in strategisch perspectief: analyse, planning en praktijk*. Deventer: Kluwer.
Wild, J. & Wild, K. & Han, J.C.Y. (2010). *International Business* (5de druk) Upper Saddle River, NJ Pearson Education Inc.
Wild, J.J., Wild, K.L., Han, Jerry C.Y. (2010). *International Business, the Challenges of Globalization* (5de globale editie). Upper Saddle River, New Jersey: Pearson/Prentice Hall.
Zuurhout, M. & Heijblom, R. (1992). *Misrekeningen in internationale marketing, twintig praktijkgevallen*. Groningen: Wolters-Noordhoff.

Articles

A taste of adventure. *The Economist,* 17-12-1998.
Brett, J. & Behfar, K. & Kern C. (2006) Managing Cultural Teams, *Harvard Business Review*, Nov.
Cadillac opnieuw naar Europa. *de Volkskrant*, 23-2-2010.
Checklist Letters of Credit, Fenedex ABN Amro.
De Exportofferte, Werkboek voor succesvol exporteren, ABN Amro.
Documentair Importkrediet en Importincasso, ABN Amro.
Kuiper, I. (5-2-2010). Habits Indonesië: Ondernemers & kenners over de Indonesische zakencultuur. *Buitenlandse Markten*, februari 2010, 8-9.
Kuiper, Ilse (17-4-2009). Vallen & opstaan: Wie een buitenlandse markt wil veroveren, moet risico's nemen: 'Eén douaneloket? Niet in Moldavië'. *Buitenlandse markten,* mei 2009, 37.
M.O.O.S. Origineel. *Schoenvisie* nr. 2, 2009.
Minimumloon omhoog. *Buitenlandse Markten,* maart/april 2010, 43.
Spreen, R. Nederlands design in Taiwan. *Buitenlandse markten,* juli 2010, 26.
The costs of celebrating. *Financial Times special,* report 3-12-2010, p. 9.
Van Grieken, M. (5-2-2010). Bulgarije distributieland?: 'Meegaan in corruptie is het begin van het einde'. *Buitenlandse Markten*, februari 2010, 32-33.

Picture credits

p. 10: Hollandse Hoogte
p. 12: Photo Amazon: Flickr, By Harlem Photography Inc.
p. 13: ANP
p. 19: Photo spices: Flickr, By Kiren
p. 22: Photo U2: Flickr, By CrossEyedCat
p. 40: The New York Times/Hollandse Hoogte
p. 53: Photo China's bike industry: Flickr, Eneko123
p. 57: Photo equality and empowerment of women, Flickr, United Nations Photo
p. 64: Karen Kasmauski/Corbis
p. 66: Photo Uzbekistan airways, Flickr, by Osdu
p. 75: Tim Graham/Corbis
p. 88: Photo Western brands Bangladesh, Flickr, by Akcurry
p. 96: Hollandse Hoogte
p. 98: Photo Ben&Jerry's: Flickr, theimpulsivebuy
p. 105: Photo Samsung article Edited source Korean Times: Flickr, Samsung
p. 107: Photo Nike, just do it: Flickr, by Kliment
p. 117: Photo The Rug Company, Flickr, by Furdis
p. 124: Hollandse Hoogte
p. 126: Photo Japanese Ikea: Flickr, by Dan & Emily
p. 136: Photo Asia, the rise of the middle class: Flickr, by cd master
p. 143: Photo Chinese girl with iphone: Flickr
p. 154: Hollandse Hoogte
p. 154: Photo BMW: Flickr, by Audunsaltvik
p. 174: Photo: Top Ten Lay's Chips: Flickr.
p. 186: Getty images
p. 188: Photo Renault and Nissan: Flickr
p. 196: Sabet Brands, Inc./Corbis
p. 199: Bernd Vogel/Corbis
p. 221: Enrico Fantoni/Hollandse Hoogte
p. 244: Hollandse Hoogte
p. 256: Photo Recall Children's Sleepwear: www.northumberlandview.com
p. 265: NOVASTOCK/Hollandse Hoogte
p. 276: Peter Hilz/Hollandse Hoogte
p. 278: Photo De-icing aircraft: Flickr by Linanneblack
p. 289: Rob Cloosterman/Hollandse Hoogte
p. 292: Rob Cloosterman/Hollandse Hoogte
p. 295: Roel Dijkstra
p. 299: Roel Burgler/Hollandse Hoogte

Index